Reviewing the Situation

Reviewing the Situation

The British Musical from Noël Coward to Lionel Bart

John Snelson

methuen | drama
LONDON • NEW YORK • OXFORD • NEW DELHI • SYDNEY

METHUEN DRAMA
Bloomsbury Publishing Plc
50 Bedford Square, London, WC1B 3DP, UK
1385 Broadway, New York, NY 10018, USA
29 Earlsfort Terrace, Dublin 2, Ireland

BLOOMSBURY, METHUEN DRAMA and the Methuen Drama logo are trademarks of
Bloomsbury Publishing Plc

First published in Great Britain 2023
Paperback edition published 2025

Copyright © John Snelson, 2023

John Snelson has asserted his right under the Copyright, Designs and Patents Act, 1988, to
be identified as author of this work.

For legal purposes the Acknowledgements on p. viii constitute an extension of this
copyright page.

Cover design: Rebecca Heselton
Cover images: gold © detshana/iStock. Curtains © JDawnInk/iStock. Set © Media Drum
World / Alamy Stock Photo. Theatre © dpa picture alliance / Alamy Stock Photo

All rights reserved. No part of this publication may be reproduced or transmitted in any
form or by any means, electronic or mechanical, including photocopying, recording, or
any information storage or retrieval system, without prior permission in writing from the
publishers.

Bloomsbury Publishing Plc does not have any control over, or responsibility for, any third-
party websites referred to or in this book. All internet addresses given in this book were
correct at the time of going to press. The author and publisher regret any inconvenience
caused if addresses have changed or sites have ceased to exist, but can accept no
responsibility for any such changes.

A catalogue record for this book is available from the British Library.

A catalog record for this book is available from the Library of Congress.

ISBN: HB: 978-1-3502-7958-2
PB: 978-1-3502-7959-9
ePDF: 978-1-3502-7960-5
eBook: 978-1-3502-7961-2

Typeset by Deanta Global Publishing Services, Chennai, India

To find out more about our authors and books visit www.bloomsbury.com and sign up for
our newsletters.

Contents

Acknowledgements		viii
1	Talents to amuse: Creating the British musical	1
	The British landscape	3
	Creative strands	7
	Looking to past and present	8
	The West End and Broadway	11
	Making it personal	13
2	*Bitter Sweet* (1929): Noël Coward	17
	Coward and the contemporary	18
	Retrospection and the creation of *Bitter Sweet*	19
	Operetta through a modern lens	22
	Subsequent musical theatre works	25
	Viewed from a distance	29
3	*Me and My Girl* (1937): Lupino Lane, Noel Gay, L. Arthur Rose and Douglas Furber	33
	Noel Gay and the popular touch	34
	The classic British musical comedy	36
	Twenty to One	38
	Playing to the crowd	40
	A class act	42
	The Lambeth Walk	43
	Props and physical comedy	46
	Distilled and reinvented	48
4	*The Dancing Years* (1939): Ivor Novello	53
	Man of the Theatre	54
	The Novello approach	57
	The screen and the stage	60
	Melody and dramatic expression	62
	Waltzes	64
	The glove and the fist	66
	Assessing the legacy	70

5	*Bless the Bride* (1947): C. B. Cochran, A. P. Herbert and Vivian Ellis	75
	The creative team	76
	The aftermath of war	79
	Ellis and elegance	82
	Post-war music	83
	Politics and the personal	88
	The perspective then and now	91
6	*The Boy Friend* (1953): Sandy Wilson	97
	Theatre and authenticity	98
	Small is beautiful	101
	A valentine to the past	104
	Divorce Me, Darling!	106
	The Buccaneer	107
	Transatlantic consequences	109
7	*Expresso Bongo* (1958): Wolf Mankowitz and the More-Heneker-Norman trio	115
	Challenges to convention	116
	Making a point	120
	Games and confrontations	124
	Promoting youth culture	126
	Teen idols on screen	129
	Striking a new tone	132
	Making history	136
8	*Oliver!* (1960): Lionel Bart	139
	The rise of Lionel Bart	140
	Impressions of the past	143
	Blitz! and *Maggie May*	145
	Music hall and musical	148
	Genre fusions	152
	Oliver! expanded	155
9	'I know what I am': The bigger picture	161
	The 3D view	161
	The musical as memory	163
	The national/international musical	166
	The end of the beginning	168

List of Shows	169
Notes	171
Bibliography	179
Index	185

Acknowledgements

It was the late John Tyrrell – mentor and friend – whose practical encouragement led me into academic research and writing. John's continual support and friendship was a joyful constant through thirty years. Stephen Banfield, the supervisor of my doctoral thesis, guided me – with a light touch that belied his perceptive helpfulness – through the early stages of my academic investigation into British musical theatre. He has since become a good friend, whose thoughtful conversations over many afternoon teas have undoubtedly broadened my skills and understanding. I owe a great debt of gratitude to both John and Stephen for their influence on my work and for occasioning so many valued memories.

This project is the direct result of the gentle, sustained insistence of Robert Gordon and Olaf Jubin, two wonderful friends and colleagues. Teaching alongside them at Goldsmiths and enjoying so many discussions around British musical theatre over lunches, in person and over Zoom calls, continues to be stimulating, exciting and a great pleasure. Olaf has helped directly through reading and commenting on the text of this book as it developed, to my benefit and, more importantly, to the benefit of you who read it. I am also grateful to Maria Lord, Zoë Anderson and Warwick Thompson, experienced writers and editors in their own right who generously took the time to offer their perspectives as the draft chapters emerged. Coming from specialist interests in music and theatre but not from within the particular repertory of British musicals, their observations and suggestions have helped keep the content and contexts focussed and, I hope, free from off-putting digressions and technicalities.

From different perspectives, Stewart Nicholls and Ken Hollings were helpful in bringing my thoughts around *Expresso Bongo* into focus. Researching Lupino Lane continued what has become many years of discussion about the lyric stage with Sarah Lenton, this time around the history of the Coliseum. Peter Viti shared his youthful memories of some of the original West End productions discussed, and Michael Burgess shared his of performing in *The Dancing Years* in revival. Discussions with René Weis and Greg Dart that began more than twenty years ago with opera have grown since into that ongoing encouragement of my research and writing that anyone who tackles such long-term and solitary projects will recognize as invaluable for the writer's spirit as much as the resulting text.

At the British Library, the Lord Chamberlain's Collection proved itself again an important, informative and entertaining source. The Sound Archive has similarly been important, notably when the staff so swiftly digitized an acetate recording from radio of *The Dancing Years* in 1949. To have such original, vital materials available and preserved is invaluable in bringing alive this particular repertory when so many of its source materials have been lost.

The strong support of Dom O'Hanlon at Bloomsbury for the whole area of British musical theatre research and writing has been essential in the progression here from an idea to a commission to a book. The anonymous reviewers of the proposal and of the final draft were enthusiastically supportive and helpful with their observations, and I thank them all for their generous encouragement. Sam Nicholls and Sophie Beardsworth at Bloomsbury have helped me negotiate the practicalities to get so smoothly from draft to print. Publishing – like musical theatre – is an essentially collaborative pursuit.

Final thanks must go to the people who made the shows explored here. The more I discover about them and their works, the more I marvel at their creativity, skill and sheer theatrical vitality.

1

Talents to amuse

Creating the British musical

In the middle of the summer of 1929, any theatregoers who found themselves in London and who sought the diversion of something dramatic, colourful and with plenty of movement and music had a choice not only of different shows but also of different types of show. The Russian Ballet was performing at Covent Garden while *Carmen* (the visiting Carl Rosa Opera Company) was a few hundred metres straight down the road at the Lyceum. But perhaps a revue was more tempting. They could see C. B. Cochran's *Wake Up and Dream* at the London Pavilion, with Jessie Matthews and Sonnie Hale, or the circus-themed variety extravaganza *The Show's the Thing* at the Victoria Palace, with Archie Pitt and Gracie Fields. For something with a story, the musical comedy *Love Lies* had proved itself a success at the Gaiety Theatre – an appropriate location given its somewhat old-fashioned style and that theatre's name in establishing the genre a few decades earlier. For a more contemporary approach, there was *Mr. Cinders* at the London Hippodrome, the other hit musical comedy from that spring's openings and which was still going strong. There was still a little time in which to catch the end of the run of Romberg's Broadway operetta *The New Moon* at the Theatre Royal, Drury Lane.

It was just too late to catch Yvonne Printemps in the short visit of Oscar Straus and Sacha Guitry's *Mariette* to His Majesty's Theatre. What about seeing the new show about to take its place there: *Bitter Sweet*?[1] It was the first full-length musical written, composed and directed by Noël Coward, the witty, sophisticated, theatrical man of the moment. In the middle of a heat wave, *Bitter Sweet* opened at His Majesty's on 18 July 1929. It was not what audiences had expected from Coward. The curtain rose on a contemporary Mayfair house, where young partygoers danced to a jazz band. 'Play something romantic', declared the singer, seeming to decry upbeat popular song even as it was vigorously presented. All was of a piece with Coward's established urbane and sophisticated style. But after a disagreement between a young woman and her fiancé, the show changed direction to focus on an elderly lady. The substance of the drama was not the present, but the elderly lady's past: London in 1880 for the beginnings of romance, Vienna in 1885 for tragedy and 1895 for a return to London. Each jump in time moved the story a little closer to a final scene back in 1929. The message of this 'opérette' (as Coward labelled it) seemed to be sentimental and romantic: follow wherever your heart leads.

The contemporary playwright was born only a few days before the previous century ended, yet he had evoked a world in story, sound, colour and movement not so much of his Edwardian youth as from decades before that – an impression rather than a memory. Lyrical waltzes and jaunty character numbers made no pretence of being in the most current 1920s dance styles. Contemporary dress in the opening and closing scenes framed the show's imagery, but the dominant stage picture was of late Victorian fashion and of the continental characters of varying degrees of social respectability at a Viennese café. The second act did not end with a concerted choral response to tragedy, or indeed any music at all. Instead, the curtain came down to the sobbing of just one character. The unexpected focus on the past rather than the present, the innovative staging and the critical acknowledgement asserted *Bitter Sweet*'s distinctiveness in 1929 as a unique work of West End origin.

Three decades later, in the summer of 1960 and during another heatwave, choices of what to see in the West End were just as varied to suit all tastes and ages. *West Side Story* had been at what was by now called Her Majesty's – the theatre name alters to reflect the reigning sovereign – for a year and a half, portraying the edgy street life of New York on the London stage. *My Fair Lady* was into its third year at the Theatre Royal, Drury Lane, endowing Edwardian London with a certain lyrical glamour just a stone's throw from the real Covent Garden Market, where the fictional Henry Higgins first encounters flower girl Eliza Doolittle. Then again, at the Vaudeville theatre Julian Slade and Dorothy Reynolds's *Follow That Girl* had already been taking its own whimsical tour round Victorian London for a couple of months. But what about the new show from that pop hit writer who also wrote the songs for the new stage success *Fings Ain't Wot They Used T'Be*, which revelled in the seedy life of post-war London? Has he really gone back in time to a Charles Dickens novel and 1830s London? Lionel Bart's *Oliver!* opened at the New Theatre on 30 June 1960.

The first-night audience took a little time to settle into the show's movement from one music number to the next, with minimal dialogue between. Swift changes within an innovative set design evoked the many locations of the story, such as a workhouse dining hall, the thieves' kitchen and London Bridge at night. Dickens's original plot was reduced to a fraction of its original scale. The London skyline was an ever-present backdrop to the central revolving performance area. The portrayals of the characters contrasted vividly, and performances were praised across the board, not least the child actors as Oliver, the Artful Dodger and all the street urchins so engagingly misled into crime by a 'pied piper' Fagin. The music had the instant appeal that had become so characteristic of Bart: effortlessly colloquial language set to song styles from Victorian music hall to contemporary pop ballad. Unusually for the premiere of a new musical, the audience even had the possibility of entering the theatre humming two of the main melodies. Common practice now, but not then, there had been a couple of weeks of advance promotion by two star singers of what proved to be hits of the score, 'Consider Yourself' (Max Bygraves) and 'As Long as He Needs Me' (Shirley Bassey). The long audience ovation given that first night was followed by huge popular success, with the show playing at the New Theatre until 1966.

The summary offered by Stephens in *Theatre World Annual* declared *Oliver!* 'an immediate smash hit, and a great personal triumph for Lionel Bart, who wrote book, music and lyrics' (Stephens 1960: 39). It was also 'a unique occasion in the history of British musicals'. Unique as a show, yes. But unique as a success? Some three decades earlier, the reviewer for *Bitter Sweet* in the *Daily News* considered – in the more restrained journalistic style of the day – that 'Noël Coward made theatrical history at His Majesty's last night. For the first time on the London stage one man has written the book and the music of a musical play, and has also produced it', Coward being 'a man who possesses such a sense of the theatre that it amounts to genius'. He concluded that the show was 'by far the best thing that London stage has seen for many a day' (Findon 1929b: vi). The experience for each reviewer was of something excitingly new, and in both cases the commercial and public responses to the shows agreed. Within a month of *Bitter Sweet* opening in London, plans were in place to open on Broadway that autumn, while the Broadway production of *Oliver!* opened when the London original was what proved to be halfway into a six-year run. Both Coward and Bart were considered to have made theatrical history, so what did they both get right? And what did the creators of the other successful shows in the three decades explored in the following chapters get right too? Between *Bitter Sweet* and *Oliver!* there were *Me and My Girl*, *The Dancing Years*, *Bless the Bride*, *The Boy Friend* and *Expresso Bongo*. Each one provides more comparisons and raises more questions for the following chapters. What informed the responses of the contemporary audiences, and how similar or different are our own to those same shows now? With collaboration at the heart of theatrical production, who and what else contributed to these successes? What wider cultural influences do the shows reveal, and how do their stories fit into the complex mosaic of musical theatre in their own times and through the decades to today? Searching for answers to these questions is what this book is about.

The British landscape

Bitter Sweet prompted the editorial in *The Play Pictorial* to comment on 'the ever recurring topic of American *versus* English musical comedy' before acclaiming Coward as marking a new national way for composers of popular musical theatre (Findon 1929c: i). A week or so after the show had opened, James M. Glover in *The Stage* considered that Coward's operette was 'another nail in the coffin of the American music play' given that 'in twelve months we have London possessed of about six musical play successes by British authors. It seems too good to be true'.[2] Thirty years later, the review headline for *Oliver!* in *The Stage* acclaimed it 'the best British musical'.[3] In between, some sort of active comparison between 'British' and 'American' shows routinely continued in the contemporary commentaries on musical theatre works that originated in the West End. Such sustained awareness indicates at the very least a sensitive nerve, while my deliberate inclusion earlier of Broadway productions of both *Bitter Sweet* and *Oliver!* plays the game of conferring musical theatre success by a geographical hierarchy: Broadway first and foremost.[4]

How appropriate is a constant weighing of the scales with London on one side and New York on the other? For a few shows it may be illuminating, but for many more it isn't. It was the failure of Oscar Hammerstein II and Jerome Kern's *Three Sisters* at Drury Lane in 1934 that provided the spur to Ivor Novello's *Glamorous Night* (1935), the first of a series of hit shows from Novello that ended only with his death in 1951. Novello's shows achieved a level of success in the West End, through extensive touring and in later amateur productions nationwide, greater than any of his contemporaries. Today his widest recognition is through the Ivor Novello Awards (named in 1956 in his memory), among the highest accolades in pop music. Yet his musicals were never produced on Broadway. Conversely, in 1947 *Finian's Rainbow* achieved 61 performances in the West End; on Broadway it ran for 725. The reviews of *South Pacific* in the West End are consistent in finding the story and script much less satisfying or convincing than they had been found on Broadway to go by the undiluted slew of rave reviews after its American premiere.[5] In travelling from London to New York, *The Boy Friend* was actively turned into a different audience experience, much to the distress of its writer-composer, Sandy Wilson, and to the pleasure of the Broadway audience. In 1956, an issue of the popular journal *Plays and Players* focussed on musicals. One article traces through the decades a popular history of 'The Musical in America'. As author Saul Colin brings the story up to date, he asks rhetorically, 'Who can forget *Too Many Girls, Best Foot Forward, By Jupiter*' (Colin 1956). In respect of these shows and the West End repertory, the question would not be 'Who can forget . . . ?' Rather, it would be 'Who knows . . . ?', and it would not be rhetorical. An investigation into West End musical theatre from the 1920s to the 1960s has to account for such differences in repertory, presentation and reception. Different and complementary perspectives can acknowledge more fully the individuality of each musical in its own place and time.

Each of the successes of the West End musicals explored in this book arose from the recognition of a good idea that suited a time and a place and an audience. Whether still in the active performance repertory or faded from it, these musicals were contemporary successes. They were the product of fortunate combinations of individuals who skilfully and imaginatively followed their ideas through the production process. Importantly, the worth of these theatre creations was acknowledged by the audiences who kept them running in the West End and then on tour round the country. All these elements – idea, manner of execution and level of appreciation – carried with them layered associations of their own, with the result that each show is distinctive. These selected works open up a complex web of traditions, influences and practices which have been mixed and matched as part of the continual reshaping of musical theatre. In describing 1937, J. C. Trewin could summarize the 'three five-star musical plays' as 'oddly sorted: *On Your Toes*, which lived on its wit; *Crest of the Wave*, spectacle upon spectacle; and *Me and My Girl*, go-as-you-pleasy, free-and-easy (or it may have been the other way round)' (Trewin 1960: 110). There is no single model to be found for a successful musical during this period, and no single strand of development that follows neatly down the years from one show direct to the next and the next . . . These musicals may constitute milestones of a sort, but they are not to be found consecutively on any single road. The shifting values of musical theatre here are untidy. Even as some of the threads weave together there are loose ends, dead ends, frayed edges and holes in a sprawling repertory.

The identification of home-grown musical theatre success has been coloured too by a fundamental lack of interest and confidence in this repertory. Transatlantic comparisons through the period examined here have consistently reinforced an underlying tone in approach stated in Findon's editorial response to *Bitter Sweet*. He praises Coward in a context that advocates musical training and support for composers of light music (Findon, 1929c: i). Three decades later, Coward could still echo Findon and with evident bitterness:

> I am convinced that the slow decay of English musical comedy is largely attributable to this complete ignorance of light music. Why should an ambitious young composer spend months conceiving and evolving a full musical score when he knows at the outset that the highest praise he can hope to get for it will be the adjectives 'Tuneful' or 'Pleasantly reminiscent'. In America, on the other hand, when a new musical is produced out of town for its try-out, the first question put to those who have attended the opening is invariably 'How was the score?' Light music is important in America, is treated with proper respect and criticised accordingly. Here it is treated with no respect and criticised, if at all, with contemptuous ignorance. (Coward 1958: xix–xx)

Vivian Ellis had anticipated Coward by a couple of years with the same points in an article called 'Give Us a Chance' (Ellis 1956): 'The main differences between the American and English Musical lies in the two countries' attitudes towards light music. In America, light music, or show music, is taken seriously. It is seriously reviewed. In England this is not the case.' He draws distinctions in style too: American shows are 'louder, cruder, slicker and more pretentious' if also 'more efficient than the British musical', while British shows were distinguished by 'wit, taste and charm'. He concludes by identifying the need for British musical theatre producers to love theatre more than chasing a guaranteed profit from the safe option of a tried-and-tested American show. In the same year, for the survey *Theatre in Review*, Sandy Wilson matched Ellis's dissection with one of his own on similar lines titled 'A Future for British Musicals'. He concludes with the hope of seeing not home-grown copies of Broadway shows, rather 'a native musical flourishing on our own soil, reflecting our own ideas and singing our own melodies' (Wilson 1956). Only a couple of years later, the shows of David Heneker and Lionel Bart were beginning to do just that.

Annuals of musical and theatre culture of the time support by their omissions that sense of neglect of home-grown musical theatre. For example, *The Year's Work in Theatre 1948–1949* has a chapter devoted to 'The West End Theatre', but it covers only non-lyric plays. Others of its short chapters have such self-explanatory titles as 'The Old Vic', 'The Year in Ballet', 'The Festivals' and even 'The Music-Hall' (Trewin 1949). Musical theatre does not figure in its coverage through individual works or as a genre. Similarly, *Musical Britain* focusses entirely on what would be termed then the 'high brow' end of the music market (Music Critic of The Times, 1951). Musical theatre in Britain is clearly something apart from arts culture. An indigenous narrative for musical theatre was being diminished even as the shows were packing them into the theatres in the West End and regionally with pre-London tryouts and post-London extensive touring. Consequently, the minimizing of these works, or absence of them, in home-grown theatrical representation sidelined them for future years too. This has not been the case with the valuing of American musicals and the construction of the 'Broadway' narrative.

Within a much narrower theatrical world, especially publications aimed at theatre fans, there was more substantial representation of musical theatre. This often came with its own subtext of West End inferiority. In the reviews of the year in successive annuals of *Theatre World*, the publication's writer-editor Frances Stephens is constantly caught between hailing British hits while distancing them from any suggestion of a pattern of musical theatre success. For example, in the inaugural volume's summary of the past year he writes, 'there was, of course *King's Rhapsody*, but Ivor Novello, it must be acknowledged, is a law unto himself' (Stephens 1950: 14). The 'of course', 'but' and 'law unto himself' turn serial success and individuality into quirks. Later, alongside the illustrated feature on the show itself, Stephens affirms that 'Novello has an unerring instinct for knowing what the public wants in musical entertainment. *King's Rhapsody* [. . .] has been no exception, and however much the carping critic may protest as he looks back over a decade and a half of Novello mammoth musicals, that this is the mixture as before, the public continues to pack every house' (Stephens 1950: 73). That mention of 'carping critics' – a minority against the majority giving generous praise – again suggests unease with the acknowledgement of Novello's success as central to the West End narrative, not apart from it.

A few years later in the annual of 1954, for Stephens the British musical theatre world could 'bolster up our morale by the reflection that *Wedding in Paris* – the all-British success, is certain to run for at least twelve months at the Hippodrome. *The Boy Friend*, that phenomenal success, and the work of one young man only, the now famous Sandy Wilson, is in a class of its own' (Stephens 1954: 12). Wilson's success again invites some form of setting him apart, not fitting the script. In the intervening years, Stephens had praised many shows individually, yet he did not allow them to constitute a pattern, so he found that morale repeatedly needed bolstering. Somewhat akin to the scepticism over the Romans in *Monty Python's Life of Brian*, one could paraphrase his approach using his own selection of praiseworthy shows as: 'Apart from *King's Rhapsody, Gay's the Word, Zip Goes a Million, Bet Your Life, Love from Judy, Dear Miss Phoebe, Wedding in Paris* and *The Boy Friend*, when has a home-grown West End musical in the past four years been a success?' And when in 1952 Stephens could report that 'The triumph of *South Pacific* and Mary Martin, at Drury Lane, was a foregone conclusion', he sidelines the widely held and strongly expressed reservations in the opening reviews already mentioned. Yet he would have been considerably more justified to take adverse comment into account for *South Pacific* than for *King's Rhapsody* (Stephens 1952: 14).

Stephens's tepid optimism that one day British musicals would succeed disguises a more pervasive underlying pessimism that prevented him changing the narrative. He was not alone in this cognitive dissonance, but rather worked within a long-standing framework of such critical assumptions around the value of these home-grown shows. This made it difficult to steer a steady course between the conflicting streams of evidence and what the popular readership expected (and for whom any brief textual element provided a framework in which to set the copious production photographs of shows and stars). Stephens's language is more the result of popular journalism than serious analysis, and it mirrors that of contemporary press reviews. Such reviews have value in evoking their times and conjuring up impressions of audience experience – but only to a limited degree, given the in-built biases of their day. Yet they have proved insidiously influential. Today we can try to be more circumspect in avoiding an unquestioned and unmodified retelling of those familiar stories and consider instead other histories. The distance we have now can lend nostalgic enchantment but, more usefully, a new critical perspective.

Creative strands

There are many ways to label the combination of play with popular music: operetta, opérette, musical play, musical comedy, musical romance and simply 'musical' are familiar options. Changing terminology is a symptom of the search for new ways to balance and shape the core elements. To varying degrees of clarity, the process of adjustment inexorably continues beyond the scope of this book with such subgenre labels as 'rock musical', 'megamusical', 'jukebox musical' and 'revusical'. Continental operetta is an influence on Coward for his 'opérette' *Bitter Sweet* (1929). It is too on Ivor Novello and Christopher Hassall's *The Dancing Years* (1939), although labelled a 'musical play', a familiar West End designation since the 1920s. Yet we have to go back to Victorian comic opera and Gilbert and Sullivan to understand its genre references for a later creation than either *Bitter Sweet* or *The Dancing Years*. The Ellis-Herbert-Cochran *Bless the Bride* (1947) uses 'light opera' in the libretto but 'musical show' in the vocal score – even though the work's dramatic themes and purposes are very much a product of the immediate post-war period. Noel Gay's music for *Me and My Girl* (1937) and the tropes of its story take us into the world of 'musical comedy'. So does Sandy Wilson's *The Boy Friend* (1953/4), almost twenty years later in creation yet a decade earlier in its stylistic tribute as 'a new musical comedy of the 1920's' (Wilson 1960a: title page).

Only a handful of years later, the 'musical play' *Expresso Bongo* (1958) is very much up to date in how it draws on the vibrant West End character and the non-musical theatre of the day. It sits within a group of shows that shared similar comically dark, urban themes and pop-related musical influences. In this respect, the 'musical play' *Oliver!* (1960) a couple of years later seems to take a small step back towards what appears with the advantage of distance a more familiar, less challenging formula in tune with Broadway values of the time. Thus, it could be interpreted within a mainstream identity and in turn become more widely and easily accepted. All these shows seek their own negotiations with the history of the popular lyric stage. Together they illustrate how a single line of chronological development cannot express the fascinating complexity they embody.

The stage does not function in isolation as a provider of entertainment. Another force begins its ascent just as the stage story here begins, and it interacts with stage shows in their creation, reinterpretation and dissemination. That force is in embryonic form in 1929 such that as *Bitter Sweet* opened, *The Stage* included long articles on negotiating new contracts for stage actors in the wake of the threat perceived by the advent of sound film. For example: 'Mr. C. B. Cochran says that he thinks the talking-film rights of *Bitter Sweet* will be worth £100,000. If so, how much more will the film be worth to its producer and to its exhibitors? On the other hand, what sum will go to the actors, singers, and musicians who make the film possible?'[6] The adaptation to the competition that sound film created with live theatre was expressed in various ways. To take one, in March 1933 Sir Oswald Stoll turned his huge flagship London variety venue the Coliseum into a cinema, but a year later he turned it back again.

Coward had the uneasy experience of *Bitter Sweet* as it was interpreted in a British film version of 1933, and the deeply unpleasant one for him of Hollywood's adaptation in 1940. For Novello, his status as a leading romantic actor in silent film influenced the style of his musical romances from conception to performance, as we will see. *Me and My Girl* has fared less well with an early television broadcast (1939) only accessible now through remaining fragments, but nonetheless vital in assessing the theatrical experience, while the near-contemporary filmed version has the advantage of retaining some central stage casting, but the disadvantage of losing almost all its musical numbers. *Bless the Bride* is marked by the lack of film representation, *Expresso Bongo* by a plethora of related 1950s 'youthsploitation' films, and *Oliver!* from 1960 owes a direct debt to David Lean's film *Oliver Twist* of 1948. Adaptations of *The Dancing Years* (both for film and television) have had an impact on the reputation of the originating stage works, while Carol Reed's 1968 big-screen version of *Oliver!* is probably the easiest gateway through which subsequent generations have formed an impression of that show. Some consideration of film, including its absence as a documenting medium, is necessary for significant parts of this repertory.

Beyond entertainment, politics creates and reflects a prevailing mood. The sublimation of the national and international into the personal is in play in the two works here that bookend the Second World War, *The Dancing Years* and *Bless the Bride*. Lyrics in *Expresso Bongo* include wry takes on intergenerational politics, while its commentary on socio-economic status and its implications for daily life runs through to another show of a similar time, *Oliver!*. Whether this is coincidence or a reflection of something wider is worth investigation. The visual signs of changing decorative fashions in clothes, hairstyle and furnishings play a part too in establishing the contemporary or evoking past periods. And even the apparent theatrical introversion of *The Boy Friend* invites the questions 'why that?' and 'why then?' The approach this book adopts to widening the context is part of seeing the identity of musical theatre works as woven deeply into contemporary experiences. The creation of each show is a pragmatic and visceral reflection of the time and place in which it happened, further shaped by the experiences of the theatre practitioners inspired to theatrical experimentation.

Looking to past and present

The awareness of a specifically national heritage runs through the home-grown, West End musicals, which lends them a different tone and purpose from shows created elsewhere and then reproduced in London. Heritage is more than 'history'.

It is an acknowledgement that the past plays a significant part in shaping the present. References to the lyric stage of the past are legion in British-originated shows. Each of the case studies here overtly exhibits this awareness to differing degrees. *Bitter Sweet* and *The Boy Friend* build the idea of genre comparison into their forms: the first frames the Victorian world with the contemporary one of the show's 1929 audience, and the second single-mindedly adopts the anachronism of an earlier period of theatre practice.

Coward's and Wilson's choices invite the theatre audience to make connections across the decade which provoke a comparison of social traits, morals, aesthetic values and performance traditions. *Bitter Sweet* opens with a song composed and performed in a manner entirely in tune with its 1929 origin. As the next chapter will discuss, the music of the second number becomes an active means of juxtaposing past and present, after which the transformations of set and costume complete a journey fully to the past. The entire theatrical experience is crucial to this effect. For those in the audience, the effect of the imagery and behavioural tone would have been to provoke in the youngest some recognition of the world of their grandparents maybe familiar from photographs or childhood encounters with elderly relatives. For those over forty it would have seemed nostalgic of the world of their own youth and possibly even their own parents'. We have a different perspective, as indeed would anyone seeing the show from only a decade or so later. To create a sense of the performance effect without taking into account the changes time will have made to the audience baseline for views, values, fashions and even different types of physicality, is to lose valuable, contextual information. Some imagination is required as well as the gathering of thoughts well beyond the confines of the theatre world. It is a revealing process that plays a large part in this study.

With *The Boy Friend*, some of the audience's time travel work already seems to have been done through the style of a particular type of musical theatre of some thirty years before. Yet, the apparent clarity of plunging the audience straight into the Roaring Twenties brings complications. The invitation was not to compare 1920s past and 1950s present but to be within a filtered, reconstructed 1920s past for its own sake. Its subsequent reception demonstrates the difficulty of unpacking a growing layering of 'then' and 'now'. When the residue of first-hand knowledge becomes second- or more likely third-hand experience, a two-dimensional view of the past replaces something more three-dimensional, the original intention is progressively lost and the drift is towards the parody of cliché.

Other musicals in this study draw on the past through association, even if not their primary thematic core. The past–present tension in *Me and My Girl* is built into its setting, with working-class Lambeth in London rubbing up against the grandeur of a stately home and a title. As the show demonstrates, family lineage can be strong for a working-class Londoner, but it is the aristocracy who display it through ceremonial robes and honours and claim it through the day-to-day social expectations and privileges of their status built into history, law and convention. Tensions around social class are still with us, but we do not experience them the same way as in 1937 or even at the time of the show's revision in the mid-1980s. Novello's shows take a different tack with their musical associations implying a world of turn-of-the-century operetta but within a total package that mixed the self-evidently contemporary with scenes of seemingly timeless fantasy. And in *The Dancing Years*, Novello starts forty years in the past and progresses chronologically up to his present day of 1939 and the implications of the Anschluss. Without the present-past-present effect of Coward's framing device in *Bitter Sweet*, the straight chronological progression in *The Dancing Years* gives the audience no clue as to when the story will end. The romantic tension of two lovers who repeatedly miss their chance ends with an intrusion from the outside world that is all the more chilling for it. The show is in part a lesson in historical consequences, prescient in that it was only six months after the show opened that the hostilities of the Second World War commenced. It would be easier for us to judge the effects intended by Coward and Novello if they had been accurately represented in the filmed versions. But they weren't. Indeed, the representation on film of British musicals that originated on stage is sparse and mostly makes clear the thinner resources afforded it than for the Hollywood equivalents of American stage repertory.

In *Expresso Bongo*, the past is ignored: it focusses on youth and the contemporary. The staged show had a cynical edge in tune with the time. This was the British musical freeing itself from the pre-war world through the conscious creation of a new direction and new values. Lionel Bart emerges out of this setting, but has his biggest success with *Oliver!* in an accommodation of the literary and theatrical past with contemporary sensibilities in a way that freely played with, and thus acknowledged, both. Again, film adaptations only partly suggest the mood and tone of the originals. In the case of *Expresso Bongo* on film, the score lost some of its most pointed numbers while some of what remained was given a cosy gloss that removed its bite. With *Oliver!*, the pared-down nature of its staging became on film lavish and detailed, and the score and script were changed too.

All these film versions increase or add a romantic gloss to their source texts and dilute the emotional force of the original stage work. The internal referencing of the context of live theatre – history, tradition, novelty, expectation, physicality – is inevitably of secondary concern in the transition to film: different genre requirements and expectations generate different practices. The past-present dialogue within a stage work is also reflected in the transient nature of the experience of live performance, with each staged iteration and each audience attendance existing simultaneous with the show's nature as enduring historical document by way of script, score, design and logged response. This shifts with film, for which the performance experience shared through the edit becomes predominantly a fixed text to be revisited even if also reinterpreted. Film adaptations offer limited help and often considerable hindrance in getting to grips with the theatrical experience.

The tension between past and present is a constant in all art. In the musical, the way in which this is made evident seems different in importance to British musicals of the period studied here than to their American counterparts. Certainty and optimism have often been identified with Broadway musical theatre of the same period – *Oklahoma!* may be set in 1908, but its thrust is on what will happen in the future with Laurey and Curly's personal future a mirror for that of a 'brand new state' that's 'gonna treat you great': in the show's final chorus, that state literally has the last word. However, the West End shows tend to focus more on the integration and questioning of reflections between past and present: in *Bitter Sweet*, Lady Shayne's past may propel the future of two young lovers, but the final image of that show is of her on stage alone as the physical embodiment of the past life the audience has followed from youth to old age. The oft-characterized Broadway optimism resulting from always looking forward has its equivalent in the more reflective questioning of identity in the West End, and it is noticeable how much the sound of Victorian music hall and Edwardian musical comedy finds its way into the shows from Coward through to Bart. Past, present and future are dynamically entangled in British musicals of this period.

The West End and Broadway

The anxiety over American domination of musical theatre has already been cited in the context of transatlantic comparison. For the immediate post-war period, the effects of this have been covered in detail (Snelson 2003), but it is worth examining the implications a little further in order to focus thereafter on other, complementary perspectives. Freed from American hegemony of value and purpose, a different, distinctive and unique repertory emerges in its own right. It is rich, varied and innovative, responding first and foremost to the concerns of its home audience, rather than being a copycat of Broadway. West End shows influenced by Broadway models are certainly in the mix. *Ace of Clubs* and *Zip Goes a Million* come readily to mind, yet both have dominant influences from other sources in their creation and reception.

Pleasing American audiences was not a concern for West End hit shows. In one rare 1940s case where this was tested by a transfer from London to New York, the outcome seems in retrospect inevitable, but at the time it was not. In November 1945, *Under the Counter* opened at the Phoenix Theatre in London, closing there in July 1947. Several factors contributed to a successful run of 665 performances. It was built around the British film and stage star Cicely Courtneidge. Its story about wartime rationing resonated with audiences in the immediate wake of the Second World War, when shortages became more severe. The unlikely and self-reflexive plot was there to harness Courtneidge's famous, indefatigable energy and high-octane comic delivery. It involved a stage performer (Courtneidge) trying to obtain the necessary materials to mount her next show through the black market – the 'under the counter' of the title – as they could not be obtained legally. The chorus and dance sequences fitted into the show-within-a-show structure. It was written by the experienced West End script writer Arthur McCrae, lyricist Harold Purcell and composer Manning Sherwin. Courtneidge, rationing and the light-headed breathing out after five years of war – the show was of its time and of its place. It delighted the British audience for whom it was intended. You had to be there to get it.

Almost no British shows had made the transfer to Broadway for around a decade, and none successfully. Novello's musical shows were never produced on Broadway, and *Me and My Girl* (London, 1937) took almost fifty years to get there. Courtneidge was encouraged by Mary Martin, Noël Coward, Katharine Cornell and Lee Shubert to take *Under the Counter* to New York (Courtneidge 1953: 147). Would this be the show to break that pattern? After just twenty-seven performances at New York's Shubert Theatre the answer was 'no'. The specificity of its context prevented it. In her biography, Courtneidge acknowledges this as she relates the advice given her by the Minister of Defence, A. V. Alexander: 'you'll have to be very careful in America or they won't understand it at all. Why don't you have a prologue explaining the "under the counter" business of shortages, or perhaps something printed on the programmes? [or] explain the plot of the show in your advance publicity.' Courtneidge reflects 'what a pity we did not take old Alexander's advice' (Courtneidge 1953: 147). Besides the different nature of that audience's daily existence from Londoners, Courtneidge did not have the star recognition in America that she had in Britain, and she was the show.

Courtneidge successfully toured *Under the Counter* round Australia for a year, where the Commonwealth connection brought a supporting level of cultural familiarity and theatrical acceptance. When she returned to the West End in 1949 in what proved another personal success, *Her Excellency*, the story involved meat rationing. The supply of meat, a strong indicator of the state of national well-being at the time, was at an all-time low, echoing the domestic practicalities that had inspired *Under the Counter*. There was no attempt at a Broadway transfer. Neither was there with Courtneidge's *Gay's the Word* in 1951, yet another personal triumph, written specifically for her by Novello as what proved to be his last completed script and score, with lyrics by Alan Melville. On Broadway, Courtneidge barely registered and Novello has a footnote as a briefly successful playwright and actor in the early 1930s. In the West End, they are central in the creation and performance of major hits and essential to any attempt to portray the character of Britain's musical theatre in the 1930s, 1940s and 1950s.

In Kurt Gänzl's invaluable and extensive chronicle *The British Musical Theatre*, the concluding summary of the 1948 hit show *The Kid from Stratford* is of it being 'a grand and funny piece of entertainment which served its star extremely well' (Gänzl 1986b: 592). The description of the show, supported by quotations from press reviews, focusses on the star, Arthur Askey, one of the most known and loved figures in British popular entertainment of the day. His status had been cemented during the war through his presence on radio – at the time the pre-eminent, communal medium nationwide for entertainment – and in British film comedies. *The Kid from Stratford* was 'a display of his talents for written and unwritten humour, for comic songs and burlesque' (Gänzl 1986b: 591). Askey's character name, Arthur Price, is indicative of the blurring of dramatic role and performer identity, in keeping with the pattern for so many of his other roles (in film as Arthur Linden, just Arthur, Arthur Pilbeam, Arthur King, Arthur Bowman, Arthur Tucker, Arthur Ashton and, on stage, as Arthur Golightly).[7] It is vital to acknowledge the performativity that Askey's persona brought to the show, and Chapter 3˙ will explore such a dynamic in relation to another star performer, Lupino Lane. Yet a 'name' is not the whole story.

Why did Askey's show include a song 'freely adapted' from Shakespeare and a parody of *Hamlet*? The conception of the show fused two elements of contemporary theatre self-evident to the audience for whom it was written, but not so today. The context of the show was borne of the arrival in the West End of new American musicals and of revivals of Shakespeare. Following the war, the crisis of confidence that affected British musicals was part of a wider issue of self-perception in British theatre-making. As one consequence, new foreign plays, especially from America (as by Tennessee Williams) and from France (with Jean Anouilh), were felt to offer more than the new plays of such pre-war British stalwarts as Terence Rattigan. A reassertion of British heritage came through Shakespeare, boosted by Laurence Olivier's Oscar-winning films *Henry V* (1944), which tied together British heritage through Shakespeare, wartime morale and national pride, and – especially relevant to Askey – *Hamlet* (1948).

When Askey's character finds an original Shakespeare musical buried in Stratford-upon-Avon, he decides to stage it. As Shakespeare's accompanying message to his script stated, 'I am mightily weary of London managements, who, forsooth, care naught for ye British musicals since "Annie, Get thy Blunderbuss".'[8] The discovery prompts Askey to quip 'This'll kill Ivor Novello' in acknowledgement of West End musical theatre going head to head with straight theatre alongside the prevalent British-American comparisons.[9] The show became a burlesque of the British theatre scene of the day, expressing anxiety around what was being performed, what was being valued, and the practical difficulties of staging a British musical – even one by Shakespeare! – because of the unsympathetic response within the financial mechanisms of production. Even if the especially topical jokes in the script were rewritten for today, that broader context of the theatrical culture of 1948 would not be accessible other than through conscious historical application by the audience. Focussing on Askey's central role only gets us so far in understanding why this show fitted its time and place.

Making it personal

The musicals explored in the following chapters were created in ways that inevitably made them of a particular place and time. The creative focus was practical, on the theatrical 'here and now', however much a lasting legacy beyond the immediate currency of increased reputational value and royalty payments may have been desired. Some of these shows consciously foreground national identity to reflect elements of the familiar world of the day to their audiences. Already in this opening chapter a mixture of descriptive terms has been used to indicate a geographically and temporally located repertory: British, English, West End, home-grown ... The most commonly used term in the literature is 'British musical' – included in this book's title for precisely that reason: it signals compactly a general area of interest. The 'British musical' and 'British musical theatre' are catch-all terms with a long-standing record of use, as quotations from critics and commentators contemporary with the period under study here have already shown. The connotations of both words are applied with fuzzy generality to a slew of variants of light, lyric, narrative stage works that originated within the theatrical system of the UK at some point from the mid-1890s on. This maintains an assumption that there is a national cultural identity within this part of the lyric stage repertory. It differs from what emerged from other geographical regions. And 'we know it when we see it'.

Collectively, the range of available labels does acknowledge that there are distinctions to be made in which national identity plays a part. Ben Macpherson's thorough investigation into the nature of Britishness in musical theatre through a repertory that partly overlaps with that of this book admirably sets out such recurring themes as gender, class and empire. His summary is clear:

> [I]t would seem that Britishness might be understood – not as a coherent ideology, cultural identity, or world-view – but as a continuing series of tensions comprised of anxiety and uncertainty. Britishness at best seems a contradiction in terms, and more accurately a plurality – a sprawling mess of anxieties, tensions and paradoxes that play off against each other and never entirely resolve. (2018: 211)

An additional refinement is to understand that in large part, 'the story of cultural identity in British musical theatre, then, is more typically the story of *English* cultural identity, operating unconsciously as Britishness' (2018: 212).

National identity is part of the investigation here, but it is not the dominant or sole focus. With such undercurrents acknowledged, the intention here is to extend the range of reference. To complement the methodology of exploration within the same trope, this book looks towards a plurality of experiences and a variety of different routes through which to explore the repertory. Inevitably in dealing with a limited selection of prominent shows as entry points, the geographical centre is London, and, within that, prominent commercial productions in mainstream musical theatre. What seemed applicable to Robert Graves and Alan Hodge in an introductory note to the first edition of *The Long Weekend*, their evocative and impressionistic history of 1918–39, has relevance: 'A criticism that we feel like making ourselves is that events in London and its environs are here treated in disproportion to events elsewhere. But this could not be helped; the tendency was for things either to happen first in London or to be first noted there' (1940: 1). Other constituencies feature only selectively as the case studies allow or, indeed, not all. This short book is inevitably limited to filling in just part of a huge theatrical mosaic currently with many gaps. The more that tiles from other perspectives can be added, the more a holistic sense of the interacting patterns will be accessible and discernible.[10]

Each case study provides its own thematic starting point, such as musical tradition, star performers, film, distanced subtexts, youth culture and performance as memory. As a consequence, new interactions and influences become part of each story, through production, performance, repertory and the push-pull between past and present. National identity is sometimes consciously interwoven, sometimes not, and where that identity is specifically important, it will be made clear. Otherwise, the use of 'British musical' is pragmatic shorthand when the focus of the investigation is mainly directed elsewhere. This avoids too some of the ambiguity that could arise in certain contexts with, for example, a 'West End' show, which without further qualification makes no immediate distinction between transfers from outside London or Britain. A variety of blurred identities will occur as the investigation moves between creative teams, production systems, performers, textual sources and film interactions. Patterns (plural) emerge through the intersection of multiple strands and through the mobility that each strand has in its own right to influence and respond to any and all other strands. In exploring the individuality of approach within Noël Coward's musical stage works, Dominic McHugh suggests that 'the transience of identity experienced by the principal characters in key works such as *Bitter Sweet*, combined with leitmotifs such as nationalism and class, provided [Coward's] personalized generic framework' (2016: 458). This book will repeatedly reveal such individuality as central to all the creative figures behind the works studied and each show personalized in its inputs and emphases. The patterns we discern across the repertory arise out of comparisons between an accumulation of these separate works. Coward's *Bitter Sweet* is the earliest of the case studies and where this exploration into identity – individual and collective – begins.

2

Bitter Sweet (1929)

Noël Coward

Noël Coward's first full-length, narrative work for musical theatre can seem one entirely of operetta convention. In *Bitter Sweet* (1929), a young, aristocratic English woman is swept off her feet by a Viennese musician. On the eve of her wedding, they elope to Vienna, where they eke out a living in a second-rate café, him heading the band and her as an unwilling hostess. A former flame of his sings at the café too, which adds tension to the situation. But the mortal threat comes from a different source: in a duel over the honour of his wife, the musician is killed by an army officer whose base desires are not to be thwarted. Years later, the widow – now a famous singer of her late husband's songs – reflects on how romance has shaped her life. Music and romance: it's a classic operetta pairing. Noël Coward was 'genuinely proud' of having written and composed *Bitter Sweet* (Coward 1953: 11). And rightly so. It is an engaging, surprising and subtle work of *musical* theatre, whose originality lies less in the ingredients of the plot than the accomplished manner of their development.

Throughout Coward's introduction to the 1953 collection *The Songs of Noël Coward* an undercurrent aims to reset the critical bearings. He stresses music above words and the completeness of a score above its constituent parts. By definition, this selection of his songs from the 1920s to the early 1950s presents individual numbers extracted from the whole shows, so his insistence is significant. By the 1950s, Coward was famous first and foremost as an actor and a wordsmith whose wry observations on life were animated in his songs by witty, densely packed rhymes. Even with his more melodic numbers, the titles, themes and carefully wrought lyrics garnered most attention. Yet almost four decades into his professional life, Coward was keen to stress the influence of the music of his youth and his musician's ear. Coward considered that vital empathic talent for music was central to his creative nature, unimpeded in any significant way by his lack of formal training in music or by his self-taught piano playing.

For the musical comedies of his youth, Coward valued the routine publishing of their complete vocal scores and the availability in the theatre of published lyrics that 'helped those with a musical ear to recapture more easily the tunes they wanted to remember and to set them in their minds' (Coward 1953: 11). The genesis in a New York taxi during a traffic jam of one of Coward's most famous songs is revealing for the way his description plays out the trope of the artist struck by inspiration more than struggling through perspiration: 'suddenly in the general din there was the melody, clear and unmistakable. By the time I got home the words of the first phrase had emerged' (Coward 1953: 14). Coward relates here how the music for one of his most enduring songs, *Bitter Sweet*'s 'I'll See You Again', came complete before the lyrics. That detail illustrates the larger theme.

Coward's choice to write *Bitter Sweet* in the form of an operetta acknowledges the centrality for him of music as its creative imperative. Dominic Vlasto highlights that 'Coward was not *also* a writer of music and lyrics', but rather that this aspect is 'often completely integral to his dramatic work' (2000: 144). At the core of Coward's first 'operette', as he labelled it, is a drama not only set to music but also about music, through which the music becomes central to any discussion of the show. In *Bitter Sweet* more than any other work by Coward, the music really matters.

Coward and the contemporary

Coward wrote of his place in British theatre through the 1920s – with perhaps only a touch of humour in the self-aggrandisement – that 'I cannot think off-hand of anyone who was more intimately and turbulently connected with it' (Trewin 1958: 7). His star status burgeoned in 1924 with his play *The Vortex*. Its central theme allied to its author acting the central character of Nicky Lancaster was all too convenient a shorthand for the press: 'I played the part of a neurotic misfit who took drugs, made sharp witty remarks and was desolately unhappy. There was my label, ready to hand and glaringly printed . . . . All that was important for monotonous future reference was the created image – the talented, neurotic sophisticated playboy' (Coward 1986: 396–7). A cover photograph from *The Sketch* in 1927 of Coward in bed, on the telephone as 'The Young Playwright, Actor and Composer Mr Noël Coward Busy at Breakfast' reinforced the label. To Coward's contemporaries Graves and Hodge, his expression intimated 'advanced degeneracy' (1940: 121). Often reproduced, this image has acquired connotations of wealth, privilege and homosexuality, and invited Coward's work to be read in parallel to such promotional, constructed biography (Clum 1999: 80, 81). Inevitably, the best-remembered works and aspects of Coward's life tend to reinforce his celebrity persona. For example, *Private Lives* (1930) remains current for performance, quotation and parody. The financial and social milieu of Amanda and Elyot combined with the verbal dexterity of their brittle, volatile sparring in one-liners on the balcony in Act I are recognizable as extensions of Coward himself. Yet Coward's sortie just a few years earlier into the different style of Ruritanian romance, *The Queen Was in the Parlour* (written 1922, staged 1926), is seldom acknowledged today. Its plot, location and language don't fit Coward's image.

The big, West End revues presented by the theatre impresarios André Charlot and C. B. Cochran in the 1920s were intended to be of their time. Coward's contributions as a writer (sketches and songs) and a performer built up his reputation as a wry, up-to-date observer of the modern world. Cochran's revue *On with the Dance* (1925) at the London Pavilion Theatre on Piccadilly Circus put Coward's name alone in lights as the author (although the music was also by Philip Braham). One of its most lasting numbers, 'Poor

Little Rich Girl', focusses on the wealthy young socialite who pursues the partying high life, but 'what comes after? Nobody knows'. The song was included in Charlot's Revue of 1926 in New York, adding a transatlantic gloss to the number and to Coward.

With Cochran's 1928 revue, *This Year of Grace!* – 'book, lyrics and Music by Noël Coward' – observations on the foibles of the modern world and pointed comparisons with an often-romanticized past were legion. Sketches and songs featured trains, buses and taxis. In 'Lorelei', the mermaid whose seductive song lured seamen in the days of sail can't compete when 'coaling steamers are belching streamers of horrible smoke, making them choke', or, worse yet, finds herself reduced to 'vamping a submarine'. The message is that 'Progress goes on, glamour has gone' (Coward 1939b: 21–2). One of the show's most lasting songs, 'A Room with a View', puts stillness and the observation of the world ahead of the hurry of participating in it (Coward 1939b: 27–30), while the addition of 'World Weary' to the New York version of the show accented this point with the urban dystopia relieved by rural relaxation (Coward 1939b: 88–90).

Stressing the contemporary in *This Year of Grace!* even more personally, a sketch of four fast vignettes called 'The Theatre Guide' gave a promotional 'brief impression of the current dramatic successes of London'. The last of them was 'Any Noël Coward Play'. An actress holding a bouquet of flowers responded to cries of 'speech' by acknowledging it as the happiest moment of her life, which elicited a staged response of 'boos and catcalls' (Coward 1939b: 15). This self-deprecation by Coward acknowledged his record of the previous year for unsuccessful plays, particularly *Sirocco*, which was booed on its opening night and lasted just three weeks. Critics were irritated by what they had come to view as Coward's precocious smugness and become increasingly harsh in their attitude towards him. They appreciated 'the delightful audacity' of his self-parody. The revue appealed and Coward was catapulted back into critical favour 'with the drum accompaniment and velocity of a Star Trap Act' (Coward 1986: 195–6). As so often, Coward invites his life to be understood in terms of a stage performance – here with a traditional pantomime flourish, propelled from below the stage into sudden view as if by magic.

The number 'Dance, Little Lady' in *This Year of Grace!* has been described by Philip Hoare as among 'the great *mises-en-scène* of 1920s musical theatre' (Hoare 1995: 193). It continues the theme of feverish and joyless activity among the young and privileged, set to a soundtrack 'with insane music in your brain'. A group of masked 'glittering macabre figures' crowded around the mimed figure of the 'little lady' critiqued by the song (Coward 1986: 195). In the same revue, another song with an apparently nostalgic title, 'Teach Me to Dance Like Grandma', still takes a sideswipe at the monotony of jazz tunes, the 'groaning' of saxophones and the longing for 'an age that has tunes' (Coward 1939b: 31). Coward's next step was to bring this emphasis on music as defining of both the *zeitgeist* and the human spirit into the foreground through greater emphasis on his talents as a composer.

Retrospection and the creation of *Bitter Sweet*

A three-week tryout of *Bitter Sweet* in Manchester prior to London sold out. The *Daily Herald* proclaimed it an 'emphatic success . . . The "operette" is not at all what one would expect from this representative of the cynical youth of the jazz age. It is sweet and it is sentimental, and it deals with things of long ago and far away. It has, moreover, a very definite story to tell'.[1] Its immediate origin lies in a weekend away, during which Coward's host played a recording of *Die Fledermaus*. A discussion between Coward and the stage designer Gladys Calthrop during their return journey to London conjured up images of Vienna in the 1880s, as Coward recalls: 'The uniforms, bustles, chandeliers and gas-lit café all fell into place eagerly, as though they had been waiting in the limbo for just this cue to enter' (Coward 1986: 196).

The triggers came from style and mood, not plot mechanics, characterizations or even genre fixtures: Vienna and operetta are part of *Bitter Sweet* but not specifically *Die Fledermaus*. Ethan Mordden notes that '*Die Fledermaus* doesn't have a single genuine love song while *Bitter Sweet* is full of them' (2021: 97). Coward continues: 'There had been little or no sentiment on the London musical stage for a long while. The Daly's operettas . . . in which the heroines dissolved in tears . . . had given place to an endless succession of slick American "Vo do deo do" musical farces in which the speed was fast, the action complicated, and the sentimental value negligible.' This is the pivot on which Coward turns away from the up-to-date manner and musical commentary of *This Year of Grace!* towards a 'little romantic renaissance'. When Coward adds that 'very soon, a few of the preliminary melodies began to form in my head' he signals that music was leading the way in filling out the detail of the world that began with atmospheric imagery.

Coward distinguishes this change of emotional emphasis in *Bitter Sweet* by the extent of its musicalization. Large-scale musical structures in popular works of the lyric stage – operas, operettas and musical comedies – drew from a range of forms. Such an approach to dramatic musicalization in a particularly successful and local variant is shown through the Savoy Operas of Gilbert and Sullivan, which provided some of Coward's earliest exposure to the light lyric stage. Here, the embracing descriptor 'opera' is a catch-all for an opera-operetta blend, often parodic or as pastiche, that also includes excursions into light popular ballads, dialogue used to minimize (but not replace) opera recitative or arioso styles of 'speech set to music', and melodrama, in which atmospheric music underscores speech and mime/gesture. The stage conventions also include choruses to set a scene and a place (the opening chorus of pretty much every first act does this), or to be a witness to a dramatic conflict reaching peak unpleasantness before an interval curtain. Other sections, whether vocal or instrumental, provide relief from the main storyline, or its suspenseful pausing (especially in ensembles), or simply move the action to another place and another mood in the spirit of 'and next . . .' or 'meanwhile . . .'. These are the musical markers of opera absorbed to shifting degrees into late Victorian comic opera, adapted for operetta and assimilated by emerging musical comedy. Coward's use of 'musical comedy' embraces this complexity, rather than reduces it to the 1920s play-song sandwiches of 'slick American musical farces', which is perhaps where we tend to place the definition today when the Princess shows of Kern, for example, are presented as more formative in a Broadway-centred musical theatre history than the Gaiety shows of the West End.

Coward considered that the success of the musical comedies of his youth was rooted in the music of such composers as Lionel Monckton, Paul Rubens, Ivan Caryll and Leslie Stuart. Moreover, 'it was in the completeness of their scores that their real strength lay: opening choruses, finales, trios, quartettes and concerted numbers – all musicianly, all well balanced and all beautifully constructed' (Coward 1953: 9–10). This accounts for the expansion of musical form in *Bitter Sweet* and the underlying attraction it held for Coward. It is wrong, though, to assume this was a return to old-fashioned practice. Such complex musical structuring was to be found in the high-profile American operetta imports in the West End in the 1920s through shows from the composers Sigmund Romberg and Rudolf Friml. Romberg's shows *The Student Prince* (His Majesty's Theatre, 2 March 1926), *The Desert Song* (Theatre Royal, Drury Lane, 7 April 1927) and *The New Moon* (Theatre Royal, Drury Lane, 4 April 1929) and Friml's *The Vagabond King* (Winter Garden, 18 April 1927) and earlier (with Herbert Stothart) *Rose Marie* (Theatre Royal, Drury Lane, 20 March 1925) were successful on the London stage in the years immediately prior to *Bitter Sweet*, with *The New Moon* opening earlier in the same year as *Bitter Sweet*.

All these Broadway operettas have historically and/or geographically distanced settings, which justify the visual excitement of elaborate costumes and scenery. In their Act I finales, in particular, they demonstrate melodrama, recitative, arioso, ensemble, chorus and solo melody in fluid, extended sections. Coward's polarization quoted earlier of older West End musical comedy versus American musical comedy is not what audiences had plentiful opportunity to experience through the 1920s. Furthermore, European operetta was not in favour in the West End in the years immediately after the First World War (Scott 2014: 62–3). American imports (albeit with continental origins through émigré composers) ably filled a gap to allow some stylistic continuity with operetta conventions (Platt 2004: 139).

Nonetheless, it is worth remembering that continental operetta was seen in large-scale productions in the West End into the 1930s. For example, Lehár's *The Land of Smiles* opened at the Theatre Royal, Drury Lane, in May 1931, with Richard Tauber as the starring tenor, who returned for the revival of *Lilac Time* at the Aldwych in September 1933 (Scott 2014: 66). The stylistic regression from 1920s dance band to operetta waltz in the opening scene of *Bitter Sweet* was as much an assertion of an alternative aesthetic that was current within musical theatre in the West End as a regressive step towards pre-war nostalgia. Cultural status played a part too, with the music of operetta considered to have a more serious intent, signalled not least by the technical musical demands made of the performers (Scott 2014: 70–1). Just as Coward's publicity photograph of breakfast in bed suggested an upper-class status, so the writing of a complete operetta laid claim to an elevated musical status, especially in swapping contemporary syncopation for period sophistication.

Coward reacted against what he expressed as a musical deficiency in English composers of light music in the 1920s in not creating 'integrated scores' (Coward 1953: 11). For the few he held in esteem – principally Ivor Novello but also Vivian Ellis – the shows he commends are of the 1930s and 1940s. Novello 'upheld almost alone, our old traditions of Musical Comedy'. Coward's emphatic repetition reinforces his point, and he continues to identify Novello's 'true quality' in 'the openings, finales, choral interludes and incidental themes he wrote to please himself ... a much finer quality than most people realized' (1953: 10–11). Solos, duets, ensembles and choruses provide the takeout melodies, but the linking sections allow the musical element to be sustained through narrative action. Importantly, this allows the music to develop its own dramatic integrity through recurring themes and melodies alongside the atmospheric qualities of varied texture and tempo. This is not the way the music flows through a revue, in which discrete sections aim for variety and contrast of material. Revue doesn't have the same sort of storytelling and has less recourse to sustained dramatic arcs heightened by musical themes that gradually intensify in significance. This characterization holds true in the general thrust of the way the music was deployed in shows that portrayed modern life in modern settings with modern dance tunes at the centre of their scores. The comment mentioned earlier from Coward regarding the 'Vo do deo do' style of American import musicals ties into his observation of the musical limitations of such shows, which have been pared down to a succession of discrete popular song melodies hammered home through repetition and separated clearly by dialogue.

A stylistic opposition had evolved from around the 1890s which contrasted the 'historical romanticism' of operetta against the 'modernity' and 'self-consciously up-to-date' content and presentation of musical comedy in which songs were interpolated into a narrative conveyed in everyday speech (Platt 2004: 29–30). It is Coward's creative persona in 1929 and his desire to expand his existing talents that creates the tension in how to approach *Bitter Sweet* as he moves from a dialogue-led genre of his present day to a music-led one with a history.

Operetta through a modern lens

By the end of the 1920s, Coward's track record invited an expectation of contemporary tendencies including American musical comedy. The rise of the curtain on *Bitter Sweet* fulfils this: the sound of the jazz band, the energy of the dancing couples and the noise of chatter and laughter from the other party guests 'should give an effect almost of pandemonium' (Coward 1933: 7). The party at Lady Shayne's house in Grosvenor Square is packed with Bright Young Things celebrating the imminent marriage of Dolly Chamberlain and her 'faintly pompous' upper-class fiancé, Henry Jekyll, and the time is 'Present Day' (Coward 1933: 7). Music, setting and tone are of 1929.

However, the operette is most readily recalled as 'swirling waltzes, lavish costumes and luxurious sets . . . – a spectacle of melody and colour which swept all before it' (Hoare 1995: 204). In the opening scene, the elderly Lady Shayne urges the young people to grab their romantic chances. Her sung message 'The Call of Life' is revealed by her story to be also 'the call of music', most intimately relayed through song as 'a call that echoes sweetly' (Coward 1933: 5–6). Coward raises the curtain on what seems to be a musical comedy, but next peels off that mask to reveal in swift stages the operette beneath. The body of the show acts out the youthful elopement of and its consequences for the now elderly Lady Shayne, taking her story back to 1875, 1880 and 1895 before returning for its 'Present Day' conclusion. There is a tantalizing misprint in the vocal score at the end of the opening jazz number, where the final word of the lyric 'play me a romantic melody' has morphed into 'memory' (Coward 1929: 5).

In Lady Shayne's youth, as Sarah Millick, she escapes her own engagement to a stuffy young aristocrat, the Hon. Hugh Devon, by eloping to Vienna with her singing teacher, Carl Linden. The first scene of flashback is a house in Belgrave Square in 1875, where Carl gives Sarah a singing lesson. Their desire to acknowledge openly their love is constrained by the formalities of Victorian class and gender roles but facilitated through song. As this is to be the last lesson before Sarah is married, it is also Carl's last chance to be alone with her. In a quasi-improvisatory song (with which Coward declared himself especially satisfied), Carl implies an escape that would lead Sarah 'secretly away' to his Austrian homeland, ending with the wish 'If you could only come with me'. The duet that follows, 'I'll See You Again', is a seduction in music, inevitably in waltz form, which anticipates musical Vienna too. The final phrase again ties love with sound in the 'echo of a sigh, Good-bye' (Coward 1933: 14–19). True love is musical. At exactly the wrong moment for the lovers, Sarah's mother and fiancé arrive, and the lesson ends.

At the ball later that same day, Sarah's anxiety over her imminent marriage is evident to her family and friends. Rejecting Hugh's stuffiness she launches into the waltz song 'What Is Love?' The music releases a new vibrancy within Sarah, and the words again link music and passion: 'play for me, set me free', her heart is 'beating' and an 'insane melody' is driving her on. In the refrain, 'voices echo' as they question 'what is love?' (Coward 1933: 17, 1929: 26) This is a classic waltz song, in which 'the quality of vertiginous momentum of the waltz's seemingly endless turning becomes an analogue for heady, unexpected feelings' (Snelson 2017: 246). It is noticeable just how many sections in the rolling 3/4 of waltz time are spread through the first act of *Bitter Sweet*, which reinforces why the title of the show in France became *Au Temps des Waltzes*. True, in Vienna in Act II there is an instrumental waltz and Manon's song 'Kiss Me' (again, on the subject of love), but there is so much more 4/4 time ('Dear Little Café', 'If Love Were All' and 'Bonne Nuit, Merci') and the bouncy energy of compound 6/8 rhythms ('Ladies of the Town' and 'Tokay'). Once past the framing devices of the fast 4/4 syncopated jazz melody for the song 'That Wonderful Melody', Act I advances musically through a near-omnipresent three-time pulse. The dominant metaphor for love is music: love makes couples in time with, in tune with and irresistibly appealing to each other.

At the show's opening, Dolly is enamoured of the jazz band's pianist Vincent rather than her fiancé. She asks Vincent to 'play something romantic', quoting the show's opening song. The resulting 'few bars of a swift jazz tune' is a trigger for Lady Shayne who hears not romance but something 'hideous'. To her, the music is proof that the young people's romantic dreams are 'nightmares' and their 'conception of life grotesque'. To demonstrate her point she insists they 'listen' (Coward 1933: 10). Her critique of the young's misguided notion of romance is set to a waltz rhythm. The young guests challenge her by cutting in with the duple time of a lively Charleston, followed by a slow 4/4 blues. This is a contrast of modern and period dance styles as well as emotional associations. In Lady Shayne's next waltz-time riposte, she condemns the late 1920s view of romance as 'a fire without a flame'. Again, the party guests challenge her perspective – back in 4/4 – as they have 'no time to waste on / Love ideals'. Lady Shayne counters – in waltz time – with her idea of love as something that can last as 'a memory when / Youth is gone' (Coward 1929: 4–9).

Coward's use of music is dramaturgical. The temporal and stylistic polarity is the dramatic centre: 'We have the foxtrot and its extremities, and the "Blue Danube" valse as its centrifugal force, or to put it in simpler terms, we have an old lady in this present year of grace telling her history in the days of her youth' (Findon 1929a: 38). But the stylistic significance goes further than that contemporary critique suggests. Through the juxtaposition of periods in the story, Coward uses music from popular America for the 1920s and styles of European operetta, dominated by the waltz, for the nineteenth-century part of the story. *Bitter Sweet* is thus a turn away from American culture and a return towards a European focus. With that at its core, the waltzes roll through the flashback to Sarah Millick's youth and her own elopement with her musician, Carl. The progression is led by 'I'll See You Again'. 'What Is Love?', a performance at the engagement ball, follows the pattern of the waltz of emotional discovery established through opera, comic opera and operetta (Snelson 2017: 247–8). The ball ends with 'The Last Dance', which – in 3/4 time – concludes with a reminder that often 'the last waltz / Is the birth of romance'. The youthful guests waltzing at Sarah's party in 1875 are a musical and visual counterpoint to those dancing the Charleston in the 1929/'present day' opening scene.

The finale of the act begins with a scene of Blind Man's Buff during which Sarah catches Carl. As the game is prepared, the music is dominated by a bright waltz whose spinning energy reaches Sarah as an enthralling sound that echoes in her heart and calls to her 'like a melody far away'. The musicalization of the textual imagery is again prominent. A slower section in 3/4, anticipatory with its chromatically drooping melody, prepares the way for Carl's entrance and capture. A restatement for both Carl and Sarah of the waltz 'I'll See You Again' marks Sarah's decision to leave her fiancé and seek a new future with Carl. The deal is sealed. The interruption by a quartet of footmen begins a musical coda that, now that love has found its way, moves the pace to 4/4, in anticipation of the concluding musical statement of the act, a reprise of 'The Call of Life', the show's 'big tune' of optimism for the future.

The symbiosis between love, life and music continues throughout *Bitter Sweet*. Significant moments are not just musicalized but about musical performance. In Act II, Sarah – now named Sari Linden – is a singer, Carl is a violinist and composer, his jealous friend Manon is a singer, and they all work professionally as entertainers in a Viennese café. In Act III, now in 1895 in Lord Shayne's house in London, the singing star Sari Linden is expected. Her career has been made in Europe performing the songs of her dead husband, killed in a duel in the Vienna café in which they worked. The upper-class guests recognize Sari as Sarah Millick from their youth. In her rendition for them of a passionate waltz song by Carl, 'Zigeuner', love, biography, reminiscence and performance come together: it tells of a princess wooed from loneliness by the music of a gipsy, which makes her spirit soar, and whose 'barbaric tune' calls to her. Despite its clear three-in a bar notation, the performance character includes marked changes of pace and pauses that help emphasize by contrast the stricter rhythmic accompaniment to the title word and the central portion of the main refrain. Contemporary recordings made by the original performers of the role – Peggy Wood (London), Evelyn Laye (New York) and Jane Marnac (Paris) – share a highly stylized manner of musical presentation. With a nod from Coward to such operetta siren songs as 'Vilia' in Lehár's

Die lustige Witwe (*The Merry Widow*), the fairy-tale scene of 'Zigeuner' mythologizes Sarah's enduring love for Carl, set within a performance by Sarah of Carl's song in a return to a social and physical situation that recalls Act I, when the audience first encountered the young lovers.

In a final twist, the show ends back in the 'present day' to round off the flashback that constitutes the body of the show. The conclusion is provided through music. Dolly is ready to elope with Vincent. Vincent is completely taken by the tune of 'I'll See you Again', but he hears the melody, not the meaning. He finds his 4/4 syncopated version more fascinating than Dolly. This confirms Lady Shayne's criticism: modern jazz-style love lacks the depth and endurance of her waltz-time love with Carl. The music switches to 3/4, and the final words are sung by Lady Shayne: 'I shall love you till I die, Goodbye.' As the full orchestra repeats the phase 'loudly and grandly', Sarah-Sari-Lady Shayne walks slowly off stage.

The message of *Bitter Sweet* is easily understood as the fondness for a fading or lost past, an exercise in nostalgia. Time is a recurrent theme, made explicit through the lyrics of many numbers in the show, as Dominic McHugh has noted (2016: 453). But Coward – aged only twenty-nine – was writing for his day, not trying to magic away the previous thirty years, as the contemporary framing device shows. Rather, Coward is commenting on shifting values through the comparative juxtaposition already evident in *This Year of Grace!*. Ben Macpherson captures this aspect of being tethered to the present rather than released completely into the past when he notes that 'Far from being outmoded, the very title of *Bitter Sweet* is perhaps symptomatic of the popular culture of the era – caught inexorably between prewar nostalgia and interwar reality, in a double bind that echoes the tensions between urban modernity and rural traditions in *The Arcadians* or *Our Miss Gibbs*' (2018: 186–7).

Subsequent musical theatre works

Coward's variations on the features of older musical comedy and operetta in his later works have been widely seen as the response of a composer increasingly out of touch and unable to adapt. Yet there was no single style of musical theatre in the 1920s and 1930s, but rather a mixed active repertory year on year. Audiences were mixed in age and taste. To cater for this range, shows were too. Coward's experimentation in the 1930s happens against a backdrop of considerably more than a slew of new light musical comedies. Prominent within the West End repertory were the Continental operettas of Franz Lehár and Robert Stolz as well as the developing home-grown operetta hybrids of Ivor Novello and George Posford.

To have European characters played by European performers of considerable reputation in recently created operetta-style shows was not unusual. For example, to Richard Tauber in Lehár's *Land of Smiles*, Coward added Yvonne Printemps in *Conversation Piece* and Fritzi Massary in *Operette*. Settings that were historically or geographically removed were routine, as with the travel brochure images of Austria in *White Horse Inn* or of Hungary as portrayed in *Paprika/Magyar Melody* (Snelson 2017: 252–5). Regency Brighton for *Conversation Piece* is exotic in its own way as is

Coward's invented island of Samolo in *Pacific 1860*. The show-within-a-show device was familiar in musical theatre too, such that the onstage-backstage-offstage affairs around an Edwardian musical comedy in *Operette* fit a wider West End pattern that was to continue in 1940s shows that included Novello's *Arc de Triomphe* and Harry Parr-Davies and Harold Purcell's *The Lisbon Story*. Taking all this together, to view Coward as an independent maverick stuck in the past is to diminish both the West End narrative and Coward's contemporary theatrical awareness.

Coward's theatricality becomes intensely self-reflexive in *Operette*, which was conceived to present in London the German stage star Fritzi Massary. Coward admired her as a performer, but she was also Jewish, and the show created an opportunity for her to leave Berlin. *Operette* had its West End premiere in 1938. The music-led core of *Bitter Sweet* has its parallel in a theatre-led core in *Operette*, in which the backstage lives of a theatre company are juxtaposed with scenes from the show they are performing, an (imagined) Edwardian musical comedy, *The Model Maid*. References to theatre life and to styles of musical theatre were thus the focus. It was not a success with audiences. It lacked the memorable musicality of Coward at his best, and audiences were confused by the dual identities of the actors in *Operette* who also played characters in *The Model Maid*. The biggest melodic success of the score, the waltz song 'Dearest Love', comes within *The Model Maid* and thus consciously is presented as a song from an Edwardian show, even though its musical style is that of the 1930s.

This theatrical reflexivity is Coward through and through – a meditation on what he knew best and loved most. While *Operette* could be interpreted as an introspective indulgence it can be appreciated more positively as the single-minded sharing by Coward of what made him tick. Twenty years before, Coward was briefly called up for military service. He spent most of it unwell. When finally discharged, his journey home passed familiar sights. Before he had achieved any of his 1920s success, his sense of where home was and what mattered to him was clear:

> The hot August sun . . . beat down upon the Gaiety, the Vaudeville, the Savoy, and the Adelphi theatres and I pictured as I passed them the cool pre-matinée gloom of their interiors: cleaners swishing dust-sheets from the boxes and dress circles, under-studies meandering about their stages under a working light, clutching scripts and mumbling inaudibly with an occasional sharp interruption from the front of the house, and strong shafts of alien sunlight striking down from open doors, and from the flies on to forlorn detached pieces of scenery; backings and flats against white-washed walls, unfinished staircases and shorn fragments of balustrade waiting about untidily to be set in Act One symmetry by the staff at two 'o'clock. I almost wept with sentimental love for it all. (Coward 1986: 62–3).

Summing up this life consumed by theatre, in 1958 Coward wrote, 'I am still, and probably for ever will be, incurably stage-struck' (Trewin 1958: 6). With this in mind, *Operette* has the impetus of a personal manifesto in how it uses onstage–offstage parallels between life and art – challenging the values of 'the usual Chorus Girl and Peer business' – to address the significance of theatre (Coward 1939b: 261). As the leading lady Liesl says to the up-and-coming Rozanne, for whom heart or career has become a painful choice, 'We are in the theatre now, and the theatre comes first' (Coward 1939b: 313). The end of the show mirrors that of the final exit of Lady Shayne in *Bitter Sweet*, with that earlier operette's focus on the centrality of musical expression redirected to Coward's parallel love for dramatic expression: 'Rozanne walks slowly into the wings as – the curtain falls' (Coward 1939b: 317).

Coward controlled his theatrical vision across writing, composing, performing and directing. The silent, monochrome filmed footage made in 1930 by Pathé of sections of the original stage production of *Bitter Sweet* documents Coward's stagecraft in positioning the cast and animating the drama. Movements are clear, deliberate and measured – 'Ladies of the Town' involves minimal gestures at what are clearly the ends of stanzas, leaving the vocal delivery as the focus, played straight out to the audience. In 'Green Carnation', the line of four young aristocrats reproduces the familiar aesthetic pose, described in the similarly titled novel that scandalously satirized Oscar Wilde, Lord Alfred Douglas and their set: 'left knee slightly bent, and his arms hanging at his sides, gazing as a woman gazes at herself before she starts for a party' (Anonymous [Robert Hichens] 1894: 1). Jumping forward a decade, a detailed description of Coward rehearsing the cast at the Music Box theatre for the Broadway opening of *Set to Music* records his attention to detail and precision in every part of the performance and staging.

> You have only to watch Coward once rehearsing to realize that, for better or worse, the show that bears his name will be a 100 percent Noël Coward show when it is introduced to the public – even though, as in this instance, he is not appearing in it. His versatility, his theatre sense, is nowhere seen to better advantage than in the grind of day and night rehearsals. He is everywhere; he does everything; he knows exactly what he wants.[2]

It is then not surprising that everything from text to props list is essential in imaginative recreations of Coward's original intentions and how they were implemented. We have Pathé's filmed extracts of *Bitter Sweet* in 1930 and production photographs in newspapers and such theatrically dedicated magazines as *Play Pictorial* (vol. lv, no. 330). To these we can superimpose such extra details as the women's chorus dresses in Scene iii, in the Millick's ballroom. Rather than a Beaton-style 'Ascot Gavotte' before the event, the suggested colours for the dresses – different for each woman – head more towards *Joseph and the Amazing Technicolor Dreamcoat* in a list that includes pale blue, red, pink, mauve, grey, white and cerise, terra-cotta, pale pink and apple-green as well as some duotone shot silks, and all with different tones of trim too (Coward 1933: 50). We too easily forget that monochrome, still photography needs to be reimagined with all the movement, colour and sound of performance to bring us anywhere near an appreciation of the theatrical experience.

The Second World War prevented Coward from presenting a new, large-scale musical work. Popular music moved on too. After the war, Coward's *Pacific 1860* (1946) seemed dated. There are many contributory factors to the lack of success of the show intended to reopen the Theatre Royal, Drury Lane, after its wartime use as the base for the military forces' Entertainments National Service Association (ENSA). Coward's great patriotic hit *Cavalcade* (1931) commenced what was to prove an impressively memorable decade for home-grown musical theatre at Drury Lane (including Novello's first four shows). Wartime work in entertainment had bolstered Coward's reputation for embodying 'Britishness'. The pairing of that theatre and a new musical created great expectations. Insufficient rehearsal, miscasting, technical problems, including with the fabric of the theatre, and even a bitterly cold winter played their part, as has been described elsewhere (Payn and Morley 1982: 69–71, 73; Morley 1987: 109–10; Hoare 1995: 369–70). For this chapter, the significance comes with problems in the work itself, notably the musical structure. Where *Bitter Sweet*'s structure signalled its purpose effectively at each stage, *Pacific 1860* lacked flow. Some numbers, for example, 'Dear Madame Salvador' and the opening musicalized encounter between Elena Salvador (Mary Martin) and Kerry Stirling (Graham Payn), suggest Coward was building on the natural musical fluidity of *Bitter Sweet*'s 'If you could only come with me'. Others have Coward's characteristic wit and attention to detail but are so reminiscent of previous Coward numbers as to seem at times generic – witness the lengthy, wordy song 'His Excellency Regrets'. Overall, the music proceeds as a succession of discrete numbers. It is not the type of holistic score to which Coward aspired.

More credit could be given to *Ace of Clubs* in how Coward actively changed towards a different model of musical theatre more directly related to recent Broadway practice. He signals musical comedy, not operetta, through the formal pattern of ballads for characters set against chorus numbers mainly led by the nightclub showgirls and alternating throughout with dialogue – no recitative-inspired vocal setting and no use of extended musical forms for finales. And instead of adopting a setting that had been distanced by period or location, *Ace of Clubs* reflected a localized London of its own day (Snelson 2023). Coward was moving towards what we can recognize as a *Pal Joey*-*Guys and Dolls* mash-up of tropes set in contemporary Soho although – as his diary entry for 27 December 1949 makes clear – before Coward had seen either American show (Payn and Morley 1982: 138).

With *After the Ball*, a musicalization of Oscar Wilde's *Lady Windermere's Fan*, Coward reverted to previous form in his search for a connection with the post-war audience. He was drawn again to subject matter whose Victorian setting invited the aura of the musical theatre of Coward's youth. Again, Coward did not generate a hit. Again, the music is more defined by interpolated individual numbers than by an overarching musical construction. The ebullient verbal play in the lyrics draws attention from the opening 'Oh What a Century It's Been' (another characterizing quartet in the manner of 'Green Carnations' and 'The Stately Homes of England') through to the late song 'Something on a Tray'. There is also an engagingly fluid and lyrical style in such songs for Mr Hopper as 'May I Have the Pleasure' and 'Faraway Land'. However, the more dramatic numbers for the leading ladies lack the emotional charge Coward had generated in *Bitter Sweet*. As with *Pacific 1860*, there are narratives that explain the failure of casting, structure, rehearsal issues, orchestration and so on in valid and theatrically pragmatic terms, but the result was what it was. It was Coward's last attempt to recapture something of the musical sweep of his initial operetta success. Coward's final show, for Broadway then revised for London in 1962, is *Sail Away*, firmly approached as a post-war American musical.

McHugh concludes that the 'vibrant colours' of an 'individualized palette' are what distinguishes Coward's style, with the result that 'his musicals are not anachronistic but sui generis' (2016: 458). We can see a steadfast pursuit of individuality in Coward's use of the familiar in unfamiliar combinations – and with steps back as well as forward. This can be appreciated too as a problem of timing that also influenced the works of Ivor Novello, as we will see in the next chapter. Coward's birth set him uncomfortably on the border between nineteenth-century established ideas and emerging twentieth-century popular styles from the other side of the Atlantic: he was not quite old enough to be entirely subsumed by the former and not quite young enough to exist solely within the latter. That Coward was never quite to recapture so whole a conception of the lyric stage after *Bitter Sweet* does not, however, detract from its skill, appeal and significance. Rather, it could point to a time, just on the border of the 1930s, when the balance between looking back and embracing the new was in happy equilibrium for Coward's musical theatre talents.

Viewed from a distance

As early as 1934, Coward explained that *Bitter Sweet* had given him

> more complete satisfaction than anything else I have ever written up till now. Not especially on account of its dialogue, or its lyrics, or its music, or its production, but as a whole. In the first place, it achieved and sustained the original mood of its conception more satisfactorily than a great deal of my other work. And in the second place, that particular mood of seminostalgic sentiment . . . did seem to me to be well done, and I felt accordingly very happy about it. (Coward 1934: xii)

For Coward, the integrity of the work and the sincerity of its emotional portrayals were crucial. With that in mind, the distortions the work underwent on film alone within a decade of its premiere have not sustained a fair impression of what satisfied Coward or appealed so effectively to those first audiences on both sides of the Atlantic. The New York production opened at the Ziegfeld Theatre on 5 November 1929 when Evelyn Laye had a great success as Sarah-Sari-Lady Shayne. The simple figure of the length of run of the show is of limited value in assessing artistic success or significance of the work – in this case, 159 performances to 22 March 1930. The Wall Street Crash at the end of October impacted Broadway theatre for some time, and *Bitter Sweet* was one of the casualties. A production in Budapest followed swiftly on 6 December 1929, while a Paris production opened on 2 April 1930.

The first film version was made in Britain with Michael Wilcox as director and released in 1933. Its opening minutes capture well the central generational identity conveyed through music. As a jazz band plays, the camera pans round to capture mostly feet and hands of some of the dancers and then across the line of musicians, whose nervous energy is conveyed through fast tapping feet, moving fingers on woodwind, strumming guitars, the fast plucking of a double bass and hands moving over the piano keyboard. The scene shows youth, energy and modernity. The camera pans further round, then zooms in on the tapping foot of a lady in a black dress seated on a terrace, her face hidden by her fan. It is a small change of focal centre and neatly done cinematically. However, the tapping foot belongs to the elderly Lady Shayne, the last person to indulge modern music. The film's conclusion retains the stage show's return to the present and the 'jazzing' of 'I'll See You Again' so that – despite that distraction of the wrong person's foot tapping – the intention behind Coward's framing device is maintained.

The use of 'The Call of Life' for the transition from 1929 to 1875 is less successful in the film, as the frail singing of the elderly Lady Shayne proves to be that of the young Sarah Millick too. Costume, hair and set indicate the transition backwards in time, but the thin-toned, quavering voice of Anna Neagle – she was not quite thirty when she played the part – did not. The script retains the elopement from the party and the Vienna section of the story but skips the 1895 return to London. The resilience of Lady Shayne, which is to be shown as her past life is played out for us, is lost in the delivery of her first lines, which exchange the barb and irony of the character in the script for the ingratiating charm of the film actress. The focus is on the distant, tragic romance of a harmless elderly lady more than the character growth from Sarah to Sari to Lady Shayne in the stage show. The film undercuts the progression to admirable strength that the stage show portrays powerfully through Lady Shayne's final, slow and solitary walk off the stage. Coward's script and score are recognizably the basis of the film, if edited, but the tonal force is weakened throughout as Coward's 'seminostalgic sentiment' becomes sentimental nostalgia.

The Hollywood film version was built around the bankable pairing of Jeanette MacDonald and Nelson Eddy. It was released in 1940, and Coward considered that it was 'vulgar, lacking in taste and bore little relation to my original story' (Coward 1986: 419). In it, 'seminostalgic sentiment' is subservient to the construction of star brands through comforting Hollywood clichés. It is thus particularly unfortunate that its original distribution, prominence as a lavishly produced MGM film musical and its longevity (available on DVD or streamed online) make it the dominant audiovisual reference for the show today. It has almost nothing of the bite of the original dialogue and little of the music in the situations for which it was intended. New lyrics imposed on Coward's music lack the precision of imagery, vocabulary and execution of the originals – for example, 'Dear Little Café' includes such replacement couplets as 'My little princess / For dessert we'll have blintzes'. Indeed, the production seems obsessed with food, using the acquiring of it in Vienna (a shortcut signal to the American audience of European poverty) as the pretext for comic routines for Carl and Sari (both attempting to give singing lessons in exchange for a chicken) as well as for Carl's Viennese friends Max and Ernst (with, inevitably, prominent continental sausage).

Where the film tips into a whole other level is in the finale. This presents the conclusion of the stage premiere of the late Carl Linden's operetta *Zigeuner*, with his widow Sari Linden in the starring role. The song 'Zigeuner' is given the full Technicolor MGM makeover, with elaborate, stylized Hungarian costumes – MacDonald wears a headdress reminiscent of an albino peacock – and a stage set that extends by film magic into a village packed with dancing locals. The premiere is a huge success, a triumph for Sari's performance and a fitting memorial to Carl's musical talent cut short all too soon.

Still in her full Hungarian stage costume, Sari returns alone to the tiny flat she shared with Carl. She sings the final lines of 'I'll See You Again' in duet with his ethereal voice and floating head. The only indication of temporal shifting comes at the start of the film as an elderly lady reminisces on the love of her youth in order to flashback for the whole of the rest of the film. The film is an exercise in being sentimental. It packages up emotion for its own sake, bereft of any sensitivity to the musico-dramatic construction that powers the original stage show.

Almost a decade later on radio, MacDonald as a guest performer on 'The Railroad Hour' played Sarah in a heavily edited version of *Bitter Sweet* opposite the radio show's regular presenter and star, Gordon MacRae, as Carl.[3] The broadcast on 31 March 1949 was one of the condensed musicals in a series that routinely prioritized the music over the narrative. The story was kept as the barest prop for the songs, with the focus completely on Sarah and Carl, the only two dramatized characters, although a chorus occasionally adds to the musical depth. Inevitably much is lost, although Manon's poignant song 'If Love Were All' is retained through its reallocation to Carl, as a comment on his life as a performing musician. The series was sponsored by the American Association of Railroads, which accounts for a third of the forty-five-minute show being taken up with the promotion of railroads as a national asset and an investment opportunity. Consequently, the identity of Coward's operette was yet again distorted, with this adaptation prioritizing the clichéd period romance and a few self-contained hit songs above any wider generational and cultural commentary or musico-dramatic development.

On disc, recordings of some of the main songs were made in June 1929 to be commercially available for the show's opening (advertisements for Columbia recordings from the current shows and with their original casts were a regular feature in programme books and theatre magazines of the time). The original London cast included are Peggy Wood (Sarah-Sari), George Metaxa (Carl) and Ivy St Helier (Manon) accompanied by the orchestra of His Majesty's Theatre. Jane Marnac (Sarah-Sari) and Raymond Bussy (Carl) recorded a few numbers too in Paris in April 1930 in conjunction with the opening of the French production. These early recordings allow us to hear the music as first presented to the public and with the original theatre orchestrations. Jumping forward to the studio recording of 1958 with Vanessa Lee and Roberto Cardinali, the musical romanticization of the sound is clear in the slower speeds, broader rubato and the considerably more indulgent, instrumentally prettified arrangements. Luxuriating in the quality of the sound takes precedence over dramatic impetus, unsurprising in a studio recording of 'hit tunes'. In 1958 it played – literally – to its immediate commercial audience, and both addressed and reinforced the sentimentalization of the sound, which reflects back on to the understanding of the work. The love story is made consistently warm and inviting. For example, in the duet 'Dear Little Café' Lee and Cardinali's performances are intimate but taken at a very slow pace in comparison to the evidence from 1929, in which the double bass (placed too near to the microphone to judge by the more subtle sound balance of the same arrangement in the French recording) can be heard making clear the regularity that identifies the song's origins in a 1920s foxtrot. The extensive TER recording of the *Bitter Sweet* score that came out of the 1988 stage production in London at Sadler's

Wells conveys, despite a few cuts and rearrangements, the importance of Coward's structural conception.

The various adaptations chart the progress from Coward's own work to the reputational golden glow of what it is assumed Coward intended. Unfortunately, the chance of correcting this through the experience of a professional performance today is unlikely, although one would hope not entirely impossible. A vital process with several of the works studied in detail in this book, and the even less familiar repertory that accompanies them, is to use what resources there are to establish what the work was at first, not what it is thought to have become. *Bitter Sweet* is better served than many with some silent footage of its original stage production and the recordings from original casts. Filmed adaptations and later recorded interpretations allow for constructive comparison. As we will see with the following chapters, despite the significance or fame of the works, few have quite the range of resources to draw upon as Coward's *Bitter Sweet*. It is only with the last and most recent of the case studies – Lionel Bart's *Oliver!* – that we reach an equivalent and accessible range of materials to evoke the original stage show.

Within Coward's musical theatre repertory, *Bitter Sweet* has the advantage of being known because it was a formative hit. This is also a disadvantage. It set an expectation of what could have followed, which influenced judgements over what did follow. There is no comparable lyric-stage success for Coward after *Bitter Sweet*, although his last show, *Sail Away*, comes closer than any of the others. That first–last opposition illustrates how Coward straddles the evolution of musical theatre in form, itself related to the changing nature of popular music. In short, *Bitter Sweet* was of its time, then became out of date. *Sail Away* was of its time, but that relative modernity has fared better down the years. It has styles of music, an approach to language and a series of character types that if not current are nonetheless still familiar: mid-century musicals rather than pre-war operetta. That said, for both shows, it is still individual songs – 'I'll See You Again', 'If Love Were All' and 'Green Carnation' or 'Sail Away', 'The Passenger's Always Right' and 'Why Do the Wrong People Travel?' – rather than the entirety of shows that have kept them in the minds of musical theatre enthusiasts while fading from the memory of a more general public.

3

Me and My Girl (1937)

Lupino Lane, Noel Gay, L. Arthur Rose and Douglas Furber

Two names are indelibly associated with the musical comedy *Me and My Girl*: star performer Lupino Lane and songwriter Noel Gay. The lilting title song became a hit, but another number, 'The Lambeth Walk', has overshadowed the show's identity ever since the 1937 premiere, even when the show itself fell out of the repertory in the 1960s and 1970s. The show is a vibrant container for complementary elements of light entertainment: contemporary caricature, popular song, farce-led script, and verbal and visual low comedy delivered true to type by an established performer (the 'name' on the poster). It was created to give Lupino Lane a second outing for his character Bill Snibson from *Twenty to One* (1935) but not as a continuation of that show's story. *Me and My Girl*'s popularity was sustained by Lupino's name and performing presence through to the 1950s (West End in 1941, 1945 and 1949) as well as extensive touring and repertory productions, and even with Lupino's son Lauri taking over from his father. After a couple of decades in the shadows, it was given a new lease of life by a revival in a revised form in February 1985 in the West End. It ran at the Adelphi Theatre for a month short of eight years. The same production became a hit on Broadway, at the Marquis Theatre from August 1986 to December 1989. Further professional revivals and amateur performances have made it one of the most familiar of all British musicals written before 1960.

The story of *Me and My Girl* comprises familiar elements. Bill Snibson is a working-class cockney from Lambeth in London who discovers he is heir to the title Earl of Hareford. To inherit he must satisfy two trustees that he is a proper person to do so and will marry accordingly, or else he will be given a small allowance in exchange for retiring into obscurity. One trustee, the formidable Duchess of Dene, wants the family line to continue, so Bill must be turned into an upper-class gentleman and marry someone of the right class, regardless of love. But Bill loves Sally, also a cockney. Sir John Tremayne, the other trustee, is more realistic: Bill should follow his heart, not the title. When provoked to best the Duchess, Sir John secretly arranges to have Sally transformed to pass as upper class. Bill gets the girl and the title. Curtain.

The plot has remained constant from the first script in 1937 to the revised version of 1985, but details have changed. The ideas are not original, with Gänzl describing 'a story particularly redolent of *Over She Goes*', from 1936, in which one member of a music hall trio inherits a title, 'as well as a whole stretch of theatre from *Peg o'my Heart* to *Pygmalion*' (1986b: 469). That comparison signals how an originality of plot and script was not the driving force behind this show. This chapter explores what was.

Noel Gay and the popular touch

James Dillon White deduces in his biography of Lupino Lane that the essence of musical comedy is 'lilting tunes, a good comedian, and plenty of pretty girls', citing this 'usual musical comedy formula' in respect of *Silver Wings* (London, 1930) in which Lane appeared (1957: 202). The definition fitted *Me and My Girl* too when it first opened in London: 'Lupino Lane and George Graves see to it that their busy business of fun-making, interspersed with song and the sunniness of pretty girls in athletic and graceful dance and movement, runs with admirable smoothness and expert timing.'[1] Instead of the holistically conceived musical concept that informed Coward's *Bitter Sweet*, Noel Gay composed songs for the show, with lyrics by Douglas Furber, that put the performer, the tune and an engagement with the specific performance moment at a premium. The script provides the structure and generates a narrative pretext that allow for popular songs and personalized comedic style to be contained within what is otherwise a straight farce. Such shows were conceived to satisfy the popular taste of the day and to divert in the theatrical moment. *Twenty to One* was for 'a music hall audience come for straightforward low comedy and some good marked tunes' (Gänzl 1986b: 430). This was the target audience for *Me and My Girl* too. The purpose explains why so few shows conceived in so localized a way have lasted much beyond their first productions, original personality casting and swiftly following revivals unless repackaged for a new audience and a new moment.

It took skill to fuse the disparate elements together in a satisfying way. The combination of script, music and performers had to be right, as did the balance between the comfort of genre convention and the detail of execution. The content needed to be distinctive too in providing takeout songs that contributed to branding the show, the ones you would have left the theatre humming, heard played by dance bands and on the radio, and probably recreated at home through singing and/or dancing to the piano (the domestic ubiquity of pianos and the amateur's ability to play them through to the 1940s and even the 1950s is something too easily overlooked). Songwriters had long sold numbers direct to music hall performers, who guarded their material as part of their unique stage identity and who spread familiarity with these songs through their tours round music halls the length and breadth of the country. The practice extended into recording, broadcasting and film as the technology for musical and visual dissemination expanded in the early decades of the twentieth century. Band leader Billy Cotton described the usual way songs made their mark in the interwar dance band repertory: 'You needed the writer, but you also needed the occasion and the man who had the opportunity to make it go straight away' (Cotton 1970: 99).

The programme for the original West End production of *Me and My Girl* at the Victoria Palace theatre (December 1937) lists for the first act an opening chorus and six named songs, and for the second an opening reprise, two named songs and a reprise finale. This would not constitute the necessary critical mass for the score of a two-act musical today. Even by 1954, when Samuel French published an acting edition, the show had acquired several more numbers. One main change for the 1985 revision was to replace some of the earlier songs with those from other sources and to expand the musical content into a 'jukebox' of Gay's output: 'The Sun Has Got His Hat On', 'Leaning on a Lamp-post' and 'Love Makes the World Go Round', and 'Hold my Hand' added for Broadway. With generous reprises, the new package has brought the composer as well as these songs to new generations of theatregoers.

Noel Gay was the professional name adopted by composer and lyricist Richard Moxon Armitage (he also wrote under the name Stanley Hill). He was trained as a musician, especially in church music as an organist, then contributed songs to West End revues including *Stop Press* (1926), André Charlot's 1926 revue and *Clowns in Clover* (1927, with Cicely Courtneidge and her husband Jack Hulbert). Gay's ability to hone appealing and memorable popular melodies led to his songs quickly being taken up by bands and consolidated in the public ear through radio broadcasts. His catchy successes tended towards such novelty numbers as 'Ali Baba's Camel' (1931), 'I Took My Harp to a Party' (1932), 'Run, Rabbit, Run' (1938) and 'That Started It' (1939) alongside those with an infectious cheerfulness, as with 'The Sun Has Got His Hat On' (1932) and 'Let the People Sing' (1939). Celebrity performers on record or in films contributed to the materials dissemination and prominence, such as Courtneidge's performance of 'There's Something About a Soldier' in *The Soldiers of the King* (1933), which annexed her own male impersonation persona from music hall. Courtneidge highlights the power to spread the word – or the song – through 'a film which people saw more than once; in fact, it was usually not so much a question of "Have you seen *Soldiers of the King*"? But how many times' (Courtneidge 1953: 119). Similarly, Jack Hulbert introduced Gay's upbeat 'Who's Been Polishing the Sun?' in *The Camels Are Coming* (1934) – catchy, repetitive, and animated on screen by Hulbert's loose-limbed dancing.

Romantic texts were matched by Gay with elegant lyricism within the familiar contours of structure, rhythms and speed that dance-band music required. There is an easy and compelling flow to the refrain of 'Melody Maker' (1939). The diatonic tune's easy roll gains a subtle propulsion through chromatic lines within the harmony. 'You've Done Something to My Heart' (also 1939) has similar appeal. Rhythm provides a key to Gay's approach to songs that capture the communal spirit of 'ordinary' people. This is heard in the martial assertiveness of 'The Fleet's in Port Again' (1936) from the London Palladium stage show *O-Kay for Sound*, and echoed in its film adaptation (1937, with the Crazy Gang) by 'The Fleet's Not in Port Very Long' as a finale appropriately assisted by the Band of HM Royal Marines, Chatham Division. The common touch is also conveyed in the jauntiness of dotted rhythms as in 'All Over the Place' (1939, *Sailors Three*, film with Tommy Trinder) and, relevant to *Me and My Girl*'s revision, 'Leaning on a Lamp-post' (1937, *Feather Your Nest*, film with George Formby).

Gay worked with many different lyricists, with his songwriting credits covering composer, composer and lyricist, co-lyricist and co-composer/lyricist. The creation of popular music from conception to performance is a collaborative process. With the extent of Gay's collaborations, he inhabits a different end of that creative scale from the methods of Noël Coward and Sandy Wilson (script, music and lyrics) or the clear delineation between author and musician of A. P. Herbert and Vivian Ellis. Over some twenty years, Gay's collaborators mostly as lyricists included Jos[eph]. Geo[rge]. Gilbert, Desmond Carter, Harry Graham, Clifford Gray, Frank Eyton (lyricist for *Twenty to One*) and Douglas Furber (lyricist for *Me and My Girl*). The collaborative aspect derives from the multiple outlets Gay's work exploited: for revue, within the structure of a musical comedy, for interpolation into film (with a known performer) or as a possible addition to the roster of free-standing popular songs for dance bands and presented by associated singers. With 'The Lambeth Walk' in *Me and My Girl*, he and Furber hit the bullseye on all fronts.

The classic British musical comedy

From the vantage point of the twenty-first century, *Me and My Girl* presents a musical comedy archetype on the lines of the formative 1890s–1900s model, which Len Platt summarizes as 'quaint, small-scale and "British" in a stereotypical way'. Crucially, Platt places this repertory in the time for which it was written, when such shows had 'a very different registration, one that resonated with important cultural concepts' (Platt 2004: 3). While *Me and My Girl* was written a few decades after the heyday of musical comedy creativity in the West End, it is driven by the same well-established qualities. It has too a contemporary side that plays directly to its own audience through the container of a familiar model comprising plot, narrative, script and musical register. These characteristics are heavily bound up with, even dominated by, an essence rooted in the live event. For what may appear a straightforward 1930s theatrical package, there are many points of influence and interpretation to untangle.

The structural markers of musical comedy are present in such song basics as an opening chorus to set the scene, takeout numbers for the romantic leads, lively comic ones for the subsidiary leads, and something for the chorus who generally acts as a body to witness events rather than provoke them, especially at the ends of acts. The dramatic basics begin with scenes that alternate between full-stage scenes and smaller-scaled ones that can be played in front of the tabs to allow for a set change to take place behind – with fewer songs than we would expect today. Scenes also alternate between different character pairings, which keeps the various strands of the plot in play, varies the onstage presentation and allows performers recuperative breaks offstage. The sentiment revolves around genuine love between the romantic leads, with other characters providing points of contrast and obstacles to be overcome. Older characters hold power, younger characters buck the system and win. Winning is always in the face of adversity and achieved only in the final moments before the final curtain. This approach to the light lyric stage was developed in comic opera and operetta, which carried through to emerging musical comedy. With the rebalancing of music (less of it) and script (more of it), the song-and-dance numbers gained more individual prominence that provided memorable anchors for characterization but also contributed less to the dramatic arc.

In plot, script and format, *Me and My Girl* can be read as a series of clichés. The first script submitted for licensing by the Lord Chamberlain dates from September 1937, only days before the first Nottingham performance. The Reader's Report for the licence picks out in its first line the perceived quality of what was on the page: 'One doesn't expect much from a Musical Comedy, but really the humour in this is positively abysmal.'[2] Such a judgement misses the centrality of the performer–audience relationship: the nature of this type of entertainment was of performance in the moment. There was an ease of acceptance for familiar situations and relationships that allowed the performers and audiences to focus on the instance of execution more than the theme and to revel in that familiarity. Performance personality mattered more than depth of script. Transient performance experience was the core focus. The decoration around the genre markers was more important than any novelty of form. After all, British comedy has never been above a satisfying groan at an old joke knowingly delivered, and pantomime still revels in it. The Lord Chamberlain's Reader did get it right in his final sentence: 'So all ends as usual.'

We can see this in action in some of the central performance pairings. In his book *How to Be a Comedian*, Lupino Lane devotes a short chapter each to 'Low Comedy' and 'Light Comedy'. Lane defines the low comedian through elements that match the portrayal of lower-class Snibson:

> Bad taste in clothes, saying the wrong thing at the right moment, and unconsciously building up trouble for oneself can be carried on to its full extent. The use of funny falls is an asset . . . The verbal side of low comedy is always on the broad side and, generally speaking, fairly obvious. . . . Being bullied and knocked around and always getting the worst of it, should always be the low comedian's lot. He should always be the round peg in a square hole. . . . He should never be able to learn his lesson, but should go on blithely asking for more trouble. At the moment of success, it should always be arranged that the result is a complete failure. . . . A low comedian should have up his sleeve – Acrobatic tricks, Funny falls . . . and have a general knowledge of slapstick comedy. (Lane 1945: 78–82)

High comedy – 'I should call this class of comedy, "Evening Dress or Drawing Room Comedy"' (Lane 1945: 83) – aligns much more with the upper-class role of Sir John Tremayne in *Me and My Girl*. It was created by George Graves, a veteran performer of high-status comic roles in operetta and musical comedy. Lane notes that 'laughs that are got in light comedy are not so big as in low comedy. In this method one goes in for a more subtle kind of gag.' He also implies the higher status of such characters when he lists the preparation he would have undertaken if a high-comedy style had suited him: 'Had my voice trained; been taught elocution; . . . studied repose; developed a certain amount of culture; gone to a good tailor; developed an air of light-heartedness and being irresponsible (on the stage); and last, but by no means least, got myself generally well-groomed' (Lane 1945: 86–7). Although neither Lane/Snibson nor Graves/Sir John sits at an extreme of the comic scale – Charlie Chaplin in contrast to Jack Buchanan, to use Lane's example of range – their personas are on opposing sides.

Sir John functions as a light comic foil in two directions. First, he provides a cross-class counterpoint. We see this as Sir John matches Snibson in alcohol consumption and parries with him in dialogue. This class dynamic between two leading male characters mirrors Lane's summary of the core of any comic double act, 'a light comedian and a low comedian working together' (Lane 1945: 119). Sir John also brings saucy innuendo to his conversation in Lambeth with Sally's landlady (which drew the censoring attention of the Lord Chamberlain). He is a benign avuncular figure too as he convinces Sally to let him facilitate her transformation (superficially, at least) into an upper-class lady appropriate for a lord. Second, within his own class, he can face down the pomposity of the Duchess of Dene and her scheme to marry Snibson to someone with parallel aristocratic pedigree to propagate the family line, with the concomitant need to remove Sally from Snibson's life. Sir John does not want history to repeat itself:

> Do you think it is right to part a couple of nature's children like you [Sally] and Bill. I won't have it! . . . I was in love once – and who do you think it was? The old haybag – the Duchess! Hang on to love! Do you want to become hard and cynical like her, – and your Bill to become a crotchety old bachelor like me?[3]

Twenty to One

The obvious choice of a writer for *Me and My Girl* was L. Arthur Rose.[4] He had written the script for *Twenty to One*, in which he established the Snibson character initially to be played by Lane's brother, Wallace Lupino, who fell ill as the show was to open, jeopardizing the production. Lupino Lane took over the role on the regional tour and developed Snibson verbally and physically into the show's dominant character. *Twenty to One* was revived on a grander scale for London, opening at the Coliseum on 12 November 1935 (White 1957: 248–56). The script identifies the show as a 'musicalized farce' – not a 'musical farce' or a 'musical comedy' – which signals how the few choruses and songs arose as diverting interpolations within an otherwise workable stage play.

The first scenes of *Twenty to One* set up a well-to-do social circle at Epsom with pro- and anti-gambling factions. Snibson's introduction in Act I scene 3 – creating the anticipatory delay for the main character – is a compendium of class-related traits as 'a middle-aged cockney, a master of the art of living on his wits. He wears a grey bowler cocked over his right eye, a horsey collar and tie, and an old-fashioned, sporty, tapering, big-buttoned, fawn cover coat, dark trouser and black boots.'[5] He speaks unlike any of the other characters: the cockney accent is roughly notated in his lines throughout ('bought 'em', 'my 'orse', ''Ow I remember'), he uses street slang ('a bundle of boodle, oof, spondulix, splosh, dinaley, money!')[6] and he introduces cockney rhyming slang ('Hampstead Heath'/teeth, 'Ivor Novellos'/bellows, 'butcher's hook'/look).[7] He is verbally animated from the outset, placed centre stage to deliver an extended commentary to convey the thrill of a horse race. This speech also introduces a touch of the meta-theatricality we will also note later when it concludes with 'Well, they said no race could excite them. And you're not the first audience I've excited with it.'[8]

Snibson is physically animated too, with set-piece scenes involving the comical demonstration of how to play musical instruments, a running gag of hiding bottles of whisky and an end sequence of Snibson drunk. Physical 'business' is central, for example:

> [Lucretia] gets hysterical. She falls into settee. She laughs, [Snibson] laughs. Her legs go. He holds her legs. Her arms go. He catches her arms. He slaps her palms. He smacks her cheeks. He grabs silver salver, fans her with it, and then applies it to her brow. She sends it flying. He runs here and there for something . . . anything. He sprinkles water at her from the carafe. He holds flowers to her nose. He uses syphon. All in vain.[9]

The script also establishes Snibson's unclear parentage, which is the crux of *Me and My Girl* and of the explicit dramatization of the social implications of lineage. A list of the varied and dubious behaviour in his past concludes with 'I'm good inside – but out of a bad stable. Bit of a crossbreed. I was sired wrong. Can't stay any course. Go lame in my morals. Must turn a dishonest penny.'[10]

When *Twenty to One*, with Lane as the star turn, ran for 383 performances at the Coliseum, Sir Oswald Stoll sensed the commercial possibilities of a follow-up for his theatre and suggested another 'Snibson' outing. Rose wrote the synopsis for *Me and My Girl* and drafted the first script. Stoll's organization turned that down, so Lane became the producer and brought in Douglas Furber to help develop the script and contribute lyrics alongside Noel Gay for the music (White 1957: 267–8). Rose and Furber had worked together on a show as early as 1919, *Pretty Peggy* (which became the name of the winning horse in *Twenty to One*). Rose directed it and co-wrote the script with comedian Charles Austin, one of the show's leading performers; Furber contributed lyrics. It was a small-scale venture that Cochran brought into the West End in February 1920. Rose and Furber continued to work together, for example with Furber's lyrics for Rose's revue *Cock a Doodle Doo*. Indeed, during the 1920s Rose was best known as the director and writer for a series of touring revues that also included *Splinters*, *New Splinters*, *Super Splinters*, *Stars and Stripes* and *What Price the Navy*.

Furber also had a strong revue background, writing sketches that were performed by such performers as Jack Buchanan, Beatrice Lillie, Gertrude Lawrence, Maisie Gay, Cicely Courtneidge and Jack Hulbert. Furber sometimes performed in them too, including in some he wrote for Charlot's revue of 1921, *A to Z*. Other prominent revues to feature his sketches included C. B. Cochran's 1919 revue (later titled *Wake Up and Dream*) and *The House That Jack Built* (1930). Furber, self-taught as a writer, was also well established as a lyricist by 1937. He had first come to notice in 1915 with Australian composer Archie Emmett Adams through the songs 'God Send You Back to Me' and especially 'The Bells of St. Mary's', with other early popular successes in 'Bless You' (music by Ivor Novello) and 'Limehouse Blues' (music by Philip Braham, from *A to Z*) (Furber 1950: viii–ix). All the sketch performers mentioned earlier sang his lyrics, as also did Paul Robeson ('Roll Away Clouds') and John McCormack ('The Far-Away Bells').

Furber's association with Lane dates from the same time as Rose's, when Furber was co-scriptwriter on Cochran's 'Arabian Night' extravaganza at the London Pavilion, *Afgar* (1919), in which Lane had appeared. Jumping forward a decade, they were co-scriptwriters on the 1932 British film adaptation of *The Maid of the Mountains*, which Lane also directed. Even from the selective and necessarily short career summaries described earlier, a circle of collaborative contacts emerges in musicalized comic light entertainment created in Britain across stage, record and film. Gay, Lane, Rose and Furber intersect at multiple stages with each other and with fellow performers and theatrical producers. Lane assembled his team for *Me and My Girl* from a circle of experienced creatives he already knew. He wanted to make the result as watertight as he could – especially when his own money was backing the venture. Rose's writing brought continuity of character and a particular approach to play with language – confused exchanges between Timothy Quaintance and Snibson in *Twenty to One* presage the linguistic mangling Snibson employs in attempting to draw on the events and figures from English history in preparing his maiden speech for the House of Lords (of which more shortly).

Furber's writing caught character well but was especially strong at hitting a punch line. See, for example, the final exchange of a sketch (from *The House That Jack Built*) between a pushy Pittsburgh wife and her rich, long-suffering husband: SARAH [Cicely Courtneidge] 'Is everything shut up for the night?' SAM [Jack Hulbert] 'Everything but you, dear' (Furber 1935: 39). In constructing his sketches, Furber considered not just verbal content but visual and physical representation too, as with the image of Jack Buchanan 'wearing the green velvet riding habit, the gaily plumed hat and the golden wig. etc of the famous Flora Macdonald' to the punch line 'Ramsay? I thought you said Flora!!!' (Furber 1927: 49) or the use of props in ever-faster succession and manic confusion in 'Let Us Fight the Talkies', described as 'a stunt for a star Comedian or Comedienne' (Furber 1935: 27–31). Coward's operetta-led approach for *Bitter Sweet* was well served by a single, central creative force. The compendium-style musical comedy of *Me and My Girl* required a more collaborative method to bring it to the stage.

Playing to the crowd

An understanding of *Me and My Girl* has Lupino Lane at its core. The show was conceived around him. Lane didn't only bring himself to the show, he brought an entire dynasty. The family line of descent is described by Lane in *How to Be a Comedian* and provides the source material for White's summary, which opens his biography of Lane in a chapter headed 'The Fabulous Lupinos'. It begins: 'The Lupinos are one of the oldest theatrical families in the world. For more than three hundred years the name Lupino has appeared continuously in the world of entertainment, and the family line can be traced through the whole rise and growth of English theatre' (White 1957: 1). It is an aristocratic lineage in its own way as significant as that any Earl of

Hareford could claim, but for real. The earliest mention of the family Lane cites is from 1642 at St Bartholomew's Fair in London, with an advertisement for 'Signor Georgius Luppino, Motion Master, and his life-like Puppets performing jigs, sarabands and country dances' (Lane 1945: 51). The Lupinos (now with a single 'p') became clowns in English pantomime from its origins with John Rich and his reinvention of the Italian *commedia dell'arte* as the British harlequinade. The family tradition was passed down the generations to Lupino Lane himself, born 1892 as William George Lupino. His name was legally changed in early childhood by his parents in deference to Sara Lane, a relative through marriage and owner-manager of the Britannia Theatre in Hoxton – a last home of British pantomime tradition – and an employer of the whole Lupino family (White 1957: 15–20).

The Lupino family of physical clowns was a mainstay of nineteenth-century music hall and pantomime the length of the country, and in the twentieth spread into musical comedy, film, radio and television. In the 1920s on the London stage, the family was represented by brothers Lupino Lane and Wallace Lupino, brothers Barry, Stanley and Mark Lupino, and Cissy Lupino, not to mention at the end of their careers the respective patriarchs Harry, George and Arthur Lupino. Given the seeming ubiquity and prominence of the youngest generations on the stage in the 1920s, 'The very name Lupino was like a trade-mark of success' (1957: 162).[11] Lane and brother Wallace were successful in silent films in Hollywood, with a prominence alongside Charlie Chaplin (a friend from a shared childhood in British music hall). Lane had an extraordinary command of the most demanding of physical movement in the pursuit of entertainment and a laugh. This was a practical demonstration of the Lupino family's training in the comic arts from childhood, drilled for hours each day by the older generation who passed down the skills of its trade in a form of guild initiation.

Unfortunately, so many of Lane's performances for silent film have been lost with the destruction of early film stock. That which does remain, often damaged, shows the specialized techniques of the expert clown. One tantalizing fragment from the short film *Joyland* (1929) captures the set and pantomime routine being used in a theatre tour. In it, the speed of the chasing and tumbling is staggering (even allowing for the undercranking of manual cameras of the time), with use of the 'grave' and 'star' traps, once standard (and dangerous) devices in stage pantomime for disappearing into the stage and emerging rocket-like from out of it.[12] Lane's early experimentation with film and his performing skill made him an ideal assistant director to Ernst Lubitsch in the seminal sound film *The Love Parade* (also 1929) as well as an actor, and Lane's performance as the manservant Jacques in the dance routine within the duet 'Let's Be Common' gives a further glimpse of his impressive technique.

To so many of the 1937 audience, if not all, the name 'Lupino' brought a wealth of first-hand associations covering decades on stage and more recently on film with Stanley Lupino, Wallace Lupino, Lupino Lane and the family's striking newcomer Ida Lupino, who was quickly taken up by Hollywood. To *Me and My Girl*, Lupino Lane brought his music-hall reputation, his many pantomime appearances, his double-act experience whether with his brother Wallace or in pantomime with Nellie Wallace, advanced comic gymnastics, an association with musical comedies and revues in the main West End theatres, the specific identification with Bill Snibson from the success of *Twenty to One* and the reinforcement of his stage personality through recent film performances. How could the show written for him not draw on that mixture of elements? The reviewer for *The Stage* acknowledged that 'Lupino Lane has seldom found better material for his well-known gifts of genial and genuine humour and surprising acrobatics [. . . and] sustains with unfailing gusto his reputation as a fun-maker'.[13]

From the themes addressed in the narrative, the show has justifiably been read as 'Carnivalesque' (Burrows 2016), centred on the crowning of 'Lord and Lady Misrule', as Light and Samuel captioned an image of Bill in his regalia embracing Sally (1989: 263). It can also be understood from the angle of the 'star vehicle' as a compendium of performance techniques across the spectrum of music hall, pantomime, musical comedy, revue and farce. For example, in February 1938, only weeks after 'The Lambeth Walk' had been catapulted to public prominence on the radio, Lupino Lane was recorded leading the audience in a rendition of the song. He divided the audience into men and women to practice their individual 'Oi' shouts, before bringing them all together to join in the chorus.[14] Such breaking of the fourth wall for the encouragement of audience participation is still a set piece of seasonal pantomime, and more broadly it flags up that a knowing awareness of the presence of an audience by the onstage characters is part of the show's nature.

A class act

Musical comedy routinely dramatized a contrast of status, whether social, financial or moral. Strands of modernity and its associated shift towards a consumerist-led society provide driving forces in such representation (e.g. see Platt 2004; Platt, Becker and Linton 2014; and Macpherson 2018). The prominent example of *The Arcadians* (1909) gives a summary comparison when the operetta music of the innocent and honest Arcadians is juxtaposed with the demotic musical comedy numbers of the materially acquisitive, morally compromised Londoners, and the corrupting power of the city and commerce is shown in action on the visitors from an idyllic, pastoral land. There is a certain reflexive element in one classic situation of musical comedy that highlights privilege and the relativity of value systems. The supposed respectability and reserve of the peerage is pitted against the uninhibited behaviour on many fronts of the theatrical profession (a centuries-long reputation): the innuendo tag 'as the actress said to the bishop' is one manifestation of this. The reflexivity arises in considering quite how many ladies of the stage became Ladies, Marchionesses, Baronesses and Countesses in reality. C. B. Cochran lists twenty-two elevations from the ranks of Edwardian musical comedy onwards such that 'even in those bygone pre-war days the lighter stage supported the titled ranks nobly'. He quotes Sir Arthur Wing Pinero, 'The musical comedy girls will be the solution of the aristocracy in the country', and adds, 'To bring this quotation up to date, for "musical comedy" read "revue"' (Cochran 1945: 27–8). Fred Astaire's sister and performing partner Adele, with whom he made his mark on stage in London in the 1920s, married to become Lady Cavendish. For repertory closer to this study, we could also add that Beatrice ('Bea') Lillie became Lady Peel, and after marriage (not as an immediate consequence of it) Vanessa Lee became Lady Graves and Lizbeth Webb became Lady Campbell. In Chapter 2, this society–theatre contrast is a running preoccupation through *Bitter Sweet* and *Operette*, and reframed in *Pacific 1860* as the son of an island's leading family enamoured of a visiting famous singer.

The progression from working-class girl to upper-class woman recurs frequently within early musical comedy. Ben Macpherson highlights just how many shows incorporate this 'Cinderella' trope at some level as a central theme, even to the extent of the formulation of titles, as in *A Gaiety Girl* (1893), *A Country Girl* (1894) and *The Girl Behind the Counter* (1906). Despite such 'near universality' of the theme, this was not unmoderated repetition but rather presented 'more complicated and challenging versions of femininity' (Macpherson 2018: 65–6). Jump forward to the late 1930s and the class-related 'Cinderella' scenario of high–low contrast in *Me and My Girl* is expressed in several ways readily spotted by the audience, even while jumbled up. Snibson is the figurative beneficiary of a *deus ex machina* as he inherits a title and wealth (his fairy godfather is the family solicitor). This highly public version of a male Cinderella is catapulted to centre stage at the outset, which contrasts with how Sally is constantly pushed to the side, especially by the Duchess for whom out of sight is out of mind. Sally's Cinderella transformation to an upper-class lady occurs offstage and is facilitated by Sir John. The evocation of this element of his pantomime alter ego is made explicit: 'Do you know, I feel a warm Christmasy glow coming all over me – I feel like a Fairy Godmother . . . And Cinderella you shall go to the ball.'[15] In this way Sir John's 'Good Fairy' contrasts with the Duchess's 'Bad Fairy', as she attempts to control Snibson and separate him from Sally permanently, but – as convention dictates – she fails.

Class is a major trope in British musical comedy, with the contrast of upper and lower classes dominant until the rise of the middle class post-war and its presentation in more 'suburban' musicals – as with the commuter-belt focus of *Twenty Minutes South* (1955) and even the professional classes more than titled ones in *Salad Days* (1954). Class is built into *Me and My Girl* from the outset, with a cockney costermonger inheriting a title that brings with it a stately home, land and money. Ken Platt's analysis of class as central to Edwardian musical comedy has been extended by George Burrows to show how the theme remained 'vibrant, current and engaging' for audiences into the 1930s (2016: 172). Burrows registers how the popularity of *Me and My Girl* indicates 'a high point in social relevance' for musical comedy in the 1920s and 1930s, rather than a hangover of a dated theatrical form. Lawrence Napper similarly identifies the show as of its time, 'expressly organised around the anxieties and pleasure of social dynamism and cultural fluidity – around the modern experience of moving for one class into another with all its attendant cultural hazards' (2014: 135–6).

The Lambeth Walk

The iconic definer of class focus that has come out of *Me and My Girl* is the Act I finale song, 'The Lambeth Walk'. While the show's story explores class-related themes throughout, this takeout number captured the essence of the show's message, which was not so much the contrast of lower and upper class, but a levelling out of the whole social scale. Everyone could do 'The Lambeth Walk'. The Mass-Observation movement that began in Britain in 1937, in its own words, 'exists to study everyday behaviour in Britain'. A summary of material from around 2,000 volunteer observers across the country was published in 1939. It includes the chapter 'Doing the Lambeth Walk' that describes in detail how 'The Lambeth Walk' became a social dance phenomenon (Madge and Harrison 1939: 139–84). The song gained wide attention after a fifteen-minute radio broadcast on 4 January 1938, which also catapulted indifferent box office bookings to a sell-out. Frequent radio broadcasting of the catchy number caught the public's ear, and it became a hit. Next, an accompanying dance was developed by Adele England, a dance teacher at the Locarno Dance Hall in South London's Streatham. She created a communal novelty number for dancers of all abilities to serve the socially inclusive function of the dance hall. Once established, the dance evolved such that 'It's not much good learning it properly. There are ever so many ways of doing it, and in any case you have to follow the pair in front of you', as 'Girl, 19' told an observer (Madge and Harrison 1939: 167). 'The Lambeth Walk' even became something of a concluding free-for-all at a short series of massed dancing in large open-air events in parks in London. As one of the observers reported: 'Final dance – "it's 3 o'clock in the morning". Words sung. Joke made about title. Dance ends. Announcer says, after pause: "Wait a minute: there's one thing more. Can anyone tell me what it is?" Small boy somewhere: "Lambeth Walk!" Others take up the cry. Lambeth Walk begins' (Madge and Harrison 1939: 181).

The significance of 'The Lambeth Walk' in sociological and political terms has been examined by Light and Samuel (1989), Napper (2014) and Burrows (2016). In this chapter, it is the physicality of what constitutes a 'Lambeth walk' that is especially relevant. There are two helpful descriptions around Lupino Lane on the origins of the number. In his biography, Lane's contribution comes as he sits with Noel Gay to formulate the musical style needed for the show. Lane suggests slight amendments to Gay's prototype for 'the *kind* of melody this cocky, irresistible story needed'. The result is 'a slow, cocky sort of march, a cockney walk' (White 1957: 269). In an interview in his dressing room at the Victoria Palace prior to a performance, Lane elaborated on this to one of the observers for Mass-Observation. 'I got the idea from my personal experience and from having worked among cockneys. I'm just a cockney born and bred myself. The Lambeth Walk is just an exaggerated idea of how the cockney struts. The cockney is well known for his wit, grit, guts and humour, and these are expressed in his walk.' In continuing to claim sole responsibility for instigating what became such a phenomenon, Lane added, 'No, there's no cockney dancing.' He also relates the idea to a song in his repertory from some twenty years earlier, by his father Harry Lupino, which was about 'the different ways in which different people, different kinds of people, walk' (Madge and Harrison 1939: 159).

Lane was conscious of his image, as would be any popular star, so his promotional claims inevitably need to be treated with circumspection in the detail if reasonably accepted in their generality. Indeed, both his claims to the cockney nature of the walk and its origins in his own heritage were questioned in the Mass-Observation chapter. But for all that, Lane was the public symbol of 'The Lambeth Walk': it was the hit song led by his character in the stage show, carried onto the cinema screen in 1939, and thereafter associated with him. When Lane officially visited Lambeth Walk (caught on Pathé newsreel footage), a huge crowd blocked the road, and he was obliged to lead them all in a mass rendition of the song before he could get away for his performances that evening of the show that kicked it all off. In the middle of a Saturday afternoon, 15 January 1938, fifteen minutes from the show were broadcast on BBC Television.[16] On 1 May 1939, BBC outside broadcasting returned for 'one of the big television occasions of the year – the first time that a musical comedy has been televised in its entirety from a theatre'.[17]

None of this televised material exists today apart from a small section at the conclusion of Act I, showing 'The Lambeth Walk'. It is fascinating to see how Lupino Lane, Teddie St Dennis (Sally) and the cast presented this iconic number. There is no impression of a formal dance overall. Rather, Lupino demonstrates his 'cockney strut', a subtle bearing that involves a rhythmic tilting of the shoulders, arms held with the elbows slightly out and the chin up. The physical characterization is of casual confidence and self-assertion, occupying the space with a certain genial authority. It is this manner that the onstage ensemble emulates as they pair up on their way into a formal dinner at Hareford Hall at the end of the first act with possibly something of a nod towards, rather than a model for, 'The Lambeth Walk' as it had become beyond the show by the time of that 1939 television filming.

As the contemporary perspective of Mass-Observation interpreted it, 'The point of the show is essentially the contrast between the *natural* behaviour of the Lambethians and the affectation of the upper class' (Madge and Harrison 1939: 157). The physical relaxation that the walk engenders is a visual representation of a shift of social status downwards. The staging manifests a song with a swagger, not a tightly choreographed dance. This is the infectious invasion of the cast with an attitude that stems from the physical lead of Lane and from the musical lead of Gay paired with the demotic expression of Furber. There are no jerked thumbs over shoulders, no slapping or bumping of knees, no 'Oi!', all of which originated with Adele England. The conclusion of the filmed stage performance is significant. The Duchess struts her way to dinner arm in arm with Snibson – who has grandly replaced his bowler on his head – manifesting in movement his triumph in provoking social accommodation. Mass-Observation noted a subversive variant in stage performance when 'the Duchess finally goes into dinner on Bill's arm, wearing his bowler hat on her head', adding that 'the gags change from one performance to another' (Madge and Harrison 1939: 157).

In the film version of *Me and My Girl* (aka *The Lambeth Walk*, 1939) just two of the show's original songs are retained: the title song and 'The Lambeth Walk'. For the latter, a huge party in evening dress produces a mass demonstration of something more in keeping with the Locarno dance version to fulfil the public expectations of what the number had become. The progression into dinner still makes a feature of pairing up the aristocratic guests with their lower-class interlopers. Social differentiation is shown through movement rather than dress (all are formally smart). The pairings generate a range of responses from an eagerness to participate (mostly the aristocratic men linking arms with younger Lambeth women) to disdain (the upper-class wives). To conclude the sequence, Snibson's invitation and the Duchess's capitulation with her own exaggerated swagger – her face suggests reluctance while her motion implies the opposite – unmistakably signal the upper class accommodating the lower, even if temporarily and possibly through the politeness of a hostess. Again, Snibson goes into dinner wearing his bowler hat in sartorial accommodation with, or possibly in victory over, his white tie and tails. Dress code is formally observed, but whose?

Props and physical comedy

The bowler hat was symbolic of Snibson's character, but also an integral prop that brought physicality to the role. In the 1939 film adaptation, with Sally Gray (as Sally), Lane performs the title song wearing the bowler, during which he adjusts the angle four times, replaces it on his head once and flourishes it at the end. There is no reason to assume that Lane did not incorporate such physical aspects of his stage performance into his film performance for continuity of character for the audience and as part of his essential armoury as a physical comedian. In the filmed original stage rendition of 'The Lambeth Walk', Lane begins the number without the hat, puts it on to physicalize the class contrast, swaps hats with Sally so that he wears her fascinator as a visible disruption of his tail suit, while she wears the bowler as a further parodic class modification of her evening dress, before Bill regains the hat for his exit with the Duchess as further counterpoint, now with her tiara. The first extant script, for the pre-London run, describes Snibson on his entrance as 'a perky little cockney, with a cocked grey bowler, which he does not remove'.[18] In *How to Be a Comedian*, Lane states that 'Hat tricks are most essential. A top hat seems to be the one most used; it takes the air better, but you should be able to manipulate with any other kind of headgear. I, personally, favour a bowler.' He describes, with illustrations, thirteen different forms of hat manipulation to master, including two different ways of throwing it onto the head (Lane, 1945, pp. 103–6).

Such comic skills were inevitably built into the show given that it was constructed around Lane. The bowler as a representation of Snibson became an essential prop. In the first 1937 script, there is a sequence in which Snibson is being instructed in polite manners by the Duchess. She gestures towards her head to prompt him to remove his bowler, which he interprets as her indicating that she is mad. When he does take his hat off, he 'starts in several directions with it, offers it to her, looks foolish, puts it on settee and sits'.[19] Rose wrote in the situations and spaces for 'business' that suited Lane. To which end, that script included in Act II scene 2 business with glasses and bottles that leads to a parody of a chess game as Sir John tries to stop Bill drinking.[20] The scene ends with a manic sequence presented through stage directions (rather than dialogue) which subverts the formality of afternoon tea: Bill's appearance is dishevelled as he tries pouring tea simultaneously for multiple footmen, crams cake in his mouth only to spit out crumbs, drinks tea from a saucer and sweeps crockery off the table with a sword.[21]

When the show was relicensed for London a few months later, and in the light of development in rehearsal and performance, the revised 1937 script had replaced that afternoon tea scenario with a classic routine that strengthened the show's affinities with pantomime (seasonally appropriate – it opened in London on 16 December 1937). The new scene is heralded with a stage instruction loaded with expectation: 'Also three maids bring on tea waggon [sic] with cream pies.'[22] The consequences are inevitable, given the slapstick heritage of the performer at the centre of the show. Bill 'hits Gerald in face with cream tart', then 'slaps tart on Jasper's head'. When 'Parchester surreptitiously hands Bill the large cream tart and urges him to let the Duchess have it', Bill is hesitant. Finally, he aims the flan at Gerald, who ducks, resulting in the flan hitting – who else? – the Duchess smack in the face. Blackout.[23] Such scenes confirm that mime and slapstick were central to the conception of this particular musical comedy, and the cream pie sequence is happily included in the 1939 film.

During the weeks in Nottingham, Glasgow and Manchester, prior to the West End, the physical action of the work evolved. The most prominent change was the insertion of Snibson practicing his maiden speech to the House of Lords, dressed in the coronet and ermine-trimmed robes appropriate to an earl. It became a signature scene of the show as Lane manipulated the cloak as though it was something with a life of its own, battled with it and mastered it. In that first script, pre-Nottingham, the only references to any such business are the stage directions for the entrance of Snibson in Act II scene 1: 'Bill appears on the balcony, he is wearing robes, coronet and carries the book of ancestors. Bill staggers forward, trips over his robes and lands in a heap downstage.'[24] In Nottingham, an accidental swirl of the robes gained a laugh, which prompted Lane to develop a whole routine with them (White 1957: 278). It is only with the playscript submitted for licence in 1949 that further stage business (marked as 'Bus.') has been added, including 'Bus. BILL falls flat on his back – covers himself right over with cloak and puts coronet on his chest like lying in state'.[25]

By the time of the 1954 acting edition from Samuel French, the 1949 stage directions have been filled out to mark a nine-stage progression of battling the robes into submission until a final exit in which 'Bill marches round and round with the greatest grandeur, making the cloak billow more and more. The orchestra drummer rolls out the beat crescendo. Bill makes a magnificent exit up R with the cloak flying out behind him like a waving flag' (Rose and Furber 1954: 43). He is off to tell the Duchess that he has had enough of trying to be what he isn't. Through the manipulation of the cloak, the scene enables a master of physical comedy to demonstrate his way with props in building up humour for, and gaining the admiration of, the audience. Symbolically, Bill is shown to have gained the upper hand over the upper-class element of his identity. For those who have no first-hand knowledge of Lane's performance, these later stage directions log a transient a part of the show's performance identity. They match well the scene as performed by Lane in the film adaptation of 1939, a source that is difficult to access even in the DVD and download age.[26] It was only with Lane ceasing to perform the role and the show being made available to other companies that it became necessary to convey the physical essence of the scene in detail.

Importantly, class is literally embodied in performance, made physical. In particular, low class tends towards low comedy traits (such as physical jokes and the belly laugh) and high comedy towards its defining traits (clever observations and witticisms). In respect of the British musical comedy *Mr. Cinders* (1928, London 1929) George Burrows has related comic physicality to the chores accruing to the changes of status with Jim as the poor relation/dogsbody (the male-Cinderella 'Mr Cinders' of the title) and Jill as the rich daughter (of a wealthy American rather than a king) masquerading as a housemaid. The 'glass slipper' is transmuted into a hat that has to fit the right head. Jill

> is always breaking things – not least the social rules – and generally subverts her role as the maid to highlight Lady Lancaster's class-orientated bullying and social pretension. Similarly, Jim, who is forced to be a handyman and to tend the grounds of Merton Chase, shows by comparison with [his entitled step-brothers] Guy and Lumley that leisure-class affectations are never a substitute for seemingly more bodily, 'natural' and simple working-class values of hard work, directness, honesty and integrity. (Burrows 2016: 177)

The film *Mister Cinders* (1934) captures how the physical work of Jack and Jill affords them access to props to carry, trip over, drop, catch and spill. Their cross-class identity expresses itself in the idea of subversion that carnival permits them, which shifts them physically towards low comedy. It's a pattern we can see repeated in the accident-prone clumsiness of George Formby's film roles, extending through to the physical confusion and discomfort of Arthur Kipps's uncomfortable elevation to 'society' in *Half a Sixpence* (1963) and even to elements of *Charlie Girl* (1965), another class-and-money story set in a stately home.

Distilled and reinvented

On 12 February 1985, after being tried out at the Leicester Haymarket Theatre, a new version of *Me and My Girl* opened at the Adelphi Theatre in London. On 16 January 1993 – the final night of the London run – Stephen Fry, who had revised the script, delivered a speech. Part of what he said is reproduced as a forward to the vocal selection from the show (Gay, Rose and Furber 1994: 2–3). Fry describes the difficulty of finding any script to work from, drawing first on a version that combined the memories of Richard Armitage – Noel Gay's son and the producer of the new version – with 'the very bastardized French's amateur acting edition' of 1954. To that material was added a 'pre-rehearsal script . . . that had been submitted in 1936 to the Lord Chamberlain's official theatre censor'. In fact, the censoring of the word 'Cissy' Fry cites identifies this not as the pre-rehearsal script submitted for licensing (LCP 1937/43, licensed 7 September) but as an amended script (LCP 1937/57, licensed 8 December) submitted for the London opening which thus includes the changes made during the out-of-town tour pre-London.[27] In that light, this London-licensed script seems to be as authoritative as one could get for the 1937 London premiere. But it's not that type of show: a fixed, authentic text for the show was never on the cards.

All the material we can consult today is reliable in its own way for its own time. Here, four pre-1985 script sources have been cited: three from the Lord Chamberlain's collection (LCP 1937/43, LCP 1937/57 and LCP 1949/37) and the 'bastardized' published edition by French (1954). There is also the 1939 film, which includes large amounts of verbatim stage script and Lupino's own characterization. Additionally, there were scripts submitted to the Lord Chamberlain for licensing in 1953 and 1954. Today we have the commercially available script from the 1985 revival, also published by Samuel French. Many speeches, jokes and gestures remain scripted as they were at the outset. For example, on learning he is to inherit a title Snibson seems to pass out. When Sir John calls for water, Snibson replies from his apparent unconscious state lying on the floor, 'I didn't faint for water.' It is present in the first 1937 script (LCP 1937/43: 19) and still there in the same place in the current Samuel French edition (Rose, Furber and Fry 1986: 11). Similarly, Snibson's early description of living in a single room and having to bathe his body in the sink in daily instalments is reproduced almost word for word in all versions.

Other elements have evolved in stages, as with the examples of physical presentation discussed earlier. Some of these changes have been motivated by topicality, as when Bill plucks up the courage while taming his robes to confront the Duchess to give her (1937/57: 86) 'the sailor's farewell' – which is 'Same as the soldier's, only surrounded by water'. Reflecting new technology, in 1949 (II-1-12) this became 'the Airmen's farewell' – 'The same as the soldiers [sic], only jet propelled'. By 1954 (43), the sailor's farewell had returned. Other changes are more significant: all versions to 1954 begin Act I at Hareford Hall, whereas the 1985 revised version uses additional words in an extended opening chorus to stage a journey by car of house party guests from Mayfair to Hareford Hall.

An additional complication arises with performance 'ad libs', by their nature neither recorded nor formalized. In 1938, a complaint was made to the Lord Chamberlain's office over inappropriate language in *Me and My Girl*. It was investigated. Correspondence with the producers shows an escalation from warning to near-prosecution for breaching the terms of the show's licence and includes the report of an official who visited a performance. The interesting part here is the willingness – not carried through to the communication with the show's producers – to accept an element of in-the-moment performance inspiration, in this case in respect of George Graves, playing Sir John: 'generally speaking, I should not be inclined to be too austere with George Graves, who is in the [George] Robey class of comedians, and being a famous gagger invariably adds to the licensed script, and must I think be allowed some licence.'[28]

There was always a tension between the legal requirement to have precise wording licensed and the demands of live theatre, especially in areas where a more direct relationship with the audience that broke the fourth wall was a central feature of the genre, as in pantomime and low comedy. Officially the Lord Chamberlain could not condone such changes, but unofficially it was a fact of theatre. However, the visiting inspector noted a small number of precise deviations of minor detail from the licensed text. Unless his memory was astonishing, the inference is that he followed the performance with a script and that compliance was – complaints about the odd word notwithstanding – high, or at least raised no concern. We can never quite know: musical comedy of this type does not have a wholly fixed text, a big difference from all the other case study shows here. A script cannot be 'bastardized' when versions under the control of the originating creatives can vary significantly, to which it is worth noting that the 1949 script, so close to that of French's 1954 version, includes for the first time the credit 'Additional dialogue Lupino Lane'.[29]

In this light, many of the revisions made to the known script sources for the 1985 production make theatrical and commercial sense. The changes continue a process that had started between the two versions of 1937 and continued when Lane controlled revivals of the show. One description of Edwardian musical comedy in its emergent state holds relevance almost a century on in the context of the revival of *Me and My Girl*: 'An important prototype "mass" culture, it was one of the earliest "star" vehicles. It utilized the most modern forms of technology, distribution and marketing available, and was intensely consumerist in its design, execution and general orientation' (Platt 2004: 3–4). The 1985 revision demonstrates facets of these values still in action through style, branding and celebrity casting, amplified in the commercial replication of the same production on Broadway, with Robert Lindsay reprising his London role of Snibson.

Yet a pattern of regular changes does not give a free hand for any and all changes. Some central integrity of the core idea has to be retained, although some changes impact the show's identity more than others. The changes of songs make this clear, not least because the original cast recordings of individual numbers and later of albums encourage a wider familiarity than is practical for the script and the stage image. Song changes were made early on. For example, when the show started and as licensed for London, it included a pessimistic song for Snibson 'Life Is a Bowl of Raspberries', a parodic take on the optimism of 'Life Is Just a Bowl of Cherries' (by Ray Henderson and Lew Brown from *George White's Scandals of 1931*). Snibson sang it in his Act II return to Lambeth, when he has failed to find Sally.[30] By the time of the London opening, the song had been taken out. In the 1985 revision, this is where a new song was added, 'Leaning on a Lamp-post', which characterizes Snibson's hope to see his 'certain little lady', Sally (Rose, Furber and Fry 1986: 64–5). The original song was downbeat: 'Life is just a bowl of raspberries, / Nothing but a bowl of raspberries, / And we always find that our ones / Are large ones and sour ones.' Its replacement is optimistic, 'Leaning on a Lamp-post' (dating from the same time as *Me and My Girl*), which redirects the characterization of Snibson at this point towards cheery charm with star quality.

In Light and Samuel's assessment (1989: 268), the interpolation of 'Leaning on a Lamp-post' provides one instance that shows the revision not as 'a faithful rendering of the original', but as 'a self-conscious play with nostalgia, and a whole pastiche of "period" effects'. Given the issue of establishing authenticity and the different frame of reference for audiences fifty years later, it could hardly have been otherwise. The dominant example of the change of tone comes, not surprisingly, with the show's defining number. In 1937 the Lambeth dinner guest at Hareford Hall 'enter in party clothes, some evidently made and some obviously hired for the occasion'.[31] Their discomfort is made visible by an attempt to fit in that nonetheless fails to disguise the class difference. For the 1985 production, that difference is made as clear as possible, with Pearly Kings and Queens playing up the cockney tourist business to the hilt. The subtle insinuation of a cockney swagger spreading up through the aristocratic contingent evident in the 1937 staging has become not the physicalizing of class and character, but rather the choreography of cockney cliché, with Lane's easy sway now a chicken strut of pushed-out behind, angular elbows and thrusting chin. Adele England's arm-linking, thumb-jerking, 'Oi'-shouting steps have been magnified and costumed into a riotous celebration of class difference through a full-frontal display of oppositional pride.

Where Act II had in 1937 opened with the upper classes trying to get the hang of 'The Lambeth Walk' as a show of good intentions but poor skills in crossing the class barrier, the 1985 revision starts instead with an interpolated number, 'The Sun Has Got His Hat On'. This rousing, lively start evokes carefree, distant times and 'bright young things' who 'match the vitality of Lambeth with their own' (Light and Samuel 1989: 268). The different message is clear. In 1937, the work was contemporary, the reflections of class equality current and the upper hand seen going to the lower class in a social comment delivered in carnivalesque manner. The 1985 adaptation is more aligned with a cartoon of a fictional world with which we may identify through a range of such sources as the television adaptations of the 'Jeeves' novels of P. G. Wodehouse and Bert from Walt Disney's *Mary Poppins* (1964) alongside its cartoon pearlies by the racetrack. What was a contemporary show has become a period postcard. Yet *Me and My Girl*, as all the shows investigated here demonstrate, cannot be fixed in meaning by the time in which it was created, even if that is where the investigation started. The world changes, audiences change and their points of reference change. In this show more than any of the other case study works here, the significance of the work is bound up with the incomplete or contradictory records we have of this type of theatre text and the transient essence of the live performance event that it serves.

4

The Dancing Years (1939)

Ivor Novello

Ivor Novello's musical play *The Dancing Years* is remembered mainly for the song 'Waltz of My Heart'. Yet it was one of the most successful shows created for the West End of its day. The length of the first London run does *The Dancing Years* few favours – it lasted only 187 performances – but the detail gives another perspective. On 23 March 1939, *The Dancing Years* opened at the Theatre Royal, Drury Lane. Upon the declaration of war on 1 September, West End theatres closed, with the show not quite six months old. Almost all theatres and shows reopened within a few weeks, but the Theatre Royal, Drury Lane, was co-opted as the headquarters of the entertainment wing of the armed services (Entertainments National Service Association – ENSA) and Novello's hit show was homeless. After a year, *The Dancing Years* went on a long national tour. It returned to London and the Adelphi Theatre in March 1942, where it ran for 969 performances to July 1944, when war again forced its closure ('those charming doodle bugs', in Novello's own ironic words).[1] So it went on tour again – for five years. The show also returned to London in a new production at the Casino Theatre in March 1947 for a further 96 performances.

The Dancing Years was the most seen and the most known home-grown work of musical theatre of its day, 'to London in the Second World War what *Chu Chin Chow* and *The Bing Boys* had been in the first war' and its title 'a household word' (Macqueen-Pope 1954: 219). Extensive wartime touring with, for the most part, an A-team West End cast had added to the glow of popular success, as Novello explained:

> The provincial public were not expecting anything more in their particular theatres than shows with one set and a few characters. Suddenly *The Dancing Years* burst upon them in all its pre-war glory, and hundreds of theatre goers assured me it had made them feel a new hope that things were not quite so bad as they seemed.[2]

As for that 'pre-war glory', the opening months of *The Dancing Years* had proved it a major hit for Novello and the Theatre Royal, Drury Lane. It came with a fine pedigree, following *Glamorous Night* (1935), *Careless Rapture* (1936) and *Crest of the Wave* (1937) as the fourth musical play Novello had created for that theatre. Those previous shows evolved an expectation of what a Novello show would deliver. From the Drury Lane theatre's heritage came stage spectacle, exoticism and romance. For the rest, Novello contributed memorable and lyrical show melodies, his own identity and interests as a playwright, and in performance (West End and on tour) his celebrity charisma as a matinée idol of the silent screen and the stage.

The Dancing Years dramatizes the perceived classic trope of a Novello drama: wistful romance. In Vienna in 1911, an aspiring young composer of operetta, Rudi Kleber (Novello), gets his big break professionally and personally when he meets operetta star Maria Ziegler (Mary Ellis). She passes over marriage to Austrian royalty in favour of being with Rudi in whose new operetta, *Lorelei*, she has the starring role. When an overheard conversation leaves her with the wrong idea that he intends to marry someone else, she returns to her Prince and marries him, discovering her mistake too late. Rudi Kleber pursues his music to become the most famous composer of operetta in Vienna and abroad, while Maria (now Princess Metterling) abandons her professional career to become the increasingly bored wife of a high state official. When Rudi and Maria meet again in 1927, it is clear they remain in love with each other, but while he is still free for her, Maria has a husband and a son (revealed to be Rudi's). Meeting again briefly in 1938 their thoughts are still 'far away' in 'the Dancing Years – happy ones – sad ones, but full of meaning' (Novello and Hassall 1953: 65).

Man of the Theatre

It is difficult now to bring Ivor Novello into clear focus. Only fragments of his work remain within any shared cultural memory, and writings on him have routinely employed language that gilds what was by any measure an astonishing career when curtailed by Novello's sudden death in the early hours of 6 March 1951. Novello's funeral service was broadcast on the radio as thousands gathered outside St Martin-in-the-Fields church and Golders Green Crematorium. Tributes poured in and an hour-long programme of reminiscences, music and extracts from Novello's plays was broadcast by the BBC radio on 8 March, borrowing its title from the 1951 biography of Novello by Peter Noble: 'Man of the Theatre'.[3] Noble's revised third edition of June 1951 has a foreword by Noël Coward that concludes: 'His death will be a personal loss to many millions of people – this is his greatest tribute and his greatest epitaph' (Noble 1951: 11). Noble offered that his biography of 'one of the giants of the modern English stage ... does not do justice one-tenth to the greatness and genuineness of the man himself, ... the great Welshman who brought more happiness to more people through his many gifts than possibly any other man of our century' (1951: 15–16). Praise indeed.

The second Novello biography of 1951, by W. Macqueen-Pope, judges its subject similarly: 'as great as anyone who ever trod the stage of this kingdom, be they who they may' (Macqueen-Pope 1954: 11). The author apologises for putting himself into the biography because:

> I knew Ivor so well and so long ... at first hand, as seen through my own eyes, in dressing-rooms, in theatres in London and the provinces, on stages, at first nights and last nights, at rehearsals and in all the glorious excitement and throbbing

anxiety of dress rehearsals – almost always in the Theatre. For the Theatre was Ivor's life. To him it was the only reality he knew. (Macqueen-Pope 1954: 12)

Macqueen-Pope was the publicist for the Theatre Royal, Drury Lane, in the 1930s, when *Glamorous Night* laid the foundation for what was to be Novello's musical theatre dominance in the West End. Subsequently, he acted as Novello's publicist. His theatre-based emphases are clear when, at the start of the 1930s, he minimizes Novello's significant career in film to focus on him as 'an outstanding figure in the British Theatre and a tremendous box-office draw. He was an actor-manager when actor managers were few' (Macqueen-Pope 1954: 130).

We should retain some reserve in evaluating the perspectives promoted by those who knew Novello while appreciating that their bias has led more to tactful selection and descriptive licence than outright fabrication. In particular, Novello's public image was kept as free as possible from what was in the values of the time the illegality of his private life as a gay man. Decades later, Novello's character has become further distorted. On film, *Gosford Park* (2001, dir. Robert Altman) boosted public awareness of him and his music, but misleadingly portrayed him as a charming entertainer required to sing for his supper in the social-climbing setting of an aristocratic house party,[4] yet *Benediction* (2022, dir. Terence Davies) characterizes him as arrogant, predatory and deliberately cruel. Relative to these selective portrayals, for the most part the biographical perspectives of Noble, Macqueen-Pope and Richard Rose (Novello's business partner for many years) are at least derived from first-hand knowledge and direct sources. Barry Sinclair, Novello's long-term understudy, captures the human complexity: 'Charming, sweet, generous, open minded, open handed, unscrupulous, business like, hard as nails'.[5]

Novello was born (as David Ivor Davies) in 1893 to a famed mother, Clara Novello Davies, whose singing tuition placed her among a circle of internationally acclaimed singers. Her close friends included the celebrated contralto Dame Clara Butt and the conductor Sir Landon Ronald. Novello learned singing technique through his mother and as a boy chorister at Magdalen College, Oxford. On occasion in his teens, he even deputized for his mother as a singing teacher (Macqueen-Pope 1954: 39). The first public performances of a song composed by Novello ('The Spring of the Year', 1910) and of his first commercial song success ('The Little Damozel', 1912) were at the Royal Albert Hall: he started at the top. When Noël Coward met Novello for the first time, in Manchester in 1916, Coward (the younger by six years) observed that 'I just felt suddenly conscious of the long way I had to go before I could break into the magic atmosphere in which he moved and breathed with such nonchalance' (Coward 1986: 47–8).[6] Novello inhabited the social and theatrical worlds with ease.

Novello briefly had formal music training with Sir Herbert Brewer, organist at Gloucester Cathedral, enjoyed classical music and especially opera, the love of which remained with him through his life. In 1915, he wrote, 'In some moods I like Debussy better than anyone, but usually Puccini rules me' (Noble 1951: 63). He 'adored' Wagner too and considered Kirsten Flagstad as Isolde and Brünnhilde a singing ideal: 'Wagner says something to me emotionally all the time, every musical phrase strikes an answering chord, every *leitmotiv* has all the force and conviction of a living statement that penetrates to the depths of my soul' (Noble 1951: 267). Novello quoted from the Act II love duet of *Tristan und Isolde* for the opening of the refrain of 'Same Old Moon' for the revue *Puppets* (1924), a somewhat tongue-in-cheek allusion prompted by an image in the lyrics of timeless love in moonlight.

Novello could be harmonically adventurous, as with his modal inflections in the songs 'Mr Pau-Puk-Keewis' (1916) and 'Barbary' (1924), in response to an 'exotic' text. Yet melodic balance and flow dominate, as in the song 'Dusky Nipper', which Novello wrote for Ben Travers's play *The Dippers* (1922). The melody is elegant in both the minor-key verse (with a major-key transitional ending) and the major-key refrain, the former mid-range and rising, the latter using phrases whose octave span is established in the first two notes and then used to structure the melody's slow climatic ascent. Differently elegant is the melody of 'And Her Mother Came Too', a lasting hit for Novello from the revue *A to Z* (1921). The opening melodic phrase is subject to repetitions slowly rising in pitch, then slowly descending. The steadily inflating melodic balloon which then deflates just as evenly is spot on to complement the verbal deflation towards the punch line that ends each refrain. Melody informed by an understanding of vocal phrasing defines the lasting appeal of Novello's music: he is remembered for songs, not symphonies.

Novello developed as a pianist from a young age too. Noble describes the early collision of influences, with eight-year-old Ivor singing in duet with Adelina Patti 'If You Were just the Sort of Fellow' from the Edwardian musical comedy *Our Miss Gibbs*, and with 'his *pièce de résistance* at his mother's musical soirées being "Poor Wandering One", from *The Pirates of Penzance*, which he invariably sang at the top of his voice, with "Hear Ye, Israel" as an encore – and, let me add, accompanying himself at the piano!' (Noble 1951: 25). Noble repeats uncritically an anecdote in which pretty much all the stylistic and theatrical elements needed for Novello's later big musical romances are listed: a mixture of lyric stage genres, vocal and melodic dominance, musical fluency and performance flair. Add to this Novello's childhood love of his toy theatre and the invention of stories for it, and you can find the playwright in this early mix too. It is a biographical indulgence drawn with hindsight to claim as inevitable a career in musical theatre, but undoubtedly the talent, training, interest and surroundings were in place for it to seem a plausible possibility.

In 1914 Novello composed possibly his most long-lived song, written in a hurry to words by Lena Guilbert Ford: 'Till the Boys Come Home (Keep the Home Fires Burning)'. It fast became an anthem of the First World War and has endured with poignant emotional accretions down to today. He contributed popular songs to West End shows including the musical comedies *Theodore & Co* (1916), *Arlette* (1917) and *The Golden Moth* (1921) and the revues *Tabs* (1918), *A to Z* (1921) and *Puppets* (1924). His unexpected acting break into silent film came in Louis Mercanton's *The Call of the Blood* (1920), then D. W. Griffith's unsuccessful *The White Rose* (1923). He had great success as a Parisian apache, the title role of *The Rat* (1925), the title role in Alfred Hitchcock's early silent film *The Lodger* (1926) and leading roles in *Downhill* (1927, also Hitchcock), *The Vortex* and *The Constant Nymph* (both 1928). To these two significant careers in composition and film acting, he added his linked career as a stage actor and a playwright. For example, Novello wrote and performed in *The Truth Game* (1928) and

Symphony in Two Flats (1929) in the West End and on Broadway and with the latter as Novello's first talking picture too (1930). Subsequent plays include *I Lived with You* (1932), *Fresh Fields* and *Proscenium* (both 1933) and *Murder in Mayfair* (1934).

The few monographs on Novello (none of them especially recent) display different authorial interests in balancing these professional facets.[7] The designation 'Man of the Theatre' is helpful. Sir Edward Marsh, an early patron and a steadfast supporter of Novello, uses this term 'first and foremost' in his foreword to a collection of three of Novello's plays. Marsh says of Novello that 'all through his [early] musical successes ideas for plays were continually coming into his head; he longed to be an actor'. He countered Novello's screen prominence by observing 'his heart was always with the boards and the footlights – he wanted to act with his own body and voice, to be in touch with an audience with no machinery between' (Novello 1932: vii). The shows that resulted from Novello's return in 1935 to the musical stage with *Glamorous Night* at the Theatre Royal, Drury Lane – as conceiver, composer, writer and performer – have come to dominate his reputation to the exclusion of almost all else, not least as all his talents combine in them most completely.

The Novello approach

The sequence of 'musical plays' for the Theatre Royal, Drury Lane, establishes Novello's approach to musical theatre: *Glamorous Night, Careless Rapture, Crest of the Wave* and *The Dancing Years*. The following ones consolidate a matured approach: *Arc de Triomphe* (1943, play with music, Phoenix Theatre), the 'musical romances' *Perchance to Dream* (1945, Hippodrome) and *King's Rhapsody* (1949, Palace), and finally the 'musical play' *Gay's the Word* (1951, Saville). The terminology sets the music within the structure of a play, rather than elevating the music above it as a shaping force in the manner of operetta or comic opera. Novello's first three shows experiment with ways to combine the available theatrical elements, and with *The Dancing Years* his fusion of play and music comes fully into focus.

The genesis of *Glamorous Night* – the initial experiment – lies reputedly in an opportunistic improvisation of a theatrical treatment by Novello over lunch with Harry Tennent, then general manager of the Theatre Royal, Drury Lane. Macqueen-Pope lists 'conditions' that Novello laid down in order to create *Glamorous Night*: 'I want everything my own way. I want no interference. I want a simply huge orchestra, I want a star cast and mounting' (1951: 313). Noble's biography consolidates the story: 'I want an orchestra of at least forty players, a cast of one hundred and twenty, and I want to devise and supervise the entire production, without interference from anybody!' (1951: 198). While differing in detail, both accounts stress the core qualities of Novello's concept for musical theatre as they were roughly shaped in his first show: the potential for rich musicalization orchestrally and vocally, a matching visual richness in the scale of the stage picture and the centrality of Novello as auteur.

The common elements between the Novello shows can be defined more specifically, as Stewart Nicholls does: 'a starring non-singing role for [Novello], a soprano as the female lead, a small contralto role (always played by Olive Gilbert), a comedic non-singing female, spectacular scenic effects, a plethora of soaring waltz themes, and an operetta-within-an-operetta sequence' (2016: 202). Olive Gilbert created roles in all the musicals but *Gay's the Word* (the timing of her onstage scenes allowed her to appear in simultaneous performances of *Arc de Triomphe* and *Perchance to Dream*), and the recurring use of her rich contralto may hint at Novello's early hearing of Clara Butt. Another regular in Novello's musicals and stage plays was Minnie Rayner (who died in 1941), 'without whom I could never feel that a play of mine was complete' (Noble 1951: 169). Walter Crisham, Muriel Barron, Peter Graves, Roma Beaumont and Zena Dare each appeared in more than one leading role in a Novello musical. Three leading roles were written for Mary Ellis (*Glamorous Night*, *The Dancing Years* and *Arc de Triomphe*).

Ruritania provides another line of continuity. It is a fictional state with a literary history that predates musicalized dramatization, yet the assumption of it as a Novello mainstay has become so indelible that it has even been erroneously considered Novello's own invention.[8] Only *Glamorous Night* (Krasnia) and *King's Rhapsody* (Norseland and Murania) – with *Gay's the Word* briefly adopting 'Ruritania' in deliberate parody – have such a setting. Rather, in the Novello shows we should recognize an exoticism of location, temporal as well as geographical, that invites different forms of scenic splendour. Examples range from a fairground to a Chinese temple (*Careless Rapture*, 1936), historicized Vienna (*The Dancing Years*, 1939) and Paris (*Arc de Triomphe*, 1943), and two different types of English ancestral home, one ancient and crumbling (*Crest of the Wave*, 1937), the other through the contrasting eras Regency, Victorian and present day (*Perchance to Dream*, 1945).

As with Novello's contemporary Noël Coward, the youthful experience of operetta and Edwardian musical comedy proved a lifelong influence. Novello was infatuated with Lily Elsie in the leading role of Sonia in London's first production of Franz Lehár's *Die lustige Witwe*, adapted as *The Merry Widow* (1907) (Noble 1951: 43). He eventually acted alongside Elsie in his play *The Truth Game* (1928), and in *The Dancing Years* pays specific musical tribute to Lehár and *The Merry Widow* (explained later). Writing for musical theatre was the prime focus of Novello in the years 1916–20: he contributed songs and partial scores to six musical comedies and revues before composing the whole score to *The Golden Moth* (1921). This part of his work is barely known today.

Novello continued composing songs sporadically through the 1920s, including for the revues *A to Z* (1921) and *Puppets* (1924), but he was mostly occupied with acting in both silent films and onstage and with writing plays.[9] However, he did not retreat from public view as a musician, but repeatedly absorbed this aspect of his identity into the roles he acted, whether written by him or by others. There was collusion between playwright and audience here. Consider the opening of Novello's *Symphony in Two Flats*, in which he played (on the stage and then on the screen) the role of David Kennard, a composer. As the scene gets underway a popular song is heard, 'Give Me Back My Heart', composed in the story by Kennard and in reality composed by Novello. What are we to make of Kennard only a few lines after the curtain has gone up? 'Oh but there's other music to write – I'm ambitious – I want to hear my music played on a wonderful big orchestra – it's always been my dream to conduct my own Symphony' (Novello 1932: 192). The play's action centres on a composer writing a symphony, while Novello's character Lewis Dodd in *The Constant Nymph* on the (silent) screen both composes his symphony and conducts its premiere. In *Murder in Mayfair* (1933), Novello wrote for himself the part of a love-tormented concert pianist.

In creating Rudi Kleber in *The Dancing Years* as a composer of operettas he explicitly brought his own self and his onstage character closer still, stating, 'it might be a good angle that the public should see a composer playing a composer, and that therefore when they heard my music on the stage they would subconsciously identify it with that of Rudi Kleber, and thus give an air of reality to the play.'[10] The concept is central to *The Dancing Years*, but the motivation is not as self-serving as it may appear, as we will see. This was the last of Novello's shows in which his offstage musical identity was formally written into his onstage character, but his acting presence continued to make the point. Sandy Wilson highlights this in quoting from a review of *Perchance to Dream* (1945): 'All the songs gain from the rapture with which Mr Novello listens to them' (Wilson 1975b: 242).

The success of the songs owes much to the fusion of the music with the lyrics. The heightened poetic tone of so many of the most prominent lyrics introduces the necessary justification for bringing in the music and contrasts with Novello's unfussy and often urbane style in his scripts. Novello was an adept, if infrequent, lyricist. One of the most striking numbers of *King's Rhapsody*, 'The Violin Began to Play', is entirely by him. He also wrote music, book and all the lyrics for *Perchance to Dream*, making him sole author of 'Till You Come Home Again', a pastiche of an early Victorian parlour ballad to suit the temporal setting of Act II and better known today as 'We'll Gather Lilacs'. But with the exceptions of *Perchance to Dream* and *Gay's the Word*, Novello's lyricist from 1935 on was Christopher Hassall.

As a student, Hassall was a member of the Oxford University Dramatic Society, then performed in *The Oxford Blazers* (1932) as his professional acting debut. John Gielgud recommended him to Novello, and in 1934 Hassall became Novello's understudy in a tour of Novello's play *Proscenium*. Hassall then played parts in Novello's *Fresh Fields* and *Murder in Mayfair*. He was in the right place at the right time as the idea for *Glamorous Night* arose, able to offer the right mix of interests as an actor, writer, poet and musician, although with no experience at writing lyrics or indeed of musical theatre. He had given Novello a book of his poetry, on which basis Novello asked him to try setting words to a melody. The result was what became the title waltz song of *Glamorous Night*. Besides writing for Novello, Hassall also wrote lyrics for the successful musical *Dear Miss Phoebe* (1950, music by Harry Parr-Davies), the libretto for William Walton's opera *Troilus and Cressida* (1954), and English-language versions of *The Merry Widow* (1958) and *Die Fledermaus* (1959). Add to this his own authored plays, and it is clear that theatre was the focus of his creative life, a prerequisite for admission to Novello's circle.

Novello was a demanding *force majeure* in his collaborations with Hassall, frequently driven by the need to work at speed. Often Hassall was given a melody one evening with the anticipation of the complete lyrics being ready the next morning, but when time allowed there was much more back and forth in their creative process. Novello tried out melodies on Hassall before settling on a final version. With some interplay on the detail, Hassall framed his lyrics to match Novello's completed melodies. Hassall recalled only two exceptions where the music was set to completed lyrics. 'My Dearest

Dear' in *The Dancing Years* is solely a refrain. Nearly a decade after the show's premiere and in response to a request from music publishers Chappell to turn it into a stand-alone song, Hassall wrote a new verse which Novello then set. The other example of the lyrics preceding the musical setting was the extract from the invented opera *Joan of Arc* within the show *Arc de Triomphe* (Handley-Taylor n.d. [1953]: 87–8).

The distinctive quality of Hassall's lyrics stems from the perspective he brought as a poet. His natural interests lay outside both lyric theatre and popular music. He recalled this difference from Novello in the creation of the pastiche number 'Primrose' for *The Dancing Years* as though by Lionel Monckton or Paul Rubens. Novello played his favourite songs from Edwardian musical comedies to Hassall, who otherwise would have had no idea of the appropriate style (Macqueen-Pope 1954: 384–5). Hassall was also an amateur musician with classical interests, so he could respond to Novello's ideas sensitively (in editions of *Who's Who in the Theatre* he repeatedly gave his hobby as 'musical composition'). Hassall shows a consistent capacity for the effective placement of memorable defining words and phrases – witness the natural setting in rhythm and intonation of 'uniform' within the song of that title in *The Dancing Years*. The titles were often suggested by Novello, but it was Hassall who had the job of working them into fully formed themes (Macqueen-Pope 1954: 381–2). His poetic imagery can be rich – the match of music, motion and flight in 'Waltz of My Heart', or the witty, cumulative Porter-esque repetitions in 'Why Isn't it You?' (*Careless Rapture*) – and is supported by technically secure construction that registers as effortless and natural. That Hassall did not diversify as a lyricist for other popular song composers in parallel with the Novello shows undoubtedly speaks to the special working relationship he quickly established with Novello and to the individualistic nature of the songs they wrote.

The screen and the stage

Sandy Wilson offers a provocative insight into Novello's career trajectory in the light of film. 'It is fascinating to speculate what might have become of Ivor Novello if his screen career had been better handled than it was – fascinating and also alarming, because we might have been deprived of his most important achievement', by which Wilson means the lavish stage musicals from 1935 on. Intriguingly, Wilson continues that Novello's early screen success, beginning with film *The Call of the Blood* (1919), 'whetted his appetite for the Theatre and he made his début on the West End stage in a small part in *Deburau* at the Ambassadors Theatre in 1921' (Wilson 1975b: 14). When considering Novello, the relationship of stage to screen is more complex than 'either/or'.

From a decidedly West End perspective, Macqueen-Pope assesses Novello's work in silent film in the 1920s as 'not of vital importance', 'short' and 'extremely profitable' (Macqueen-Pope 1954: 116). Napper and Williams counter that it is 'an essential element in his creation as a star of both screen *and* stage' (Napper and Williams 2001: 42), and the listings support this more nuanced view.[11] Between 1920 and 1934, Novello appeared in twenty-two films, of which the last six were sound films. In the same period he appeared on stage in twenty plays. Five of the stage plays were also filmed, two of which – the silent films *The Rat* (stage 1924; film 1925) and *Downhill*

(1926; 1927) – were by Novello with Constance Collier under the pseudonym 'David L'Estrange', and two by Novello alone – the sound films *Symphony in Two Flats* (1929; 1930) and *I Lived with You* (1932; 1933). Novello's final film, *Autumn Crocus*, is from 1934 and the first of the Drury Lane musicals that brings Novello fully back to the stage opens in 1935. There is a certain irony here: while it is impossible to see the stage shows today as they were conceived, a large part of his film repertory is available once more on commercial DVD and web uploads. It is easier than ever now to discover Novello the erstwhile distant screen star in person but not the lasting icon of musical theatre.

In the 1930s, the scenic sensation that had previously been the preserve of so many forms of large-scale theatre – whether in Drury Lane popular shows or the vast historical tableau of French grand opera – gained a serious competitor in film now with sound as well as large-scale imagery. Even a selective list of scenic elements from *Glamorous Night* is impressive: several attempted assassinations, a mob stoning a palace, a ship blown up then sinking, a huge gypsy wedding and a televised royal wedding. Mcqueen-Pope concludes, 'It was all astonishing and it was all Drury Lane' (1954: 179). But reviews caught the additional cinematic dimension: 'It is not an easy task now that the talkies have been brought to technical perfection, to invent a big-scale entertainment that will rival them in popular appeal' (quoted in Wilson 1975b: 196).

The willingness of West End theatre management to implement grand and expensive staging concepts in the 1930s was in part an urgent response to such commercial imperatives. This is also clear in the evident vacillation by theatre owners as to whether they should turn their theatres into cinemas, which many did. Novello wryly reflected this in his play *Party* (1932) in which a drama critic complains: 'my boss has got all his money in Talkies, so we've all got to say the Theatre is dead' (Novello 1932: 121). In Novello's play *Proscenium* (1933), an American theatre director goes further: 'I believe in the theatre – I believe in beauty in the theatre – I believe that in the theatre lies a road back to Sanity ... I want to give people the chance to dream again – and I want to show them that there is an art beyond the reach of mechanical devices and black and white shadows chasing each other round a white sheet' (Novello 1934: 69).

Novello understood film from a 1920s perspective. There was a marked change in film presentation at that end of that decade, where the screen had equipped actors with 'accentuated actions, highly expressive features, dramatic gestures, [which]would have looked ludicrous on the stage or indeed in any medium not entirely divorced from the stage or indeed in any medium not entirely divorced from sound' (White 1957: 172). Novello entered acting through romantic, melodramatic, silent film roles, often tinged with a sparkle of humour evident in the eyes and a wicked smile. This is the reputation he brought back to the theatre through the 1920s, where he also became an experienced stage actor, better equipped than so many silent screen actors. Novello's stage plays in the 1930s introduce an unexpected element into a domestic situation so that the emotional landscape grows out of scale with the social setting. For example, *I Lived with You* is a wonderful domestic comedy in which a Russian prince escapes the Revolution apparently with little but the clothes he is wearing. When he becomes the lodger of an aspiring lower-middle-class household, a clash of values causes havoc. *Symphony in Two Flats* sets a Bohemian comedy in one flat against a tragic romance (Novello as an increasingly blind composer) in the flat above. The characterizations are humorously mannered with the focus more on the theatricality of performance than the assertion of a social message.

This may explain the appeal for Novello of his reinvention on the musical stage at a point where his screen career lacked direction and the mechanics of film production were unsatisfying against acting a whole play in the theatre to immediate audience response. He could also 'get away from the conventional musical comedy, the kind of production for which he had written music and lyrics twenty-five years before' (Noble 1951: 199). His silent performance style from the 1920s necessitated emotion writ large for the intense storylines with bold hand gestures and facial expressions, as in *The Rat* and *Downhill*. Yet his style of vocal delivery was urbane, wry and most effective when understated. He did not play 'big' when acting on stage. The heightened gestural expression required by silent film has a parallel in the expansion of expression through music in a stage drama. The music allowed Novello to retain in his shows the scale of emotional expression of the silent screen alongside his belief in theatricality per se, which naturalized the acceptance of a hyper-realistic performative experience. As established by *Glamorous Night*, within such a scaled-up setting Novello the stage actor could be framed to his best advantage.

Novello's first three shows for the Theatre Royal, Drury Lane, created dramatically contrasting settings and atmospheres by which the audience 'travelled' as though in an epic film. Here was the big screen interpreted on a big stage. But with *The Dancing Years*, Novello distilled and consolidated that previous assortment of elements into a more integrated work unified through dramatic purpose and location rather than by using its characters to provide credibility-stretching pretexts to have one spectacular set piece follow another. At this point, any Novello 'formula' becomes specific to him rather than to Drury Lane: none of his subsequent shows were created for that theatre. Novello's concept for *The Dancing Years* redirects the visual and situational fantasy towards more believable settings of a relatively recent historical past, recognizable to anyone aged forty or more in the 1939 audience. The 'exoticism' has moved much closer to home in geography and in operetta-style staging.

The action stays in Austria: Vienna for Acts I and III, the Austrian Tyrol for Act II. The characters realistically age through 1911, 1914 and 1927 to 1938. Narratively justified spectacle is introduced too by the staging of the finale of Kleber's first operetta and by a costume ball, both set in recognizable locations in Vienna (respectively, the Theater an der Wien and the Belvedere Palace). Such staging demands are positively restrained in comparison to the previous Novello-Drury Lane shows with effects including the sinking of a liner, wrecking of a train and staging of an earthquake. What is gained is a more believable central relationship that has the quality of a close-up rather than a panorama: the relationship of Rudi Kleber and Maria Ziegler dominates. Through the music in particular, the emotions are given a large-scale presence. The drama comes from the story, not the staging.

Melody and dramatic expression

Music animates *The Dancing Years*. The stylistic contrasts between operetta, musical romance and musical comedy in the score mark the passage of time as well as the changing mood from nostalgia to relative modernity. In Act I (1911), Viennese Silver Period operetta is represented through the premiere of Kleber's debut work. In Act II (1914), Grete demonstrates the song-and-dance number 'Primrose', ostensibly from one of the latest London musical comedies. Novello's own style provides the continuity through the whole show against which these pastiche numbers appear in relief. Indeed, as he intended, Novello's musical voice becomes synonymous with that of Kleber's, especially for the intimate and private side of his relationship with Maria Ziegler. The constancy of Kleber's feelings for Maria is shown in stylistic consistency. His numbers appear in scenes in which Maria is the focus, and the dialogue makes clear that she has inspired the music and is the subject of the lyrics. As Novello did not perform singing roles – he felt the ability he had had as a boy chorister went when his voice broke – the emotional connection of the love duet is fulfilled throughout by Rudi Kleber providing the song and Maria Ziegler providing the voice. The musical commentary on the characters and the story as well as on the forms of musical theatre gives visceral depth to the show.

Formally, Novello mostly avoids the multi-section passages associated with operetta (as in Act I of *Bitter Sweet*) and earlier musical comedy finales (such as Novello's own Act I conclusion in *The Golden Moth*). However, he does introduce long-form musical construction for the finale pastiche of the show-within-a-show, *Lorelei*, where it is understood as historically distant in genre and musical style: a Viennese operetta of 1911 within a Novello musical play of 1939. Furthermore, the finale extract takes place during the period of Lehár's ascendance within Viennese operetta and in the same venue, the Theater an der Wien, where Lehár's groundbreaking *Die lustige Witwe* was given its premiere (1905). In the finale, Novello adopts the musical rhetoric of Lehár's romantic declarations in his tenor ballad 'My Heart Belongs to You'. Compare this with 'Dein ist mein ganzes Herz' in *The Land of Smiles*, introduced by Richard Tauber – with English lyrics by Harry Graham as 'You Are My Heart's Delight' – at the Theatre Royal, Drury Lane, in 1931. Novello's leading melodic phrase shadows Lehár's second, while the general pace, tone and style provoke a reminiscent association. The Lehár connections continue through the duet for Lorelei and Ceruti 'Love Calls with a Voice Loud and Clear' in the *Lorelei* Finale, which echoes the melodic shape and harmony of *Die lustige Witwe*'s Act II duet between Camille and Valencienne, with the section 'Sieh dort den kleinne Pavillon' (Novello and Hassall 1949: 150–2; Lehár 1906: 89–91).

The long *Lorelei* Finale presented in *The Dancing Years* – led from the theatre pit by Novello in the character of its composer Rudi Kleber conducting his operetta's premiere – was used in the 1945 tour.[12] This original version – along with an additional waltz song 'When It's Spring in Vienna' – is given in an appendix in the published vocal score. This finale was later replaced with a shorter, simplified version more suited to limited resources (removing the need for a strong solo tenor as Ceruti and making fewer demands on dancers and chorus). The two versions share a concluding section, but the shorter version is the one printed in the main body of the published vocal score. In this substitution, the connection with *Die lustige Witwe* becomes specific. Its opening chorus uses a melody in a bright duple time with a distinctive and catchy rhythm that matches almost exactly the march rhythms of the instrumental introduction to Act I of *Die lustige Witwe* and its return as a sung chorus at the start of Lehár's Act I finale.

Sealing the deliberate allusion (an in-joke as well as a tribute), Novello's melody is an inversion – a mirror reflection – of Lehár's (Novello and Hassall 1949: 38–41; Lehár 1906: 4, 32–3).[13]

Waltzes

The form of the waltz bridges the archetypal, period identity of Vienna and the music of Novello. Given the musical content, a more accurate title for Novello's show may have been *The Waltzing Years*, but that would not have been quite so distinctive following a number of shows that already had 'Waltz' or 'Waltzes' in their titles. Notably for London, there had been a biographical fiction on the Strauss father and son in *Waltzes from Vienna*, lavishly staged at the Alhambra in 1931. Thanks to the Strauss family, Vienna has become synonymous with the waltz. Kleber is a composer in Vienna. When asked in the first scene if he writes 'Great Symphonies – Fugues – Opera', his reply 'No – just waltzes' elicits the response 'what a relief' (Novello and Hassall 1953: 11). Rudi Kleber echoes Ivor Novello.

The associations of the waltz tie the sound of the music and the motion of the dance to a spectrum of emotions from joyfulness to romantic love to outright eroticism. These different waltz qualities of 'spirit' and 'dance movement' are readily expressed in British operetta from 1907 – the London premiere of *The Merry Widow*, with which the young Novello was so taken – and Novello's own *The Dancing Years* in 1939 (Snelson 2017). Exemplifying the waltz as a manifestation of an exuberant spirit is 'Waltz of my Heart', possibly Novello's second most famous song after 'Keep the Homes Fires Burning'. It enters *The Dancing Years* early in Act I in a way that only gradually reveals the whole thing: Kleber's piano demonstration of the opening phrases, then a chorus sing-along, a break as Maria Ziegler enters and discusses the number, then her rendition of the whole song completed with the first hearing of its introductory verse. In film terms it appears to be a MacGuffin, an early device to establish Rudi as a composer, set his style and his aspiration to write operetta, pay his debts and provide the means through which he and operetta star Maria Ziegler meet. But with that achieved, the song grows in significance through Act I from that opening piano fragment to the conclusion of the *Lorelei* Finale, with full orchestra and chorus (Novello and Hassall 1949: 60–2). It is emblematic of Rudi Kleber's spirit and indeed of Novello's too in its joyous, emotive voicing of the very idea of musical expression.

At the outset, the refrain ('The lark is singing on high') is given prominence. This makes the discovery of the opening verse ('Waltz of my heart, haunting and gay'), with as strong a melody as that of the refrain, that much more engaging. The two sections flow together wonderfully. The verse constantly teases with a slow rising in pitch and sudden drops from the high point of the phrase. Furthermore, a harmonic diversion threatens to derail the verse by heading in a slightly unexpected direction which leads to a moment of stasis that is broken by a no-fuss restart. The refrain contrasts with arc-like phrases emulating the slow swing of a pendulum from its low point up, then hesitating slightly at the apex before swinging back down. The flow between verse and refrain is the result of the blurring of composer-lyricist boundaries. Before production started, there was a lead refrain by Novello with lyrics by Hassall that began 'Waltz of my heart'. After Hassall returned from a break (his honeymoon), that original refrain had become the verse. Novello had written what is now the main refrain but had got stuck part way through the additional lyrics. Hassall completed them. This explains why the phrase 'waltz of my heart' is prominent in both verse and refrain (Handley-Taylor n.d. [1953]: 87–8). The resulting song is a fine demonstration of technical vocal command integrated with musical and poetic expression in relation to character, but also as an expression of what binds together Kleber, Ziegler and Novello.

Early in 1935, shortly before the first of Novello's Drury Lane shows opened, his play *Murder in Mayfair* was novelized by Denise Robins for Mills and Boon (previously she had novelized Novello's film *The Triumph of the Rat*). The clichés on the first page of the novel, setting scene and tone, anticipate a connection between the waltz and Novello's identity that is now indelible: 'They had danced together all night, waltzing most of the time, the dreamy enchanting Lehár melodies intoxicating them as did their close contact with each other. . . . music in their hearts, music and love drenching them, there was nothing, nobody else in the world this night but themselves' (Robins 1935: 1). Intimate, romantic and physically suggestive: it had to be a waltz.

Novello adopts such an approach to the waltz in 'I Can Give You the Starlight', which closes Act I, to convey a different level of intimacy. The refrains of 'My Heart Belongs to You' and 'Waltz of My Heart' (when first heard, without its introductory verse) start at melodic high points. Both numbers are delivered in public and observed by onstage groups. However, 'I Can Give You the Starlight' is performed in private. The phrases of the refrain begin low and only gently rise, and within each phrase the tendency is to fall away from the higher notes rather than keep soaring upwards. What may not be so obvious is that the tonic bass note that grounds the harmony – a G at the bottom of a chord of G major in the vocal score – is not heard until the very last note of the main melody. The harmonization begins on a first inversion – B at the bottom – and this creates a subtle drive in the harmonization that requires the necessary sense of completion. The verse is absolutely grounded on that tonic bass note G, and thus sets up a subliminal sense of its absence through all but the final two bars of the 36-bar refrain. Endorsing the compositional effectiveness, Novello used this same suspension of the tonic to similar effect in the refrain of 'Some Day My Heart Will Awake' in *King's Rhapsody*.

The bar count signals a further subtle emphasis in which the simple repetition of two phrases just before the end delays the expected conclusion at bar 32 to bar 36. Novello composes a slow deceleration so that the melody gently glides to a stop rather than lands with an exclamation mark as does 'Waltz of My Heart'. The tight musical focus fits the intimate situation of Maria sight-reading Rudi's latest work with him at the piano. It is personalized further by Kleber's introduction to the song in which he tells Maria: 'A strange and beautiful thing has happened. . . . You and my music have become one' (Novello and Hassall 1953: 32). Where 'Waltz of My Heart' pulls back to wide screen, 'I Can Give You the Starlight' ends on a close-up.

For the physicality of the waltz, that defining quality of perpetual movement through turning, the score includes 'The Leap Year Waltz', a ballet number during the 'Period Fête' at the Belvedere (Novello and Hassall 1949: 100–5). It adopts the standard format of a Strauss waltz, with a principal waltz melody in alternation with others that use contrasting characteristics.[14] The principal waltz melody, the first one, uses the insistent repetition of short phrases that bridge the bar lines to give the section an urgent propulsiveness that suggests the perpetual turning motion of the waltz. The second section has a long-phrased melody, little more than a rising scale in steady crotchets that drives towards the ends of its eight-bar phrases. In its constant reaching upwards, this second melody presents the gravity-defying element of the waltz. The return of the principal waltz melody is followed by a new melody in a different key whose prominent melodic characteristics are sustained melodic notes at the start of the bars and a gentle rise and fall in pitch. This is the waltz as 'effortless'. Back in the original key, the principal waltz returns as the conclusion.

The final image of *The Dancing Years* – onstage and as included in the film of 1950 – abstracts the dancing into a space out of time.

> [T]he stage was almost dark, and a gleam of blue light crept in like rising moonshine. Shadowy figures filled the stage, waltzing, waltzing, changing partners, and waltzing on until the stage was crowded with a whirling mass of dancers. The light grew stronger, but always blue – and blue is the colour of Hope. Hope was always Ivor's theme. And, through that throng, came the two lovers whose paths had parted. Here in the land of Hope, of Memory, they met again; they took each other in their arms and they waltzed through eternity. (Macqueen-Pope 1954: 331–2)

In fact, that description was written about the end of *Glamorous Night*, but as Macqueen-Pope continued, 'That was the trick of Ivor's genius. He used it several times and it never failed.' It demonstrates Novello's use of the tried and tested but alongside other recurring features – performers, musical style, his own onstage characters – is an assertion of the Novello 'brand'. The showman knew what his audience wanted. And it wanted Ivor Novello.

The glove and the fist

Any investigation into what could constitute a 'Novello style' inevitably stresses similarity more than difference, and such 'brand awareness' creates a selective blindness towards differences and innovations. Alan Bott's review of the premiere of *The Dancing Years* begins with this tack in describing 'the most glittering, scrumptious, tuneful and pseudo-passionate of all the shows [Novello] has assembled for Drury Lane. His manifold admirers will love it. . . . It neither has, nor intends, anything to do with reality.'[15] Novello had created a formula, and by definition any show with Novello's name on it must conform. Bott further emphasizes fantasy: 'The background is the old Austria, which, with its waltzes and operettas and uniforms and gaieties, has succeeded Ruritania as the theatre's Never-Neverland.' How should we then interpret a passage later in the same review that describes the final scene as presenting 'a Vienna which has been Nazified by officials with hearts of cement. They ban [Rudi Kleber's] songs, put him in "jug", and intend to do worse, since he defies them in a long harangue about the Vienna That Was'?[16] This was six months before the declaration of war with Germany. 'It neither has, nor intends, anything to do with reality.' Really?

There is a more pronounced contradiction in the *Daily News* review, in which 'the success [of Novello] was suggested early in the evening with his first waltz song, promised by the interval, and assured by the deafening cheers at curtain-fall, cheers which deafened even the still, small voice inside me which I keep trained to remind me that these musical spectacles are all nonsense'. That 'nonsense' was driven by 'the triumph of Formula, the tenth Muse' in a show set in 'the same Old Vienna'. The conventional is dismissed, yet the unexpected seems to be too when

> in the last scene of all, in the captured Vienna of 1938, Mr. Novello, now artistically decrepit, defies the conquerors (omitting only the jibe that they are wearing tactfully odd German uniforms) and brings the house down – why, this is only to show that Mr. Novello is astute enough to make the best of both worlds, the tinkles of 1911 and the tragedies of our own day.[17]

Either way, Novello couldn't win. Whatever Novello presented on stage was shaped by critical preconceptions of his work and the role of popular musical theatre: 'tinkles' must overshadow 'tragedies'.

In the build-up to war, the uncertainty of the public mood was of concern to theatre producers anticipating the reaction of their potential audiences. After war was declared, there was no ambiguity, hence those original 'tactfully odd German uniforms' pre-September 1939 were later turned to obvious literal ones. *The Dancing Years* returned to London in 1942, this time to the Adelphi Theatre. The review in *The Stage* describes Novello's characterization as leading towards the elegant white glove: 'Whether in the shorts and loose shirt of the penniless young musician or in the fancy costume of the fête or in the evening dress of the prosperous composer, he lends to every thing [*sic*] his own fine spirit.'[18] The glove is immediately paired with a reference to the fist: 'In the gaiety, the sentiment, even the tragic moment of his appearance before the Gestapo, soon to be dispelled by visions of the past, he conveys as an actor just the same message that he does as author and composer.' Novello inhabited convincingly the trajectory of Rudi's life story. However, the reviewer has no doubt that *The Dancing Years* continues that prevailing view of Novello's artistic purpose established in the previous three Drury Lane shows: 'It is a message of unfading romance. In spite of the undercurrent of sadness that runs through the play, there is no trace of cynicism or of disbelief in beauty's worthiness.' Certainly, this is what audiences took away from Novello's shows and what has been sustained through to their reputation today. But there are also 'tactfully odd German uniforms', 'Nazified' Vienna, 'the Gestapo' and 'tragedies of our own day'.

The wartime theme goes back to the inception of the show. On Christmas Eve 1949, BBC Radio broadcast *The Dancing Years* in the 'Saturday Night' Theatre' series, with several members of the 1939 cast: Mary Ellis (Maria Ziegler), Roma Beaumont (Grete), Olive Gilbert (Cäecile Kurt), Peter Graves (Fransel), Anthony Nicholls (Prince Charles Metterling) and, of course, Novello himself (Rudi Kleber). The prime time scheduling along with the celebrity cast reinforce the special status of the show. In a promotional article in the *Radio Times*, Novello described his inspiration in 1938 while on tour in Liverpool with *Crest of the Wave*:

> I had been to Venice, not Vienna, for my holiday, and had been very moved and shocked by a story I had heard from an old friend of mine who had gone into his favourite gramophone shop in Vienna and found himself unable to buy any records of music of any of the famous Viennese composers who had Jewish blood. This, of course, was after the Nazis had occupied Vienna, and it occurred to me to wonder what would have happened to me if as a composer of popular music I had also been Viennese and of Jewish descent. In this conjecture Rudi Kleber, the composer of *The Dancing Years*, came to life.[19]

The script submitted for licensing in 1939 has this scenario for its opening scene. The curtain rises on a Prologue in which an elderly, tearful woman is led away from an interrogation by two Nazi officers: 'Herr Ober Lieutenant' Goetzer says to his junior, Lieutenant Poldi, 'Sob stuff! They can turn it on like a tap.'[20] Their next prisoner is 'a man between 50 and 60. He is pale and has obviously been through a great mental strain.'[21] What an entrance Novello gave himself, the matinée idol *in extremis* – aged and worn, but defiant. What an opening to a Novello show at Drury Lane. Novello intended the identities of the fictional and real composers continually to blur, as when Novello's character is asked to confirm that his name is Rudolph Kleber and responds, 'Is it? Oh yes, so it is.'[22] The hesitation is because he is always known as Rudi, but the ambiguity for the audience – it is really Novello – is there too. The younger officer's admiration is quashed by his superior when 'A year ago I should have asked for his autograph' solicits the cold response 'And today he'll ask for mine on a death warrant'.[23]

A confrontation between Kleber and Goetzer halts with the arrival of Princess Metterling (aka Maria Ziegler). When Goetzer leaves the room to send her away – she is not allowed to see a 'political prisoner' – Poldi tells Kleber of his admiration since childhood of the composer's music. This introduces the flashback to Kleber's life from youth and obscurity to fame and success that makes up the bulk of the show. With that scene having opened the show, an 'Epilogue' closes it. Maria saves Kleber through the formidable political power of her husband's name. It is only a reprieve. Rudi intends to carry on his subversive help to those targeted by the authorities, and asks Maria to help him as long as he can. The show ends with their shared memories blurring into that blue-lit whirl of waltzing.

As conceived and initially staged, the show is framed by the political and physical oppression of the Anschluss of 1938, with the prologue casting a shadow over Kleber's growing fame through the whole work. The Lord Chamberlain's Office allowed this content because the political situation was not made explicit, with no recent names or events cited: 'Plays properly "Ruritanianised" as this is, must surely be allowed to contain this implied background.'[24] Consequently, the interrogation scenes were not censored, but by letter and telephone call it was made clear that the military title 'Herr Ober Lieutenant' could not be printed in the programme (it was not used in the dialogue) and that 'no German symbols or salutes will be used'.[25] This explains the 'tactfully odd' military uniforms. The Lord Chamberlain's Office was wary of real life intruding into the proper fictions of the stage. So, too, were some audience members. An undated and unsigned letter to the Lord Chamberlain purported to come from 'a number of people who while being quite sympathic [sic] resent the inclusion . . . [of the] Anti-Nazi scene', concluding that 'It seems a pity that politics are allowed in such plays'.[26]

There was a response as the show settled into its run, but not to remove this element. Instead, the Prologue was slightly streamlined and repositioned as the first section of the Epilogue. The brief instrumental passage that covers the scene change into the 'Epilogue' includes a distorted and threatening version of the Austrian national anthem.[27] The contemporary dimension thus cast no shadow over the bulk of the show, but it appeared in chronologically correct order at the end (which conveniently removed Novello's need to change his appearance from older Rudi Kleber to his young self between the Prologue and Act I). That Kleber is of Jewish descent can be inferred only through his name. He is not interrogated as a Jew, but as an Austrian composer who has used his wealth to buy false passports to help 'a great number of people who wished to leave a country which had no further use for them'.[28] A concluding speech calls Vienna 'a Hell for my lifelong friends' and a 'city of the dead' under 'silly little toy soldiers with your regulations and instructions and coloured shirts'.[29] With the advent of war, this last description was made more explicit as a Vienna run by a 'stupid, greedy machine . . . spitting hate and aggression' (Novello and Hassall 1953: 64). But for all such amendments and dilutions by indirect presentation, the message behind Kleber's treatment in what had become the closing scene of the play remained self-evident.

Another element used to reflect a contemporary environment is more subtle, but equally unacknowledged now. Three sequences are included in the score under the shared title 'A Masque of Vienna': Part I 1911, Part II 1914 and Part III 1927.[30] Part I is a mimed and danced street scene that portrays Vienna under the last days of the Austro-Hungarian Empire. A young girl accompanied by her governess, a flower girl, a modiste and a girl 'of high family' draws the attention of elegantly uniformed officers. A roué and an old man are enticed into dancing. An officer and his girl waltz, while a waiter 'watches the lovers intently – when they get sentimental he cries – when they are happy he reacts in the same way' (Novello and Hassall 1953: 20). Just when the officer thinks he has been deserted by the girl, the old man brings him a rose from the girl. The scene presents differing levels of blossoming romance, always suggesting a carefree atmosphere.

Part II is a fast reprise of music familiar from Part I, which is used as the introduction to Act III. The curtain rises on the Belvedere Palace in Vienna, the site of The Period Fête, a costume ball with an early nineteenth-century theme. The highlight of the fête is the 'The Leap Year Waltz', which is the fullest evocation of Johann Strauss II-infused Vienna in the whole show, and it is ostensibly danced 'by Miss Grete Schone and the entire Corps de Ballet of the Theater an der Wien' (Novello and Hassall 1953: 51). This scene has subtextual significance for many of its original audience through being set in 1914, just before the outbreak of a war many of them had lived through, and was now being viewed on stage when the outbreak of war was again feared.

The Period Fête is followed by 'A Masque of Vienna: Part III'.[31] Where Part I establishes a romantic, nostalgic Vienna, Part III presents Vienna in the wake of the Austro-Hungarian Empire's collapse. On the same street as for Part I, the mime and dance present a dystopian version of the earlier scene. A beggar is given a carrot by an old woman, the flower girl and the modiste are still present, but the officers who previously courted them have new roles as a profiteer, a chauffeur and two 'toughs'. The scene ends 'when GIRL sees WEALTHY MAN coming and proceeds to attract him. MAN looks her up and down' (Novello and Hassall 1953: 53). There is no romantic presentation of a rose. Times have changed for the worse, and charm has been replaced by a desperate pragmatism. The 'Masque of Vienna' is there 'to convey an impression of contemporary life of a Viennese street, and has no connection with the main story' (Novello and Hassall 1953: 2). Yet it does have a place in setting up the darkening historical tone that will intersect with the main text in the final scene of Kleber's imprisonment.

There are two identities for *The Dancing Years*: wartime and post-war. Novello's descriptive setting of the theme in his article for the *Radio Times* provided a balancing context given that the Christmas Eve radio broadcast excised the epilogue and (inevitably for radio) the masques. A scene-change narration by Novello established the mood of 1927 in a 'changed' city, where 'the melancholy that had invaded Vienna struck me like a tune once gay and now reprised in a minor key'.[32] Musical arrangements were taken from the film adaptation, in advance of its release by Associated British Pictures Corporation in April 1950. In effect, the show was 'Ruritanianised' to suit an audience for whom the war references were an intrusion into something that could easily be presented as escapist and nostalgic. This matched better the 'tradition'[33] of a Novello-branded show as it had developed further through *Perchance to Dream* (1945) and *King's Rhapsody* (1949). These excisions set a pattern that continued through to the 1960s and 1970s when the show was still current on the amateur operatic circuit in Britain, and in a television adaptation (1981).[34] Thus, a significant thematic element in the show's inception is now primarily acknowledged only through brief comment in studies, as here, and not as part of any shared performance awareness.[35]

Assessing the legacy

The reputation of Novello is bound up with 'Ruritania', a part of Middle Europe as colourful and dramatic as it is unreal. The association is entrenched but misleading, as Macqueen-Pope pointed out even when Novello's last two shows were still playing simultaneously in London (1951: 19). First, Novello's works did include topical awareness. This is most clear in the contemporary settings and characters of the plays through to the early 1930s. With *Glamorous Night*, the central character Anthony Allen is an inventor of television – the show was produced in the year between the first public demonstration of television in America in 1934 and the start of television broadcasts by the BBC on 2 November 1936. The show's concluding royal wedding was staged within a television surround to emulate a broadcast. This continued the 'Televariety' experiment at the Coliseum in March of the same year which had simulated 'a large television theatre of the future, watching an entertainment broadcast from various parts of the world'.[36] Furthermore, the spectacular scene of the sinking liner in the show was prompted by the disaster of the SS *Morro Castle*, which caught fire sailing from Havana to New York and ran aground on 8 September 1934, resulting in 137 deaths. The Ruritanian element ran in counterpoint to the modern, which heightened the fantastic quality that invited theatrical indulgence.

Even with *King's Rhapsody*, when Ruritania seems to be at its most fictitious, there is ambiguity. Elements of the plot mirror the life of King Carol II of Romania, who in the 1920s lived openly with his mistress Elena ('Magda') Lupescu in Paris, abdicating his throne in favour of a regency for his son, Michael, in 1927. The royal scandal was the stuff of the popular press of its day. But by 1949, another abdication in favour of a foreign mistress had rocked the British establishment, and the unspoken shadow of Edward VIII and Wallis Simpson added a frisson of recognition. Novello's reflection of the current and the political is more directly represented in *Arc de Triomphe* (1943), created during wartime. The story concerns the life and love of a French opera singer, Marie Forêt (Mary Ellis), loosely fashioned after the American soprano Mary Garden. While studying in Paris, Marie falls in love with a French actor who is subsequently killed in the First World War. The creation of parallels with the experiences of the Second World War at a time when France was under German occupation is deliberate. It is self-explanatory in the inclusion of *La Marseillaise* and an intentionally 'stirring' number in the show, 'France Will Rise Again' (Snelson 2021: 194–5). Unlike the anticipation of crisis that tints *The Dancing Years* early in 1939, *Arc de Triomphe* is explicitly about patriotism and self-sacrifice at a time of national crisis.

Novello had purpose in how he shaped his shows. He reflected dramatically aspects of the world around him, but he did not preach to further any causes. Edward Marsh described Novello as writing plays 'to please himself' as well as for a broad theatre-going public. The later plays 'have a significance beyond their outward show; but what he starts from is the fun of imagining characters and situations and action, not the desire to embody an idea' (Novello 1932: vii–viii). The inclusion of a changing social and political environment through *The Dancing Years* enriches character and situation, but it does not constitute its dramatic foundation, which remains the troubled trajectory of the love between Rudi Kleber and Maria Ziegler. The politically charged sections were uncomfortable in the first months of the show's life and became prompts to increasingly undesirable memories after 1945. The removal of these raw associations does not destroy the story line, but it does have an effect in the same way that dropping the opening scene of *Bitter Sweet* shifts that show's emphasis. Moving the original Prologue of *The Dancing Years* to join the Epilogue and then cutting that final scene in its entirety and to a lesser extent Parts I and III of 'The Masque of Vienna' has played up the Novello archetype of romance viewed through nostalgic, tinted lenses. It took two decades for another Maria, in Salzburg, to bring Nazis (and children and nuns and goats) to musical theatre and gain credit for the incorporation of such a theme. Now, when playing the subtext as main text seems to have become theatrically *de rigeur* – often with powerful results – one wonders what a director could do by taking their lead from the threatening tone of the interrogation Prologue and Epilogue and the censored military titles, uniforms and gestures rather than the nostalgic elegance.

Sandy Wilson summed up Novello's legacy: 'The world that Ivor ruled, a realm of glamorous, gaiety and romance, where everything was a little larger than life and at least twice as lovely, had gone for ever. All that was left was the music. Soaring, lilting, caressing, and as beguiling as the man who wrote them, his melodies are his memorial' (Wilson 1975b: 21). Stewart Nicholls concurs.

> Few people can boast such a successful and varied career in the world of entertainment; nonetheless he is practically forgotten today and almost unheard of outside of Britain. . . . It is the songs from his operettas which keep his name alive, but only through concert performances, newly recorded CDs, and reissued archival recordings, not because the shows they come from are performed. (Nicholls 2016: 199)

Here we encounter a recurring problem. So much of the repertory that runs through this book has faded from popular awareness as have the circumstances that gave rise to it. The importance of the people and the works in their own time is self-evidently not the same as it is today.

There is a need actively to negotiate the shifting values between an original 'present' that becomes for us an increasingly distant 'past'. Novello's final completed show, *Gay's the Word*, illustrates the problem. It is almost unknown today other than among musical theatre and/or Novello aficionados. What it demonstrates from the first notes of the Overture is an entirely different sound from what was expected, returning Novello to contemporary popular music for theatre as he had done in *Careless Rapture* and *Crest of the Wave* or even way back in his early compositions for musical comedy. The show tackles the potential of a modern British musical by problematizing 'old' and 'new' styles of show.[37] This is a difficult work to access today for an audience unaware of its historical background or Novello's reputation and the repertory specific both to him and the West End in the late 1940s. Without that context, the point of the many allusions, parodies and associated messages that make up the show is misunderstood, garbled or ignored. Instead, it becomes a good-natured and generalized self-regarding romp for theatre people. In *Gay's the Word*, Novello and his lyricist Alan Melville set out to present what a new British musical could be in 1951, but 'it discusses the issue rather than simply leads by a new example' (Snelson 2003: 228). Significantly, the central quality of 'Vitality' that Novello identifies in the Act I finale represents his own understanding of the theatre as grounded in the experience delivered by performers on stage to a live audience, not as a thematic abstraction as the show itself promotes.

In Novello's words, he is 'not highbrow', 'an entertainer', has 'no pretensions' and is an 'unrepentant sentimentalist'. He wrote 'to appeal first to the heart' and didn't use theatre for 'moralizing lectures on social behaviour', always keeping 'firmly within my *metier*' (Noble 1951: 272–3). We can see here Novello the businessman and the showman selling his brand, and if you look for these aspects in his works you will find them. Yet more technique and finesse are required to sustain so extraordinary a career to such a standard. The reputation of *The Dancing Years* shows this reduction of Novello's worth to the clichés of charming waltzes and idealized romances. His two final stage shows pose their own question in that they are so different, yet they ran concurrently at theatres literally round the corner from each other. At the Palace Theatre, Novello played his ultimate royal Ruritania role in *King's Rhapsody*, while Cicely Courtneidge sent up this very image and its association with Novello in the opening scene of Novello's *Gay's the Word* at the Saville Theatre. It takes a wily and confident showman deliberately to use their own reputation in such a way and make a success of it. It is 'theatrical'.

An anecdote Hassall includes in his biography of Edward Marsh captures the essence of Novello. Marsh met Novello in December 1915. He was a loyal, practical supporter and a close friend throughout Novello's life. Marsh loved theatre. He regularly read and commented on Novello's draft scripts and attended many first nights. Marsh 'criticized on rational grounds, although he was dealing with an instinctive artist and a showman to whose work the conventional canons of art could not usefully be applied' (Hassall 1959: 587). There is the danger of misrepresentation in claiming that the results of a distinctive talent arise in conceptual isolation. The biography of Novello demonstrates instead a wealth of talent thriving in alliance with a richness of experience, conscious development and constant effort. By definition too, the 'conventional canons' are challenged by any work of art that does something unexpected, which is to say pretty much all works that make a meaningful impression. All the case studies in this book display such a challenge in some form. However, 'instinctive artist and showman' is a more individualized observation. Hassall continues:

> There were times when [Marsh] would warn the dramatist against the improbability of speech or turn of a situation which later in performance he would have to confess was a theatrical stroke which made its effect. 'Really, Ivor, you simply *can't* say that!' he would protest, interrupting the reading. 'But the extraordinary thing is, Eddie, I can,' Novello would retort, smiling, and more often than not it turned out in the event that he was right.

In *The Dancing Years*, Ivor Novello brought together in a strikingly impressive way the influences and talents and – so importantly – an instinct that defined him so well as a 'Man of the Theatre'.

5

Bless the Bride (1947)

C. B. Cochran, A. P. Herbert and Vivian Ellis

Bless the Bride can appear as something of a curiosity in the story of the West End musical. The show is mostly forgotten to all but enthusiasts and has rarely been staged in the past three decades even by amateurs. Yet it was among the big successes of the immediate post-war years. Without the customary provincial tryout, the show opened at the Adelphi Theatre on the Strand on Saturday 26 April 1947, where it ran for more than two years. Its old-style producer was keen for a new creative challenge, so it closed on 11 June 1949 while still playing to packed houses. The show's popularity helped make a musical theatre star in Britain of its leading lady, Lizbeth Webb. It opened the way for the Broadway debut (in *Arms and the Girl*, 1950) of the leading man, George Guétary, and hence into the film *An American in Paris* (1951), for which he is most consistently remembered. The show's songs 'This Is My Lovely Day' and 'Ma Belle Marguerite' were familiar hits for decades.

The show was created under the close supervision of veteran impresario C. B. Cochran, already mentioned in Chapter 2 as the producer for Coward's *Bitter Sweet*. In a matchmaking manner reminiscent of Richard D'Oyly Carte with W. S. Gilbert and Arthur Sullivan, Cochran brought together writer and lyricist A. P. Herbert and popular composer Vivian Ellis for revue in the 1930s. Wartime service intervened for Ellis and Herbert (both in the navy), and Cochran reunited the theatrical triumvirate after the war to create three shows: *Big Ben* (1946), *Bless the Bride* (1947) and *Tough at the Top* (1949). *Bless the Bride* was the most successful.

The setting is Victorian, specifically 1870–1, when Lucy, a young English lady, runs away on her wedding day. She acts on instinct to pursue a whirlwind romance with Pierre, a French actor. In doing so, she rejects her duty to her family, previously unquestioned, of making a socially advantageous but emotionally limited marriage to an Englishman with a minor title. Before Lucy and Pierre can marry, her family tracks her down in France and war takes Pierre away to fight for his country. Back in England, and only just in time for the final curtain, Lucy and Pierre are happily reunited. The setting calls for rich period detail in the stage pictures, while the excursion to France allows for much play around English and French stereotypes – notably against what may be expected by mocking the English rather than the French.

On its surface, *Bless the Bride* adopts dramatic, lyric, visual and musical dimensions that constantly evoke with fondness and familiarity the past rather than the present. In his opening-night review, Anthony Cookman considered that 'the heavily decorated period pageant runs smoothly and cheerfully along familiar but by no means outworn lines'.[1] There is more to it than that. It is a cross-generational theatrical experience on many levels: ostensibly about the nineteenth century, the show simultaneously explores the twentieth through a complex interplay between past and present in themes and styles that continually blurs boundaries. For anyone unfamiliar with the older British musical theatre repertory, it is possibly the most challenging work explored in this book. How could this show be so significant and successful in its day and yet have become subsequently so neglected and, if mentioned at all, so often misrepresented? Much of the explanation comes from changes in cultural memory.

The creative team

The trigger for *Bless the Bride* came from C. B. Cochran – Charles Blake Cochran, known affectionately as 'Cocky'. He was an old-style impresario, immersed in the creation of theatre and absorbed by every element of it for its own sake, a creative catalyst who provided ideas, shaped shows from broad brush to intricate detail, and discovered and encouraged talent. He was whole-heartedly absorbed by 'the recklessness, generosity and good comradeship of the stage' (Graves and Hodge 1940: 124–5). Making money – and often losing it – was a side effect of the pursuit of ever-new theatrical entertainments. During a producing career that spanned half a century, he was associated with some of the biggest names in entertainment, particularly musical theatre, on both sides of the Atlantic. The juxtaposition of such figures as Harry Houdini, Noël Coward, Eleonora Duse, Cole Porter and the Ballets Russes gives a flavour of the range of those who benefited from his experience and influence across the entertainment world. His productions became characterized by scale, spectacle, high standards and star performers. Right through the 1940s and the creation of the Cochran-Herbert-Ellis shows, his obsessive, energetic work on every facet of a production belied his age, and his name on a show was the imprimatur for quality.

Cochran was born in 1872, so the period of *Bless the Bride* represents something of the world in which he grew up. This is not coincidental. His initial request to Herbert was for 'a Victorian period play' (Herbert 1970: 120). That direction towards the nineteenth century set a course with far-reaching temporal and generational consequences for the nature of the show. At the micro scale, it resulted in such detail as the opening scene of croquet at 'Mayfield' in Sussex, by which Herbert introduced a nod to Cochran's childhood in Lindfield (Ellis 1953: 228). Cochran's idea for a visit to France and Trouville resulted in the larger structural feature of Act II scenes in France at the seaside town of 'Eauville'. Bigger implications can be found in the eventual form of the show and the constant expressions of stylistic negotiation between period and contemporary that arose with a show set in 1870 and created to appeal as a new work to a 1947 audience. Herbert and Ellis were particularly well placed to tackle this in that they were both technically expert and classically educated in their respective fields but known for their output in the popular domain. Their ability to fuse heritage and convention with immediacy and novelty suited the project.

Herbert's personal and professional character was in large part set by his experiences of combat in the First World War. Moral conviction, national duty and close exposure to the awful conditions, physical mutilation and lost lives – including those of friends – most immediately found expression in his fictionalized account *The Secret Battle* (1919). The novel was acclaimed for its portrayal of war (including by Churchill and General Montgomery) and for its fine literary quality – Herbert's 'best book' in the view of his biographer, Reginald Pound (1976: 65). It was not financially successful, which encouraged Herbert to turn towards practising law in anticipation of a more sustainable living. But he quickly gravitated back to writing, this time in the comic and diversionary mode for which he became famous, not least as a contributor to *Punch*, an influential, weekly satirical magazine founded in 1841. As Pound suggests, here too Herbert's interest grew out of wartime experience: 'Laughter was a solvent of fear, humorous journalism an antidote to the terrors of the night' (1976: 65). While Herbert made his name through satire and humour, his subject matter arose from his strong sense of the place of the individual within society and nation, the values that had to be shared in sustaining this, the legal structures that attempted to uphold it and keen observation that exposed the systemic flaws that blocked individual rights.

There is common ground between Herbert and W. S. Gilbert. They both had legal training which they rejected for popular writing. They both capitalized on a love of logical absurdity, using witty dramatic juxtaposition to make a point. They both flourished their linguistic talents with brilliance and precision. It was a complimentary comparison that Herbert protested yet couldn't ignore: 'I did not want to be "another Gilbert" and resented it when people said I wasn't' (Herbert 1970: 95). The influences of Gilbert on Herbert's writing come through in the vocabulary, metres and forms of the verses as well as in his sheer delight in inverting the usual world view to comic effect. For example, in his libretto for the comic opera *Derby Day* (1932, music by Alfred Reynolds), Herbert in wittily rhymed couplets has the young, dissolute Eddy describe how his own character has been blighted by the moral and upstanding nature of his aristocratic parents. The consequence of their example is that he has not learned to recognize anything bad and thus immediately succumbs to it. Eddy pithily concludes that his tombstone should be inscribed 'He might have been much better if his parents had been worse' (Herbert 1932: 131).

Overt tribute to Gilbert and Sullivan came in the short parody *Perseverance (or Half a Coronet)* for Cochran's revue *Streamline* (1934), the earliest of Herbert and Ellis's collaborations on a show. In this send-up of familiar Gilbert and Sullivan tropes, the influence of *Iolanthe* and *The Gondoliers* on Herbert is clear, especially in plot references and versification. Ellis's music is more generically styled. Although Ellis knew from his youth of some of Sullivan's music, he did not know whole shows. The first he saw fully staged was *Patience* in 1934 specifically in preparation for his work with Herbert on the pastiche (Ellis 1953: 51). Herbert thought that Gilbert's verses lacked 'real dramatic excitement or emotion'. He considered he did much better and in *Bless the Bride* 'set out to make people cry' (Herbert 1970: 95). His analysis of Gilbert is undoubtedly in part self-serving, yet songs in *Bless the Bride* including 'The Silent Heart', 'This Is My Lovely Day' and 'Ducky' bear out his talent to convey the genuinely touching in different ways.

Vivian Ellis worked well with Herbert, and both men described in their autobiographies a shared enjoyment of their supportive collaboration of some two decades. One work spans the period. Herbert's novel *The Water Gypsies* (1930) was filmed in 1932, for which Ellis contributed the title sequence song 'Little Boat', setting lyrics by Herbert. More than two decades later the song found its way into their adaptation of *The Water Gypsies* as a full stage musical (1955). Both lyricist and composer were already well established when Cochran brought them together for his revue *Streamline* (1934). Ellis's breakthrough had come with his score for the musical *Mr. Cinders* (1929), from which 'Spread a Little Happiness' has proved the most enduring number. He claimed he read only two scripts for musicals that immediately struck him as bound to succeed: *Mr. Cinders* and *Bless the Bride* (Ellis 1953: 79). Cochran had included a few individual songs composed by Ellis in revues in the mid-1920s, beginning with *Still Dancing* (1925, a revision of *On with the Dance*), but it was with *Follow a Star* (1930) that Ellis became the headline composer for a large-scale Cochran revue. Throughout the 1930s, Ellis had music (as either sole composer or contributor) in concurrent West End musicals and shows, through which he provided material to many of the leading performers of the day, such as Cicely Courtneidge, Jack Hulbert, Frances Day, Alice Delysia and Leslie Henson.

Collaboration was paused during the war, in which time the public perception of the three shifted. By virtue of age and success, Cochran was a grand old man of theatre. Herbert's reputation was the most current with the public through his involvement with wartime politics and his regularly published writings. But Ellis had effectively dropped out of the London music scene during his wartime service at the Devonport naval base in Plymouth. He lost touch with Herbert and did not meet up with Cochran for some time (Ellis 1953: 215–19). The story was different for Ellis's fellow writers who also performed, and the war years kept them in public view. Novello continued with extensive national touring and presented his new musical *Arc de Triomphe* (1943), themed around wartime patriotism. Coward was active in official wartime propaganda (including the film *In Which We Serve*, 1943) and an often-gruelling round of performances for troops. The individual shifts and breaks in creative continuity experienced by Cochran and especially by Herbert and Ellis reset their parameters when they began working together again on *Big Ben*. They evolved a new approach characterized by a distinctive cross-genre fusion that was most fully consolidated in *Bless the Bride*.

Wendy Toye's direction and choreography contributed much to the effectiveness of the show in preparation and performance. She was a highly organized and driven theatre professional who gained the admiration of Cochran, Herbert and Ellis. Her theatrical background began in early childhood – she listed her first public appearance as dancing at the Royal Albert Hall in 1921 at the age of four and a half. Toye matured from juvenile roles to become a prominent principal dancer in London theatre, especially in the 1930s. Also, she gradually moved into choreography for musicals and revues (particularly George Black's at the Palladium). By 1945, Toye was in the top rank of West End's dancer-choreographers, and not yet thirty. Cochran's engagement of Toye as a director launched what was to become the most notable facet of her distinguished career in directing for stage and later film. As a woman director of musical theatre in a substantially male field she was following the lead set by Leontine Sagan, a former student of Max Reinhardt and the first female director to stage shows at the Theatre Royal, Drury Lane: Sagan directed all Novello's musicals from *Glamorous Night* (1935) to *Arc de Triomphe* (1943). Toye's later directorial career in musical theatre included opera and operetta, as well as being director and co-creator of the successful revue based on the works of Noël Coward, *Cowardy Custard* (1972).

Cochran's approach to Toye to direct *Big Ben* was a surprise to her as 'I couldn't see any position for dancing in it'.[2] Rather, Cochran had seen the potential in bringing youthful direction and energy to the team of himself, Herbert and Ellis. There was a symbiotic quality in the intensity with which all of them worked together. In his autobiography, Ellis spelt out Toye's thorough organization, precision and ability to charm everyone in the cast (Ellis 1953: 220–1). Toye was sensitive to the tone of this creative team, and her young and physical perspective on staging complemented the more cerebral qualities of Herbert and the smoothness of Ellis's style. For all of them, the tone of *Bless the Bride* was 'tongue in cheek'.[3] As reviewers noted, Toye's interpretation of this mood contributed lightness, stage energy and visual clarity, which brought a freshness to what could otherwise have become historical heaviness. For example, John Courtenay noted in his review for *The Sketch*, 'This is an endearing piece of Victoriana, directed (but not over-directed – mark the difference) by Wendy Toye, whose groupings throughout have the proper pictorial quality; she keeps the stage fluid; her crowds never stiffen into waxwork. . . . Miss Toye's patterning is one of the Adelphi delights.'[4]

This chapter elaborates upon an apparent contradiction in reviews, as in *The Tatler*: 'Everything has the mark of good taste inseparable from a Cochran show, and though originality has been avoided as though it were something that stung the hand that fed it, Miss Wendy Toye and her collaborators succeed in giving conventional sentiment and humour a genuine freshness.'[5] Without novelty to distinguish it, was its appeal solely that of classy production and performances? Or does such an assessment miss something significant that could account for the show's popular appeal in the West End, on tour and for some time after in the amateur repertory?

The aftermath of war

On one level *Bless the Bride* is a charming and diversionary entertainment: a sepia-tinted period romance along conventional line, grounded in staid Victorian England. A young woman on the eve of her socially advantageous marriage realizes that she is acting out of duty, not love. Her discovery is caused by a foreigner who arouses genuine emotion in her for the first time. They run away to his homeland in pursuit of romantic happiness. A selective description such as this emphasizes tropes shared with *Bitter Sweet*. Elements of the musical style adopted by Ellis to suggest the chronological setting do too.

To take another perspective, the story explores the contrast of values between the English and the French amplified through differences between the young and the old, focussed through personalized situations of love and loss. The show begins with very English pastoral idyll – croquet on a Sussex lawn – and ends with an accommodation of values across the parent–child generations and an accord across the English Channel in the reuniting of a young English lady (Lucy Veracity Willow) and a young French man (Pierre Fontaine). Herbert is consistent in how he builds 'national character' into the script:

> For the English characters, instinct is to be subjugated: emotions are hidden, restraint is valued, history and tradition are privileged, conformity is valued, energy is suppressed, and the environment is tamed. By contrast, for the French, instinct is to be followed: emotions are expressed openly, restraint is not valued, but change and especially individuality are valued, energy is released, and the environment is to be responded to. (Snelson 2003: 149)

Herbert's usual introduction of social and political purposes into his work is expressed in *Bless the Bride* through these deliberately caricatured and polarized national identities. The English–French contrasts lead to understanding between both sides when faced with Prussian aggression: war between France and Germany becomes a means of uniting English and French perspectives.

Contemporary reviews present the surface image of the charming Victorian setting and the happy ending, revelling in that distance in time and that diversionary aspect of the tone. By the accepted criteria of the genre and the time, successful musicals were diversionary and thematically light. Theatre reviewers passed silently over the multiple scenes and the explicit dialogue that seem to be reliving experiences that resonated with the Second World War and its aftermath. The conversation the show had with its first audiences through the constant subtext had the potential to make it a very personal experience. It seems so when viewed from the distance of many decades in a parallel with the minimizing of the Nazi representation in *The Dancing Years*. It was even easier to distance the themes of *Bless the Bride* from the recent experiences of the 1940s audience to whom it was aimed through a historical setting of almost eighty years earlier, and thus beyond direct memory.

A summary of the wartime references woven into the show makes the relevance of approaching *Bless the Bride* from this angle clear (for a detailed analysis see Snelson 2021). The quantity and cumulative effect of these references go beyond the addition of period detail. For example, photographs of the production show Lucy in her generous bridal gown, with veil and long train, and accompanied by her many sisters in equally lavish bridesmaids' dresses. Today, the image reads simply as a literal staging of the scene. Yet the sheer quantity of material on display in the stage costumes made something of a statement after the wartime rationing of clothing through coupons and the utility clothing scheme. It was only in 1946 that clothing controls began to be relaxed (Zweiniger-Bargielowska 2000: 48–51). Consequently, the stage image of 1947 was even more dream than reality than ever for brides of the previous seven years, unless it was the 'something borrowed' from one's mother and even grandmother, as Lucy was able to do (Herbert 1948: 28). The stage picture is not just that of an idealized wedding image but also an extravagant contrast to the audience's contemporary experiences. An extra twist is given to this, albeit anecdotal. Wendy Toye remembered the audiences for *Bless the Bride* as generally younger than those at the same time at the Coliseum for *Annie Get Your Gun* (in which she appeared as Winnie), not least because of the number of bridal parties ('hen nights') in the audience.[6] Moreover, production photographs illustrate the elaborate and generous costume designs throughout the show.[7] The dressing in period of the cast of a new large-scale musical acts as a reminder of the impact stage costuming alone could make after a period in which resources for theatre performance were not a priority, which contributed to the dominance of musical theatre revivals in the 1940s.

One dramatic intervention in the final minutes of the show bluntly puts the consequences of war centre stage. The French actress Suzanne appears during Lucy's twenty-first birthday party. She sees the happy, beautifully dressed family and friends and the centrepiece cake. This is in stark contrast to her dishevelled and lean appearance. She berates them for their dancing and their comforts set against her recent experiences of the Siege of Paris, searching for food among the rubbish, eating rats: 'the hunger, the famine, the cold' (Herbert 1948: 62). Placed so near the final curtain, the contrast is dramatically bold and the reminder of wartime deprivation unavoidable, even 'consciously provocative' (Snelson 2021: 195). The last scene of the show is the focal point for an accumulation of such war-related events and themes as the declaration of war between France and Prussia, the military cowardice and belated bravery of Thomas Trout (Lucy's erstwhile fiancé), the call to arms in France, the subsequent reported death of Pierre in battle and Lucy's growing obsession with France's fate. Even Grandpapa in Act I introduces French-English-Prussian wartime contrasts in a semi-comic vein, mistaking the 1870 threat of war with that from Napoleon: 'Ah, Waterloo . . . Good old Blücher. The Prussians saved the day!' (Herbert 1948: 20). He dreams of the wars of his youth: 'Now the Yankees are against us. War with America! . . . Why, there's old Wellington!' (Herbert 1948: 21). At the end of Act I the double blow of Lucy eloping and with a Frenchman is enough to kill him off 'from grief and shame' (Herbert 1970: 121).

Herbert leaves his audience with a plea to reject past factionalism. Pierre presents his reunion with Lucy in terms of national cooperation when he rewrites some of the lyrics of their earlier romantic duet 'This Is My Lovely Day' as 'This is the better way, the flag of England the flag of France together flying' (Herbert 1948: 63; Ellis and Herbert 1947: 174). These are almost the last words the audience hear before the curtain falls on the entire show. The context of 1947 gives a visceral, electric charge to those lines and the finale's wider celebration of reunion and reconciliation. Significantly, the action of the show bookends the Franco-Prussian War and thus avoids presenting any of it. There are no scenes of Pierre as a soldier, no ongoing reports of the war's progress and no staging of Suzanne in Paris during the siege. It is a wartime show that sidesteps the actual war. The focus is on Lucy reuniting with Pierre: girl meets boy, girl loses boy, girl finds boy again. It's just a light, romantic piece, isn't it? Any emotional effect at the end can thus be deflected as the result of a conventional happy ending, rather than any more personal and recent themes. That duality was the show's strength in its day but a weakness as time passed and the generational associations waned.

Ellis and elegance

Vivian Ellis was a sophisticated musician from a classical background. His grandmother Julia Woolf was a concert pianist whose own compositions included the comic opera *Carina*. His mother was a classical violinist who had studied with Ysaÿe. Ellis himself was a concert-standard pianist who studied with Myra Hess at the Royal Academy of Music. For comparison, Coward was untrained but instinctively musical. Novello had moderate technical training but was immersed in the particular qualities of the voice and song pretty much from his infancy. Gay is nearer to Ellis in having had early musical education at the Royal College of Music and as a church organist. What they all share is an ability to come up with natural, memorable and communicative melodies. This is the essence of popular musical theatre throughout the whole period explored here, and indeed beyond. Ellis honed his skills working for the music publisher Francis, Day & Hunter, where his responsibilities included the assessment of the manuscripts of new songs sent in and the demonstration of them to the publisher and to well-known performers in search of new material for their acts. For an inquisitive and analytical composer, this practical contact with so many new songs proved an ideal training ground. Through it, Ellis worked out what suited him best and began to have songs published and adopted by performers. His own songs were not always the most immediately commercial, but they had class, and Ellis stuck with advice given him by Jerome Kern: 'Go on being uncommercial – there's a lot of money in it' (Ellis 1953: 52).

Ellis's music is detailed and subtle. In common with Coward and Kern, he admired the work of Paul Rubens, who 'became my ideal. Here was a kind of light music I *could* compose, graceful without being vulgar' (Ellis 1953: 51). Ellis's style is distinguished by a flowing lyricism allied to an inventive rhythmic approach to word setting. His work is always that of the craftsman, and often delightfully so in making unexpected details seem both surprising and natural. By way of example, the opening of the refrain of the song 'Sweep' uses rhythmic variants that in turn elongate the opening word as a though in a street call, 'Swee--p any chimneys today, lady', with the lilt of syncopation to the bottom of a diatonically descending phrase before a little upward flick on the word 'lady' completes the phrase. The word setting is engagingly unpredictable but unforced. In 'I'm on a Seesaw', the leading song success to come out of *Jill, Darling*, the up-and-down motion of the emotional metaphor is neatly encapsulated through an injection of bouncing octaves into the otherwise smooth undulations of the refrain.

In the more emotionally driven numbers, the unfussy, direct and elegant style conveys sincerity. Within *Bless the Bride*, the context and lyrics of 'This Is My Lovely Day' create a calm centre in Act II, but especially so with Ellis's setting. The first phrases slowly rise up to be balanced by the emphatic, descending shorter phrases of the melody's conclusion. The structure is standard, but Ellis's pacing of melody and harmony in conjunction is masterly. Where Novello so often wears his heart on his musical sleeve, Ellis tends to place his just visible between a well-tailored jacket and a neat cuff. A similar comparison can be made with the lyrics of Christopher Hassall for Novello and those of Herbert for Ellis – expansive for the former pair, and precise and targeted for the latter. It reveals the different theatrical natures and throws light on why these collaborations were so effective, their work so integrated and their shows so different in theatrical tone.

Before the Second World War, Ellis was the most successful of British popular songwriters and one of the few to achieve some success in the United States after his first transatlantic hit, 'I Never Dreamt' from the revue *Will o' the Whispers* (1928). Ellis's pre-war catalogue includes a succession of beautifully phrased numbers, many of which became popular with dance bands: for example, Ellis's 'She's My Lovely' (from *Hide and Seek*, 1937) was the signature tune adopted by the British band leader Billy Ternent. Between 1927 and 1939, Ellis wrote the music to fifteen shows, twelve of them for major West End theatres, along with numerous contributions to revues and several songs for films in the 1930s. Almost all adopted a distinctly popular tone, yet signs of Ellis's classical background were there. Examples include the incorporation of whole-tone modality in 'The Wind in the Willows' (*Cochran's 1930 Revue*), in which the unusual inflections of the melody are underpinned by the propulsion of a slow, sequential harmonic lift, and the almost improvisatory, art-song quality of 'Little Boat' from the film and stage adaptations of Herbert's novel *The Water Gypsies*.

Post-war music

After the war, Ellis's shows sound different. The elegance and detail are magnified through larger-scale musical numbers and character contrasts. While the scores feature the takeout songs that could be popular hits, they sit within a greater emphasis on structural completeness, from overture to final curtain. The music is an integral part of how theatrical drama is created in the whole show. Coward emphasized this approach to whole-show musical construction and identified it as important within Novello's whole scores. Herbert's librettos provided the spur for Ellis to put this approach into practice in a way that the pre-war revues and shows had not. And Ellis had the skill and breadth of imagination to realize it. Herbert constructed his librettos with an eye towards comic opera verse forms, including notably Gilbertian constructions, and the inclusion of moral and social purposes already familiar from Herbert's authorial voice and formal political activity as a Member of Parliament. More layers within the story and the text allowed for more layers in the music than a pre-war script-and-song sandwich so familiar from musical comedy, as with Ellis's first big hit, *Mr. Cinders* (1929). In fact, Ellis thought the label 'musical play' for *Big Ben*, *Bless the Bride* and *Tough at the Top* a convenient genre disguise to placate the expectations of the times. He used the term 'light opera' (Ellis 1953: 220) or even – in a further parallel with Coward – 'operette', as he explained:

> In operette music ceases to be merely a series of tunes accompanying songs. It becomes an integral part of the play, colouring and developing the action, possessing a dramatic life of its own by which it expresses the thought and feeling of its themes. (The most striking example of this faculty in *Bless the Bride* is when Pierre returns after being given up for dead. Before he appears the orchestra gives the theme of his love song and Lucy's face clears as though the music expresses her

premonition that he is alive.) Instead of chaining the composer to a lyric, the music of operette gives him a free world for creative development of his own.[8]

There is no clear, shared definition of the term as distinct from 'operetta', and it is often taken to be simply a French-language synonym. Coward's choice of word creates a little distance between his own works and the familiar operetta repertory of Lehár, Straus, Fall, Kálmán and Stolz. However, when used to describe post-war shows, 'operette' seems to be a more loaded term than it had been pre-war. That at least seems to be Ellis's view when he continues that '*Bless the Bride* is as different from the high-pressured and much trumpeted *Oklahoma*[!] as a rose is from a prairie flower reared in a Broadway hot-house. But the home-grown product has elegance with its simplicity, wit and charm of lyric and music, which give it a most attractive character of its own.'[9] Ellis draws a distinction in style and approach between a specifically British form – 'home-grown' and described with the consciously European term 'operette'– and an exemplar of contemporary American musical theatre style. Such a focus towards the Continent rather than across the Atlantic builds on the stylistic tendencies in the 1930s shows of Coward, Novello and Posford. British musical theatre is never best dealt with solely in terms of contemporary Broadway comparison.

Ellis's command of music within numbers and across the arc of the entire score of *Bless the Bride* is such that the show makes an impression greater than the sum of its individually impressive parts. This can present a barrier in appreciating the show today: the extracts of the original cast recording do not convey the contrasts, transitions and cumulative effect of the musical drama. In this century, the opportunity to experience the contours of a complete performance in real time, even at an amateur level, has been rare. Consequently, imagination must be brought to reading the script and playing through the score. This is an unfortunate barrier, as the show was a turning point for Ellis. The subject matter benefited from a style rooted in a specifically English past and theatrical tradition in a more concentrated way than *Big Ben* had afforded. The pull between contemporary and past drives a bigger musical architecture whose layers of contrast reflect on and deepen the dramatic arc of the script.

The show is a performance of musical theatre memory in how it melds together different elements of the popular lyric stage of some eighty years. This was not historical awareness on Ellis's part, more a reflection of the range of styles actively performed in the repertory. For a new show of 1947, *Bless the Bride* is unusually eclectic, but there would have been recognition for such variety across the age range and lyric references of the whole audience. Herbert fashioned generational conflicts into the script, which Ellis was inspired to represent and expand upon in large part through genre contrasts: the score is integrated through the studied use of difference in genre styles, not from stylistic homogeneity. Different lyric forms that Ellis draws upon include the nineteenth-century coloratura waltz song ('I Was Never Kissed Before'), Gilbert and Sullivan patter song ('Too Good to Be True'), Victorian parlour ballad ('The Silent Heart'), the sentimental solo of Edwardian music hall ('Ducky'), madrigal ('The Englishman'), Gallic folksong ('Mon Pauvre Petit Pierre' and 'Ma Belle Marguerite'), musical comedy chorus ('Bobbing–Bobbing') and contemporary popular song (the ballad 'This Is My Lovely Day' and the tango 'A Table for Two'). Operatic forms of recitative and arioso are also woven into the multi-section Act I finale. The café scene in Act II adds yet more variety when it alternates the sections musically to bring out Herbert's rising tension that in microcosm replays an all-too-familiar progression for the early audiences: the denial of war, then the threat of war, then a declaration of war.

The Victorian family is shown as staid, backward-looking and patriarchal, and in large part it is the source of Lucy's problems. It embodies tradition and it values continuity. It stifles individuality in expecting the subjugation of the self to the group. Herbert's view is not wholly damning, for he also portrays an affection for the unity and strength it generates. Ellis portrays this venerable institution in music in the number 'God Bless the Family' (Ellis and Herbert 1947: 61–6). The main refrain is cross between a four-square hymn tune and a national anthem, which captures the patriotic elision of God with Nation. An arpeggio ostinato in steady crotchets suggests the ritualistic, slow march quality heard in 'Land of Hope and Glory' (the trio from the first of Elgar's *Pomp and Circumstance Military Marches*). The ostinato bass line is the more meaningful for having been first heard as the main motif of Lucy's earlier song 'Any Man but Thomas T'. When Lucy sings the refrain 'God bless the family' she asserts her family's collective will, not her own. Toye took her cue from the music and directed this number with the grouped formality of a Victorian family photograph, a deliberately overserious and stylized approach that surprised Herbert when he first saw it.[10] The family is presented throughout the show from both affectionate and critical points of view.

In Act II, Pierre anticipates Lucy's arrival at the restaurant in Eauville with the tango 'A Table for Two'. The recurring rhythm here is springy and propulsive, not weighty as with that 'family duty' ostinato figure. The melody is lyrical and expressive, not four-square and formal. A contrasting middle section speeds up, and Pierre fires out words that convey his joyful impatience waiting for Lucy's arrival. It is not just that this is an extrovert solo, but the tango for 1947 is up to date and fits with the Paris-Latin Quarter exoticism that was part of the developing performance persona of George Guétary, the creator of the role of Pierre. More generally, Ellis uses contemporary musical styles for Pierre's solo numbers 'Ma Belle Marguerite' and 'A Table for Two'. Lucy's family is musically tied to the past, while Pierre sounds like the 1947 present. For Pierre, Ellis adopts the most relaxed musical styles of the score, with contemporary rhythms or folk-song formats. Pierre always sounds so natural in comparison to the Willow family (that hymn-tune formality, the pseudo madrigal of 'The Englishman' in Act II), Thomas Trout (a comic character out of Gilbert and Sullivan, complete with patter-song style) and Grandpapa (who dreams of waltzing).

Qualities of emotional restraint and freedom are allied with English and French characters, respectively, when Lucy's and Pierre's natures are juxtaposed through consecutive solo numbers. The text of Lucy's 'The Silent Heart' is a pastiche by Herbert of Tennyson, which Ellis sets in the manner of a Victorian parlour ballad 'simply, but seriously' (Ellis 1953: 233). On the face of it, Lucy's presentation of this pointedly titled song as a drawing room performance to the family suggests composure, yet the uneasy undercurrents are clear in the sound. We know that Lucy's heart is definitely not 'still' as the words state – Pierre's kiss in the shrubbery saw to that – and the music conveys her unease. Melodic disquiet is created through oscillating 3rds that descend through the vocal phrases along with 9th suspensions stressed at the phrase end. In the accompaniment, the disturbed undercurrents are further voiced by chromatic descents in the middle of the texture. In short, Lucy's emotional sense of isolation is distinguished by a musical otherness peculiar to her. Despite audiences not according the number any special recognition, it was Ellis's favourite of his score, and he included it as a prominent piano solo (played by himself) in an orchestral selection of the show recorded with the Adelphi theatre orchestra.[11]

Lucy's solo is in the learned musical language of the art song and is introverted through its self-reflective theme. In contrast, Pierre's 'Ma Belle Marguerite' is folk-influenced and extrovert, with Marguerite as an alter ego for Lucy released on many levels from the constraints of English propriety to tread grapes and drink wine. The tune bounces along infectiously, with a sense of the French nursery rhyme 'Alouette' as a possible model behind the dotted rhythms, phrasing and cadences. When the 'ting-a-ling' refrain is taken over by the chorus at the end of the second verse, Pierre's melismatic counter-melody adds to the sense of emotional and physical release. Where Lucy's 'Silent Heart' solo is an internal struggle not to reveal emotional truth, Pierre's 'Ma Belle Marguerite' is extrovert and celebratory.

The influence of British comic opera of the later nineteenth century, including some specific spin from Gilbert and Sullivan, is present in Herbert's libretto, and on that account is traceable too in Ellis's score. The influence is predominantly formal (verse structure, metre and rhyming pattern). There is a more personal model for Ellis, who thought of his grandmother's comic opera *Carina* often as he worked on *Bless the Bride* (Ellis 1953: 15, 227). Some similarities arise through the plots, although these are as much the generic tropes of the comic opera genre as anything more individual. In *Carina*, the disruption of marriage to the 'wrong' person by the 'right' one in disguise and a certain contrast of national types and values (Ireland and Spain) could have triggered some recognition by Ellis.

More pertinent are the musical forms of comic opera, also found in *Carina* – but then anything with brides scheming to get the husband they want rather than the one they are given inevitably evokes such Italian repertory classics as *Il barbiere di Siviglia* and *Don Pasquale*. The link between *Bless the Bride* and comic opera is most evident in the ensemble and finale-style sections. In these, the flow between action and reflection is paralleled in multi-section structures that address different qualities of dramatic pacing and delivery through musical settings that range from recitative to choral ensemble. In this regard, the finale to Act I of *Bless the Bride* owes something to Gilbert and Sullivan in the appropriation of nineteenth-century models, especially Italian.

The Act I finale is long, fluid and eventful. The action on stage makes the narrative clear, further enhanced by changes of setting. It begins with an uneasy passage in 4/4 time in which Herbert voices through the bridesmaids and sisters the disquiet around Lucy's impending marriage to the Hon. Thomas Trout and their concern that it could be a mistake. Ellis conveys unease through unexpected harmonic shifts on the second bar of the main phrases allied to a melody that is regular in its rhythm but unpredictable in its unexpected, prominent semitones. Contrast is the point here. The indecisive melodic and harmonic character of this portion of music makes it suitable as a bridging section between main sections of the finale. First it introduces a lively waltz, the title song of the show. The music is uplifting through the prominence of the widening rising leaps in the melody. It is a more conventional expression of wedding-day joy than the tongue-in-cheek opening has been. After the waltz, the opening bridging music provides a transition into Herbert's comic description of happy marriage as exemplified by Grandmama and Grandpapa, set by Ellis in a jig-style 6/8.

Next the bridging passage articulates another transition. The addition from the chorus of ritualistic, sustained 'Ah's expands the sound ready for the sudden deflation of Lucy's three screams as she fakes being unwell to get out of the ceremony. Pierre's entrance disguised as a doctor is in a fast duple time appropriate to setting up a speedy escape for him and Lucy. In the middle of this, the underscore comes from the introduction of the earlier number 'Any Man but Thomas T'. Ellis's choice of musical recollection here adds context to Herbert's practical script to get Lucy's Nanny (constantly protective of the child she has helped raise) in on the action. Nanny aids the deception, and the music switches to a reprise of the polka used earlier in the act for tennis. As Pierre is in the act of eloping with Lucy, the music amplifies the earlier expressed disapproval and distrust of things French by focussing it on Pierre. The bridging passage from the very opening returns as Pierre in his disguise declares to Lucy's father that the wedding is off. A return of the waltz 'I Was Never Kissed Before' reasserts the emotional freedom and honesty Pierre has brought to Lucy, who comes back dressed as a page and ready to flee.

At this point Herbert inserts a short reflection for Lucy on what she is leaving behind. The awkwardness of this delay is reflected in the interjected urgings of Pierre ('Come on!') and Nanny ('Go on!'). It's a classic genre trait of nineteenth-century opera that the leading lady (or man) will stop and sing something reflective and sustained to express their emotional state just before the final activity that closes a scene. It is the lyrical aria that comes before the fast cabaletta. We see that form here. Pierre's and Nanny's urgings provide the tongue-in-cheek quality to comment on the mismatch of genre convention and literal action. What makes this clear is Ellis's setting, which returns to the nineteenth-century parlour ballad style associated with the unawakened Lucy (chromatic harmony, emotionally leading semitones in the melody, repeated accompanying chords to animate the chromatically decorated harmony). A further twist comes with the concluding instrumental passage, marked 'molto espressione'. This underscores the entrance of the page boy dressed as a bride decoy to be laid out on the sofa by Nanny – a funny juxtaposition of Victorian sentimentality in sound and a Sleeping Beauty parody on stage, which sets up the comic reveal for the climactic 'discovery' by the family of the plot.

The chorus and family creep in to check on the indisposed bride. Their tiptoeing 2/4 section provides momentum and dramatic character more than melody to allow the situation and lines to carry the point. This is interrupted by Suzanne, who has seen Lucy and Pierre flee down the garden. The music is still focussed on text (exclamatory and accusatory phrases), not tune, and the bouncing 6/8 reflects the onstage energy and action. A sudden break into unaccompanied choral singing gives another nod to operatic genre conventions. Via a swift hunting horn 'Tally ho!' from Thomas, the music of 'God Bless the Family' returns in a display of Victorian formality in grouping and choral sound: 'The Family will fight and win or die.'

Exuberant stylistic interplay is prominent in all of Ellis's subsequent musical theatre scores. *Tough at the Top* pushed the mix of *Bless the Bride* further, but it did not cohere as a stage show to the same extent. Novello wrote to Ellis to praise its music, but he identified the central problem of characters who were not sufficiently interesting (Ellis 1953: 248–9). The score had compositional integrity but at the expense of any sufficiently striking takeout numbers that could be the 'hits' to sell the show. *And So to Bed* (1951) is a musical adaptation of J. B. Fagan's play about the domestic life of Samuel Pepys. Ellis rose to the occasion through lovely numbers inflected with English period musical references. Where that Ellis elegance comes into its own is in the effortless melding of historical pastiche and contemporary appeal. This demonstrates Ellis's fine ear for stylistic analysis and creative absorption in fashioning effective reinterpretations that balance past–present references. Ellis's final work with Herbert, *The Water Gypsies* (1955), again uses music to heighten the generational and societal contrasts in the story: the nostalgic, slow world of barge life on the one hand – flowing, lyrical, measured – and on the other the faster paced, modern aspirations of 1950s life – energetic, rhythmic. For example, the score juxtaposes the Edwardian waltz 'Castles and Hearts and Roses' with the elegiac approach in 'Little Boat' and the contemporary show-tune swing of 'It Would Cramp My Style'.

In each of Ellis's post-war stage works, his contribution is much more about integrating dramatic structure, character and atmosphere into the whole score than inserting some very good tunes into a script. In consequence, each show is distinctive but unmistakably by Ellis. Like Coward and Novello, Ellis was by instinct a composer for the theatre.

Politics and the personal

Herbert was the Member of Parliament for Oxford University from 1935 until 1950, when the university seats for Oxford and Cambridge were abolished. As his biographer Reginald Pound put it, Herbert's 'chief purpose in Parliament was to ensure as respectful a hearing for the voice of reason as for *Land of Hope and Glory*' (Pound 1976: 208). A few formal honours convey something of the status he achieved in the spheres of literature and politics. He was knighted in Winston Churchill's 1945 Resignation Honours for his defence of parliamentary free speech; he received an honorary doctorate from the University of Oxford in 1958 in the same ceremony as Harold MacMillan, Hugh Gaitskell, Francis Poulenc and Dmitri Shostakovich; and he was made a Companion of Honour in 1970, the year before he died.

One of Herbert's most lasting literary legacies is his series 'Misleading Cases', published serially in *Punch* from 1910 and collected in several volumes. They describe ludicrous situations of law as though the reports from actual court cases, involving such absurdities as whether in law a golfer can be a gentleman and whether taxes can be paid with a cheque written on a cow. They are still funny. Those interested in assumed cultural hierarchies – a categorization that has frequently impacted adversely on the critical assessment of musical theatre – can find pertinent observations in Herbert's 'Trott v Tulip: Is "Highbrow" Libelous?'[12] Herbert argues, of course, for the term being understood as a reputational slur. Underpinning such humour is Herbert's assertion of the rights of the individual to justice and the necessity of justice to be clear, fair and consistent. His humour contributed to the desire for law reform (Pound 1976: 291).

Show business and politics collided constantly during Herbert's time as an MP. For example, in 1936, he was introducing to Parliament an overdue major reform of divorce law that became the Matrimonial Causes Act 1937. He was also working on a show, and described the effects of the conjunction:

> While we were in Committee, I was also in rehearsal. After lunch every day I would rush away across the river to a barn-like building near Elephant and Castle and endeavour to switch my mind to the manifold problems of Mr. Cochran's *Coronation Revue* (one of which was now, 'Will there be a Coronation?') Then, with appeals in my ear from a Hungarian composer, an American producer, and an English comedian to write more words or better words, I would hurry to the Treasury Solicitor to get the text of the new amendments and to the House to confer with [the MP] De la Bère and the [divorce Bill] team. There I would find an odd assembly of telephone messages. 'From Mr. Kent, insanity amendment on the way' – 'From Mr Collins, please send second verse of *Twilight Serenade*' – 'Please ring Treasury solicitor' – 'Please ring Miss Binnie Hale' – 'Please ring Mr. Cochran'. . . . Twice I woke up from fitful sleep and found myself trying to set divorce words to one of M. Brodszky's tunes. A weird and worrying time. (Herbert 1950: 86–7)

The same themes familiar from his writings for *Punch* are in his librettos. They include the idea of 'common sense', defined by the opposition to what Herbert viewed as errant nonsense. *Big Ben* combines this trait with other strong interests of Herbert's. The plot of the second act concerns a threat to the right to a pint in a local pub through a Prohibition Bill: Herbert was a regular at his local inn for fifty years and a campaigner for fair licensing laws. Opposition in Act II of *Big Ben* to this Bill occasions the infiltration and subversion of the Commons Chamber of the Houses of Parliament during the debate to pass the new law.

The penultimate scene of the show features the song 'London's Alight Again'. In the intentional ambiguity of that title line alone, the imagery of the fire-bombed city of the Blitz turns into the renewal of post-war London. The first verse is a roll call of landmarks, listing St Paul's Cathedral, Lambeth ('walking the same old way'), Piccadilly, the Strand and Nelson's Column in Trafalgar Square. The second verse makes the war-post-war comparison clear with a 'city of wonder suffering long torment and thunder', 'wonderful people' and 'valiant East-enders' in a 'shattered town'. Such damage is given symbolic status: 'Treasure your scars: these are your splendours, these are your stars' (Herbert 1946: 99–100). National pride and the protection of freedom are elided in a final scene in front of the Palace of Westminster. The midnight Westminster chimes are matched to the chorus finale's words by Herbert: 'Chime out Big Ben / Tell all the men / Say England will / Be England still' (Herbert 1946: 102). The lines gain significance through the contemporary setting of the story and the extra emotional charge of a simple statement of pride in national identity just after the Second World War.

In effect, the show is a thinly veiled, comic exposition on the political and moral state of the nation as Herbert saw it. The original plot is driven by the development in secret of a love affair between publicly competing political candidates against a background of comic presentations of Tory, Socialist and Communist stereotypes. Prominent elements within the show's character include royal ritual (via the King's Bargemaster, nicknamed 'Big Ben' and thus adding a double significance to the show's title), a local pub ('The Barge Around'), activity around and on the River Thames and parliamentary procedure. It is a concatenation of images and themes that signified to Herbert national identity. Such characteristics are a projection of his own character, and *Big Ben* can also be read as a biographical compendium of references to Herbert's own life and career, as noted at the time: 'The whole piece, the good and the not so good, bears the impress of a single agreeable personality. It wishes we knew more about Thames water and it is fearful lest killjoys shall dock us of our beer. To the present dire shortage [post-war rationing] it pays no heed.'[13] John Russell considered the spirit of the show distinctive for the time: 'Sir Alan . . . is a kindly man in an unkindly world. . . . Those who have sat through other musical plays may notice a welcome and unfamiliar flavour in Sir Alan's script; it is not that the jokes or the versification are always good, for indeed the wit has little edge, but that it is the work of a man to whom kindness and good feeling are important.'[14] The campaign manifesto – and waltz song – for the leading character Grace Green in her bid for election is 'I Want to See the People Happy'. The reviewer for *The Stage* distinguished the show by the importance of its text, which unusually for the time was published when the show opened: 'Herbert's lively dialogue and spirited lyrics should be read before and after seeing this stimulating light opera with its political undercurrent.'[15]

Herbert wrote shows that dissected social structures and values. His previous librettos for the comic operas *Tantivy Towers* and *Derby Day* had similarly espoused national totems with fox hunting and horse racing, as the titles indicate, with the latter also providing a strong defence of the local pub and the downfall of teetotallers. These two shows included a running critique of social status in which the aristocracy were invariably left deferring to the common sense of their lower-class betters. By their final curtains, each story had demonstrated what Herbert thought made for a better, more mutually tolerant and respectful society. This approach to dramatic purpose arose from his own character and interests, so we find it in abundance in *Bless the Bride*, where it brings contemplative depth to the erstwhile light romance.

The contemporary setting of *Big Ben* gave its message an earnestness that some commentators considered fought against the comic plot. The lesson was learned. For *Bless the Bride* Herbert integrated his message and surface plot with more subtlety, aided by the distancing of a Victorian setting. Herbert highlighted the importance of social structure through setting up what he termed the 'indomitable institution of the Family' in order to disrupt 'this fortress' when it is 'invaded' by Pierre (Herbert 1970: 121). In *Bless the Bride*, the curtain patriotism of *Big Ben* that unites all political sides in the shadow of Parliament becomes national union symbolized through the personal union of Lucy and Pierre. The third of the 1940s Adelphi shows, *Tough at the Top*, dramatized the romance of a Ruritanian princess with a British boxer. Politics prevents their marriage, and the final curtain statement from the boxer 'Battling Bart' asserts the primacy of personal freedom:

> They can wreck a man's happiness, but not a man's will:
> Little lamps of liberty will smoulder still,
> Till the trumpet sounds, and we break the chain
> And the wings of the spirit ride the free air again
> (Herbert 1970: 128–9)

Herbert was profoundly influenced by his experiences during the First World War, which made him a champion of all things personal and individual, especially in the face of inflexible, impersonal authority and the larger sweep of global politics. In 1935, his electoral address for the Oxford parliamentary seat that he won stated under the title 'Liberty' that 'I am a firm believer in the good sense and robust control of the British people; and therefore, until the contrary is shown, I should prefer to trust and educate rather than restrict' (Herbert 1970: 188). Each of Herbert's three librettos for Cochran and Ellis express positive personal responses to national and international political strife in the context of personal liberty. The shows cannot be separated from the life, times and beliefs of Herbert and his place as a national figure who spoke of justice and decency at a personal level through a comic lens. To talk about these shows without acknowledging this personal philosophy as central is to skew their theatrical and emotional strengths and Herbert's purpose.

The perspective then and now

Four days after the premiere of *Bless the Bride* at the Adelphi theatre, and only a few minutes' walk away at the Theatre Royal, Drury Lane, *Oklahoma!* opened. It played in the West End until 21 October 1950 (for the final five months at the Stoll theatre, now the Peacock). The success of *Oklahoma!* has been much fêted in stamping a particular style of American musical theatre onto how we view the whole musical theatre repertory from 1943 (Broadway) and 1947 (West End). Yet in West End terms, the contrast of the two shows, which ran concurrently for more than two years, invites consideration of how *Bless the Bride* could depart so strikingly from what have long been assumed as the requirements for a hit musical of the time and still be such a success. The need for that consideration is reinforced at the start of the runs of *Bless the Bride* and *Oklahoma!* when Novello's *Perchance to Dream* (1945) overlapped the opening of them both by some six months, and his *King's Rhapsody* (1949) became a hit, overlapping the end of the run of *Oklahoma!*. By 1958, a similar issue arises with the opening of the home-grown *Expresso Bongo* followed within a week by the London premiere of the Broadway success *My Fair Lady*. The details of that juxtaposition (see Chapter 8) further demonstrate that no single set of criteria can account consistently for the demonstrable successes on the musical theatre stage in London at the same time as those in New York.

Herbert addressed the old/British–new/American narrative in respect of the conjunction in the West End of *Bless the Bride* and *Oklahoma!* He considered it 'utter nonsense' that the American import was pre-eminent in its innovation of the integration of song, character and narrative, and described both shows as 'very healthy infants from the same good family, that is all' (Herbert 1970: 122). Cookman's description of the *Bless the Bride* as a 'heavily decorated period pageant', quoted at the top of this chapter, could also have been included in his review of *Oklahoma!* on the facing page.[16] Londoners in the West End in 1947 were not personally involved with cowboys, the wide American plains, fields of eye-high corn or the creation of an American state in the early 1900s out of the Oklahoma and Indian territories. There was much more of a connection with the presentation of Victorian attitudes and tastes (parlour songs and morality, both still in evidence daily) and European interaction in the light of wars and their associated partings and loss. It is not surprising that an outsider show from Broadway that had been extremely well publicized long in advance of its West End opening was thus seemingly characterized as a novelty through its escapism and the attraction of its optimistic, energetic, well-fed community played by actors who were in the main young (of whom the West End had been depleted during the war). *Bless the Bride*, the home-grown show by West End names already familiar from the 1920s and 1930s, was characterized by the recognition of shared national heritage and personal experience. From the perspective of the familiar narrative of British failure and American success that became particularly entrenched in attitudes towards musical theatre after the war, Herbert asserted in 1970 that were he to write a new script for a musical, he 'should not give the slightest thought to any American model'. This was not defiance after a battle lost for a singular musical theatre identity. Rather, Herbert maintained a resolute conviction that his work reflected his own identity and did not rely on the importation of anyone else's.

Ellis repeatedly attacked the Broadway–West End comparison as simplistic, misinformed and misguided, as for example in what was introduced as 'an eloquent plea for the British composer, who is generally denied all the opportunities open to his American rival'.[17] The central disagreement comes down to two features. The British cultural context was different, and the method of production was different. Wendy Toye experienced working in both centres when she followed directing *Tough at the Top* in London with an associate director role for a version of J. M. Barrie's *Peter Pan* in New York with music and lyrics by Leonard Bernstein. She returned to London to direct Herbert and Ellis's *And So to Bed* (1951). Toye observed that the fundamental difference between her London and Broadway experiences was not a matter of style or modernity, but about better resourcing in New York theatre along with which came a greater willingness to try out new ideas.[18]

The ideas, parameters of genre and presentational style of the Cochran-Herbert-Ellis shows fit with a narrative of post-war national reconstruction which makes them introverted, anchored in the past and feeling a new way towards a future. From creative and cultural perspectives, these shows were not in competition with American imports. Rather, they played out lyric stage values from an entirely different viewpoint. Transatlantic comparison does not match like with like. Comparing *Bless the Bride* with *Oklahoma!* in a point-scoring exercise that uses the same criteria for both shows reveals little of the integral qualities of each show. Both were popular and both were successful when performed round the corner from each other at the same time. However, this direct contrast of two shows labelled as 'American' and 'British' within a few days of each other in two of the West End's largest theatres in the wake of the war set the narrative trajectory of the 'American Invasion'. Once we acknowledge that the creators of the shows had entirely different purposes in national, social and political contexts, the basis for that narrative looks tenuous. Extensive details of creative purposes, performers, nationality, contextual theme and statistics support this (Snelson 2003).

Notably, the Gilbert and Sullivan repertory provided an important touch point for contemporary audiences because it was widely known across all ages and widely performed in British theatres both by the professional home company D'Oyly Carte and by amateurs. More generally, audience familiarity with lyric stage repertory was broad, from opera (full productions or as 'popular classics') through to musical comedy. Knowledge was strengthened by touring companies and amateur performances which also included the circulation of highlights at everything from domestic gatherings to community events. Cinema had only become dominant during the 1930s, with the result that audiences in their thirties and older had been raised on performances of live lyric theatre when it was not in competition with film musicals from the Hollywood or British film industries. Besides being acquainted with popular numbers from opera, operetta and musical comedy, audiences had a wide range of styles of social and religious music making in their style vocabularies. The eclecticism of the score of *Bless the Bride* should be understood in the light of this variety.

At the time of its first performance in London, *Bless the Bride* represented a compendium of elements drawn from the status quo of the lyric stage of the past century. Today, through its text and musical structure, it is probably most accessible to audiences with some grounding in operetta and Gilbert and Sullivan. For those attempting to slot it into a post-Rodgers and Hammerstein, American-dominated repertory, it will read as alien to the genre of the modern musical. One reviewer of *Bless the Bride* signalled a divergence of genre expectation: 'Wit, music, setting, performance all admirable. What is missing? As in *Big Ben* I feel, some more robust comedy. True, this might be hard to interpolate without breaking the pattern.'[19] This was echoed in a recollection by Herbert of being introduced by Cochran to an American impresario – Herbert thought it was one of the Shubert brothers – with a view to an American transfer. The 'very high American theatre man' advised Herbert to 'give the comedian some more robust humour'. Herbert firmly rejected the idea as against the Victorian tone they had keenly maintained throughout, and the role of Thomas Trout was not that of a 'comedian', as he ended the play nobly, no longer a 'silly ass' (Herbert 1970: 123). This contrast between applying a genre formula and letting a work define itself is telling.

A large-scale revival in London at Sadler's Wells in 1987 failed to transition into a full West End run. Reviewers seemed to have agreed upon the problem of casting star names at the expense of decent singers – this is not a score for which personality alone is sufficient. The bigger problem was in knowing how to approach the work forty years on. On the one hand, the show has 'some archly witty lines and two irresistible songs in a score that believes in the simple virtue of hummable tunes'.[20] On the other, the 'rapidly implausible plot, oddly too-early period setting (1869) and almost instantly forgettable score lack the energy of contemporary American hits'.[21] A betwixt-and-between stylistic identity confused any strong sense of how it sat in the musical theatre repertory of the 1980s: 'I derived moderate but fitful enjoyment from this well-staged musical, which I fear may have been revived about ten years too soon. As yet, *Bless the Bride* is old enough to seem *passé*, but not so old as to have acquired the quaint charm of a completely forgotten period.'[22] The show highlights the difficulties of viewing works through the lens of an established narrative and its associated hierarchy of criteria. To assert in respect of this show that 'musicals took a long time to journey from amiable idiocy to cohesive drama, and in 1987 one expects a little more' is a fair perspective if one assumes such a clear, single-minded evolutionary direction for genre and values.[23] That is a very big 'if'.

In 1999, the pub theatre The King's Head in Islington, London, staged a short revival in a heavily revised form. Revision was necessary for practical reasons because the pub theatre was very small. Still, a large cast was crowded into the tiny, shallow if wide stage with a single set that could be minimally tweaked to suggest different locations (a green carpet in a drawing room also functioned as a croquet lawn, for example). The Eauville scenes were relocated to a Parisian café. The score was cut down and the accompaniment reduced to a piano with some solo instrumental colour. The script was heavily altered in structure and detail. It started in 1940 with a ninety-year-old Lucy recalling her youth: cue the flashback that constitutes most of the show before the closing return to 1940. The device copies *Bitter Sweet*. American director Martin Charnin adapted the script to focus mostly on the love interest and reduce some of the detail of Herbert's Anglo-French rivalry.

The show was described widely in reviews as old-fashioned, and some reviewers noted the tonal shift of the production with Charnin's rescripting 'clumsy when not downright vulgar' and which 'altered much of Act II, and improved nothing'.[24] Charnin was a noted Broadway and off-Broadway lyricist and director for musicals (best known for *Annie*, 1977), and his updating is understandable as a way of reframing a show of one generation to make it connect with another. However, Charnin stripped out the contextual core, which no longer matched the genre expectations of audiences or indeed directors. The near-simultaneous opening in 1947 of *Oklahoma!* and *Bless the Bride* was noted by many reviewers in 1999, who rehearsed the 'old-fashioned/British' versus 'new style/American' party line. The comparison addresses only musical theatre. That in itself risks distortion: 'When in the second half, the action shifts to 1870 Paris as the Prussian siege is about to begin, you feel that historical reality somewhat dwarfs the romantic problems of a runaway Englishwoman.'[25] This minimizes the significance of the English-French romance for the time in which the show was written. Atypically in 1999, one review focussed on why the show had been successful and why contextual dissociation made such an impact in appreciating the show in later decades:

> Watching this revival almost half a century later, you can just imagine the Adelphi Theatre packed out with Londoners in austerity clothing who all knew of some young man who went to fight the Nazis and never came back. With an *entente*

cordiale plot ... AP Herbert and Vivian Ellis' musical comedy must have resonated with that common experience of loss. The show also upheld good old-fashioned family values ... at a time when broken homes were often part of the war damage. But as time goes by, the pure Americana of *Oklahoma!* has endured ... where the thoroughly British *Bless the Bride* ... now looks like the last gasp of the dying British musical theatre before Lionel Bart introduced a pop sensibility and Andrew Lloyd Webber beat Broadway at its own game.[26]

However, the judgement in that final sentence turns on a British–American comparison that reflects more recent values back onto a work whose creators never had them in their sights. The reviewer continues to praise the rewriting and performance, concluding that 'You'll be blubbering by the final curtain'. One way or another, the show could still pack an emotional punch for some of its audience.

The show was significant in its day. With an imaginative understanding of the themes, the stylistic mosaic of their execution and what the audiences brought with them into the theatre in 1940s London, it is an impressive and engaging work. Dissociation from that time and from that understanding has inevitably grown, and audiences reasonably expect a visceral experience in the here and now, rather than an archaeological excavation in theatrical form. Updating any show that was heavily tailored to a time and a mood can all too easily remove what made it resonate in the first place, resulting in a set of stereotypes and genre pastiches. Is *Bless the Bride* still performable to a wider audience than those already comfortable with the genre conventions of operetta and the Savoy Operas, who can thus bring to a performance some appreciation of the original stylistic loci? Debatable. Is it an important work in the canon of British musical theatre that deserves to be fittingly represented in the story of the home-grown West End musicals? Absolutely.

6

The Boy Friend (1953)

Sandy Wilson

From small-scale origins, *The Boy Friend* became a large-scale surprise success. Script, lyrics and music were all by Sandy Wilson, who conceived it as part of an evening's entertainment at a theatre club, the Players' Theatre. It was performed briefly in spring 1953, then expanded in stages into the three-act show performed today. It opened in the West End in January 1954 and ran for five years. A different production of *The Boy Friend* opened in New York in September 1954 – note how swiftly the show crossed the Atlantic – where it played for thirteen months and then toured through America for several years. It has been filmed (albeit in near-unrecognizable form by director Ken Russell), professionally revived regularly if not necessarily frequently, and has become a staple of community performances by all ages and abilities. Of the repertory discussed in this book, *The Boy Friend* comes next only to *Oliver!* in having maintained a consistent familiarity with general audiences from its start into the twenty-first century.

The show's appeal is self-evident: light, tuneful, swift, diversionary, nostalgic, witty, undemanding, full of charm. Yet for all its self-contained, well-defined and two-dimensional musical-comedy nature, its concept brings complexity. *The Boy Friend* has successfully negotiated the different genre expectations of, on the one hand, the specialist group for whom it was originally intended and, on the other, the vastly larger, general audience who have taken to it nationally and internationally. Sandy Wilson's 'valentine from one post-war period to another' (Wilson 1959: 14)[1] was created within a group of practitioners who prized theatrical authenticity. It has developed as though 'from one aesthetic to another' to straddle the border between period compendium and parodic camp classic.

The story is set on the French Riviera in 1926. Polly Browne is at the Villa Caprice, a finishing school near Nice. Her widowed millionaire father fears gold-digging suitors and will not allow her a boyfriend. To save face in front of the other girls at the school, Polly invents one who will accompany her as Pierrot when she goes to the Costume Ball as Pierrette. The headmistress of the school, Madame Dubonnet, guesses the truth. When a delivery boy, Tony, brings Polly her costume, they instantly fall for each other: Polly now has a real boyfriend for the ball. When Polly meets Tony that afternoon on the seafront, she pretends to be Madame Dubonnet's secretary so as not to disclose her wealth. At the end of their assignation, Tony runs off with the police in pursuit. Polly concludes that he must be a thief and only after her inheritance. Once again with no boyfriend, she resigns herself to missing the Carnival Ball. But things are not as they seem. To help Tony, Hortense, the maid at the school, persuades Polly to go to the Carnival Ball so that Tony can prove he does love her. That evening, the lovers are reunited as Pierrot and Pierrette. Tony turns out to have been hiding from his aristocrat parents, who had called the police when they had spotted him on the seafront. The Honourable Tony Brockhurst, the son of a lord, is thus a worthy boyfriend for rich Polly Browne. The happy mood that results is further sealed by the multiple acceptances of marriage proposals between the finishing school's young ladies and their beaux and between Madame Dubonnet and Polly's father: 'Our dreams just won't come true without / That certain thing called "The Boy Friend"' (Wilson 1955: 31). QED.

Wilson's public profile rose rapidly as the creator of such a hit. He was also the subject of an early 1960s in-joke when his forename was taken alongside that of Julian Slade for one of half of 'Julian and Sandy', comic creations in the national radio show 'Round the Horne'. For those who understood the subcultural references, these caricatures of theatrical men in sexually suggestive sketches – at a time when male homosexuality was illegal in Britain – became totems for theatrical camp and gay innuendo that continue still. It is no surprise then that *The Boy Friend* has long been viewed in the context of the covert and not-so-covert locus of gay subculture of the 1950s. The open secret of the sexual orientation of the writer of the show has been projected back onto his most famous creation – rightly so as the repressive conservative atmosphere of the early 1950s in Britain influenced the theatrical landscape in which the show was formed.

In August 1954, Wilson defended his musical comedy to a journalist who had characterized it as 'queer' and 'gay' solely from the title. Wilson's response was that it 'wasn't that kind of show at all' (Wilson 1975a: 238). But Wilson's defence has not withstood the varied sensibilities of performers and audiences. Since it was first staged, the show has been categorized anywhere on a scale from charmingly innocent to highly camp. Not surprisingly, queer perspectives have regularly figured in commentaries on the show (e.g. Snelson 2003: 248–59), self-evidently so with the subtitle 'Sandy Wilson's *The Boy Friend*, London Theatre and Gay Culture' of Deborah Philips's detailed monograph on Wilson's output, *And This Is My Friend Sandy* (2021). A camp sensitivity may explain part of the show's appeal but cannot account for all of it by any means. Although some aspects of a gay reading will arise towards the end of this chapter, this investigation principally takes its lead from *The Boy Friend*'s foundation in the representation of theatrical authenticity. Paradoxically for a show so often understood as mannered artifice, *The Boy Friend* began with an urge to keep it real.

Theatre and authenticity

The Players' Theatre, for which *The Boy Friend* was written, was a distinctive institution. It had been formed in 1937 to revive the idea of Victorian supper rooms. At these, convivial meetings over food and drink had been accompanied by entertainment. A

Chairman (a Master of Ceremonies) with a larger-then-life presence controlled the raucous, participatory audience and introduced a mixed programme of music, drama and variety acts. The timing of the Players' recreations was late evening to suit a post-theatre crowd that included fellow professional performers. One of its founders, Leonard Sachs, became a familiar figure through the country as the Chairman of a long-running series of televised adaptations of the Players' shows under the title *The Good Old Days*. The crucial point is that this was not a burlesque of an older style but the recreation of it in mood, content and detail. The Players' Theatre prized authenticity.

The celebratory book *Late and Early Joys at the Players' Theatre* was published in 1952. It describes the origins and atmosphere of the original supper rooms in London's Covent Garden area and the famous characters associated with them. In parallel, it records the origins of the Players' Theatre, the people behind it and the venues it occupied. It describes how the Players' finally took up what proved to be a long-lasting residency in the Hungerford Arch underneath Charing Cross Station. The location matched the historical narrative perfectly, having also been the site of Carlo Gatti's Under-the-Arches Music-Hall, which had opened in the 1860s. The Players' new residency is described as bringing 'not a new glory, but a revived ebullience and life, awakening echoes of those earlier days' (Sheridan 1952: 57). Moreover, 'the genuine Supper Room entertainment has been re-created, with all its punch and loud vulgarity, its bursting vitality and its utter sincerity' (Sheridan 1952: 64). The resurrection of the past was made explicit through the Players' performers too: 'Who in these days can listen to and sing with Joan Sterndale Bennett, without thinking of that earlier "Vital Spark", the small and lovely Jennie Lee? Or who can hear and watch Hattie Jacques without recalling instantly the great Marie Lloyd, or watch Johnnie Heawood and not think of G.H. Elliott?' In summary, 'They are not imitators, these artists of London's only Victorian theatre; in their own right they have made for themselves and out of themselves a part of that bygone age' (Sheridan 1952: 69).

Out of this aesthetic, in 1953 *The Boy Friend* arises with its subtitle 'a new musical comedy of the 1920s'. Writer/composer Wilson, director Vida Hope, designer Reginald Woolley and a cast of Players' regulars sought out what was genuine for a show of the 1920s. As Hope described, from early in the first rehearsals the cast 'were telling each other off for any hint of over-playing or burlesque business', and the physicality of the show in 'stance, posture, gesture and so on' was recreated from photographs of 1920s productions (Wilson 1955: 12). *The Boy Friend* was sincere in how it created a carefully drawn outline rather than a distorting caricature. That period accuracy was noted on the opening of the three-act version at Wyndham's, for example:

> [Sandy Wilson] has shown the strictest regard for the essentials of the style he is reproducing; and [Vida Hope] has seen to it that the company put across these essentials without the smallest suggestion that they think all this old-fashioned stuff rather nonsense. Scrupulous care has been taken with detail. Women's figures have miraculously changed since the twenties. The ladies of this musical comedy wear not only the dresses of the twenties but display (by some means known only to themselves and the ingenious costumier, Mr. Reginald Woolley) the figures of the twenties. Methods of theatrical make-up have also changed. The company

use the make-up of twenty years ago, and it is quite a shock to note how subtle a transformation of method this shy art has undergone at the hands of its devoted practitioners in this comparatively short time.[2]

The Stage is the trade journal for British theatre with a predominantly theatrical readership, which has long included a euphemistic 'theatrical' – that is, gay – contingent. Despite this, its review quoted earlier indicates no subtext beneath that authenticity in continuing that *The Boy Friend* 'has strong claims to be regarded as the gayest show in town' which 'brings to the older playgoer an onrush of engaging memories of years when the world seemed a less harassing place than it is to-day'.[3]

Before *The Boy Friend*, Wilson was known as a writer for intimate revue, not musicals. He contributed material to the successful revues *Slings and Arrows* (1948) and *Oranges and Lemons* (1949), but it was as sole author for *See You Later* (1951) and *See You Again* (1952) at the small Watergate Theatre near the Player's Theatre that he firmly established himself. Intimate revue requires each number in the programme to be precise and concise: 'Nothing – *nothing* – can go on too long' (Wilson 1975a: 130). Contrast between numbers is essential to maintain the impetus in the absence of a plot. Concerns common to all good theatre are highlighted through the miniaturist lens of intimate revue. The small cast has to act, sing and dance in whatever way is required. Wilson particularly liked this 'charade-like nature' such that 'the audience never knows what may happen next, who will appear, in what new guise, doing something quite different from his previous appearance' (Wilson 1975a: 130).

The Boy Friend was commissioned from Wilson as the latter two-thirds of a 'Late Joys' performance, each of whose three sections were around thirty minutes long. Wilson has described how easily all the elements of the characters and story came together (Wilson 1975a: 173–9). The fluency is understandable in the light of Wilson's familiarity with the elements of the 1920s musical comedy style and production. Writing for intimate revue was a training ground for keeping to a brief. The cumulative effect of these elements defined the direction of the show: small scale, with the contact between performer and audience that stems from intimate revue. Leading players would include those known to the Players' audience and familiar among Player's performers. For example, the maid Hortense was conceived for the regular performer Violetta, who 'specialised in roguish French chanson' (Wilson 1975a: 174), and Madame Dubonnet was written for Hattie Jacques, although in the event it was another regular, Joan Sterndale Bennett, who created the part. The writing would concentrate the essence of a full-length musical comedy into about an hour, and the accompaniment would come from a minimal band of piano, bass and drums.

The tone came from the established Supper Room entertainment the 'Late Joys', which reinforced how essential authenticity was to period and style for the new commission. Don Gemmell, who directed the 'Joys', was concerned over Wilson's suggestion of a director who could be 'a bit modern'. This was Vida Hope, who had directed *See You Again*, but reassurance came with her expressed desire to 'do it as a serious reproduction of a period and not as a burlesque'[4] (Wilson 1975a: 185). The ethos of the commissioning institution is inextricable from the result. After the success of *The Boy Friend*, Wilson had earned a place in *Who's Who in Theatre*. It is not surprising that he listed in his entry 'Club: Players' (Parker 1961: 1177).

Small is beautiful

The Boy Friend was first seen in 1953 for just three weeks (14 April–3 May) as two acts each of thirty minutes which ran as part of an evening's entertainment at the Player's Theatre. It was expanded for a return to the Players' for six weeks (13 October–22 November), then ran for a further six weeks at the Embassy Theatre (1 December 1953–11 January 1954). It opened at Wyndham's Theatre in the West End proper on 14 January 1954 and stayed there for just over five years, closing on 7 February 1959. *The Boy Friend* was never intended to be 'big'. After short runs in small theatres off-West End it retained its original scale for what became a celebrated show in the West End. It stood out as fresh, direct and intimate when set against the big-scale production values of other musicals of West End and Broadway origins running alongside it. Musicals occupied the biggest theatres, had the biggest casts and the most lavish productions. That was – and still is – one aspect of their appeal: big can be beautiful. But here was evidence that small could be too. The cast for *The Boy Friend* is not large, the chorus requirements are limited, the stage settings are undemanding and the original band requirements are minimal. A comparison with what it takes to put on a convincing performance of any of the central works explored in previous chapters makes the modesty of its technical demands evident. The scale naturally arose out of Wilson's focus and experience as outlined, but it came too from the aesthetic of the Players' Theatre along with its production resources.

A central feature of achieving 'smallness' is how convention is harnessed. The use of archetypes of plot and character reduce the need for exposition and explanation. The recreated 1920s work of the 1950s does not need to innovate in these areas. In fact, the trajectories of the plot and subplot are clearer if they do not surprise. That way, the audience delight is directed to the manner in which character traits play out in familiar ways. Typically, the central romance will be thwarted by a misunderstanding, some true identities are disguised, and the ending is revelatory and happy. In such recycling, the audience brings its experience of the style, rather than an exact knowledge of narrative detail (Colson 2003: 44). By comparison with most new 1950s musicals being performed in neighbouring theatres, the freshness perceived in *The Boy Friend* could be the consequence of a lack of novelty in character and plot. The recognition of traits and tropes of its chosen style of musical comedy was the point. Criticisms of generic over-familiarity and a lack of innovation that could be levelled at new shows didn't apply. The audience is expected to realize at once that the delivery boy is not what he seems while knowing that the secretary is not what she told him she was. This is a direct parallel to the plot of the 1928 hit *Mr. Cinders*, yet as that Cinderella-inspired title signals, its central narrative trope had long been familiar. In *The Boy Friend*, the three-act format with a single set per act is typical of 1920s musical comedy. Even the Act II beach setting is familiar enough from London's version of *No, No, Nanette*, and had been given a nod of recognition in *Bless the Bride* only a few years before *The Boy Friend*.

Wilson's technique from intimate revue keeps the action clear and swift. French's acting edition is indicative in that the script for Act I of the familiar three-act form – stage directions, dialogue, lyrics and all – takes just thirteen pages. The opening speech is by Hortense into a telephone, so the audience hear only half of the conversation. In fewer than fifty words, we nonetheless learn the identities of Hortense, Madame Dubonnet and Polly Browne as well as the location, the institution and its social milieu, and that a special event is imminent (Wilson 1955: 23). The device to get Maisie alone for a seductive song-and-dance routine – in the middle of a drawing room – with her boyfriend Bobby van Husen is for all the other girls to leave while Maisie stays to look for her dorothy bag.[5] This is the cue for Bobby to enter through the french windows. At the end of the number he exits through the french windows – as all the young men do, it would seem, and as does Maisie.

French windows allow for a Cinderella moment when the other girls think Polly wants to be left to herself in anticipation of the arrival of her mysterious boyfriend, so they leave by the french windows. Once alone, Polly tears up the letter she has received from her father, who will shortly arrive, but which she pretended to the girls was from her boyfriend. She throws the torn paper out of the french windows, and the pieces seem to conjure up in their place a young messenger boy carrying a dress box. It is both a subliminal transformation scene in miniature in the staging and a leading man's entrance for the 'boy meets girl' moment. The audience easily registers it. Less than a page of dialogue takes them both from first contact to flirt contact in the duet 'I Could Be Happy with You'. With an afternoon assignation arranged, Tony takes his leave of Polly . . . through the french windows, of course. In a final exchange, Polly greets her father, allowing for ambiguity when Maisie asks Polly, 'Has he arrived yet?' 'He' is Polly's father, the real subject of the letter she received, but now also Tony the genuine boyfriend for the Costume Ball, still known only to Polly. A reprise of 'The Boy Friend' concludes the act.

Act II includes some comic insertions that allow for jokes, physical humour and wordplay. The short encounter on the beach between Percival Browne (Polly's father) and Lord Brockhurst (Tony's father) introduces such classic punch lines as Lord Brockhurst's mildly suggestive 'I don't want assistance in my domestic affairs. It's foreign affairs I'm talking about' (Wilson 1955: 75). This is a small diversion interpolated into a scene essentially between Madame Dubonnet and Percival in order to juxtapose Percival's reluctance to swim (for which we read engage physically) with Madame Dubonnet and Lord Brockhurst's roving eye, which is regularly blinkered by the presence of the formidable Lady Brockhurst. The scene's exit number is the summary song led by Madame Dubonnet, the 'You-don't-want-to-play-with-me Blues'. Structural elements of the typical musical comedy formula are followed: dialogue leads into song, the set-piece comic repartee is there for effect rather than plot and the scene ends with the song followed by character exits. The adaptation is observed through concision. Each element is compressed, occasioned by the original show's two-act/one-hour length – observe the formula, make the point, move on fast to the next bit, just like the speed of intimate revue.

Wilson has fun manipulating convention beyond employing it for audience recognition in the pursuit of brevity. Genre reconstruction some three decades on is also genre deconstruction. For example, the opening chorus of Act I in the drawing room of the Villa Caprice finishing school introduces four of the school's 'Perfect Young Ladies' – Maisie, Fay, Dulcie and Nancy. There is minimal dialogue to set up the Carnival Ball, Polly Browne and her mysterious boyfriend, which swiftly introduces the title song. For its second refrain, 'Marcel, Pierre and Alphonse enter by the french windows and join the Girls' (Wilson 1960b: 4).[6] How convenient that the men are on hand and that those windows are there. The moderate stage space makes the low number of performers enough for a chorus routine in the drawing room. The timely entrance of the boys does not need explanation in the dialogue as its rationale comes from the genre's requirement for a chorus number, not from the mechanics of the plot. This convention is reinforced after the number when Dulcie reminds everyone of the rules of the Villa Caprice: 'Boys, boys, you know you are not allowed on the premises. You must leave at once' (Wilson 1955: 31). The convenient entrance of the boys in the middle of a musical number emphasizes the convention of a chorus number in a show, accepted and unquestioned by those on stage and in the audience. The school rule only applies once the song and dance of the musical comedy stage is over, and the space reverts to being the drawing room of the Villa Caprice. In an intimately scaled theatre whose stage proportions suit the scale of such a domestic interior, this works with knowing charm.

Musical comedy conventions are used in truncated form such that the original genre formats are observed in outline only. A pattern of complete scenes is maintained but more at the level of revue sketches that progress through a series of scene-blackout rotations. This results in the sequence of dialogue-song-exit line recurring in swift succession, not least in the exposition of Act I. The pace can be fast because minimal information is needed to prompt recognition of what is already familiar to the audience. This is the opposite of the treatment of entirely new material, which needs to be reinforced to be retained. The duality this creates between the content expressed and the content actually understood by an audience tuned into the genre (as was more the case in the 1950s than now) works at a micro level too. At the conclusion of Act II, Tony's fast escape leaves Polly feeling betrayed, her dreams of a Carnival Ball partner seemingly in ruins. Dulcie asks Polly, 'Did he steal something from you?' She replies, 'Yes, Dulcie, he did.' Dulcie's follow-up in the onstage world is appropriate for a suspected theft, 'Not your gold bangle?' It is Polly's response that demonstrates how the audience fills in the detail: 'No, not my gold bangle. Something much more precious' (Wilson 1955: 90). The line makes sense to Polly and to the audience but not to any other character in the scene. Polly's answer works in secretive collusion with the audience. The work's self-knowing nature pervades the detail. With a large canvas, the view is better from a distance, where the broad themes create impact. But *The Boy Friend* adopts the scale of a miniature, in which attention is constantly directed to the detail. The structure, tropes and characters are already familiar. The focus for the audience is directed much more towards how the work is presented than onto what it is.

A valentine to the past

Wilson was born in 1924. He remembered almost nothing directly of the 1920s, although recalled hearing his elder sisters and friends playing gramophone records and trying to learn the Charleston. He became aware of the decade as a discrete period with its own character only in the 1930s, then post-war caught touring revivals of 1920s musicals and found sheet music of the songs (Wilson 1955: 15–16). For Wilson, the appeal of the 1920s lay in discovery more than memory. He published a collection of photographs from the period under the title *The Roaring Twenties* to evoke the mood of the decade. In Wilson's introduction he describes what had first captured his imagination: 'Despite the aura of sophistication that hangs around them, the atmosphere of jazz, cocktails and promiscuity, the Twenties seem to me an Age of Innocence, a time when Youth could truthfully say "Here we are, fresh, eager and unafraid. The future is ours to play with. Let the Games commence!"' (Wilson 1976: Introduction).

First-hand and early experiences of the lyric stage by Coward and Novello, in particular of Edwardian musical comedy and turn-of-the century operetta, fed into the form and style of their shows. But Wilson's staging of the past is not born from the reliving and reshaping of personal experience. He described how the exuberance of the 1920s became to some degree shameful in the wake of the Depression and was pushed to the back of the collective memory. He was 'drawn irresistibly' to what seemed in the 1930s to his young mind the preceding 'Forbidden Decade. Shreds of the old tunes haunted me – how *did* the Charleston go? A glimpse of a cloche-hatted girl in a photograph beckoned to me, like a Lorelei, from an inaccessible island. Where had it all disappeared to?' (Wilson 1976: Introduction).

The process was not so much one of rediscovery. Rather, it was a selective distillation of inferred tropes and characteristics gleaned from primary sources at a generation's remove. As a consequence, *The Boy Friend* gained life simultaneously in three decades: originating reference points from the 1920s were accumulated in fragments by Wilson from the perspective of the 1930s onwards, then synthesized in the early 1950s into a show. It is telling that the final sentence of Wilson's description of the 1920s quoted earlier could be just as easily applied to *The Boy Friend* in capturing youthful exuberance and delighting in the period's 'Games'. These qualities underpinned the show's reception and quickly gained it popularity. This spirit contrasts with that of the larger, contemporary shows in surrounding theatres whether created for the West End or imported from Broadway.

The music of *The Boy Friend* is principally located in American musical comedy of the 1920s. Wilson drew from general stylistic traits and from specific exemplars, the most prominent of which is Youmans, Cesar and Harbach's *No, No, Nanette* (1925). Wilson's opening chorus 'Perfect Young Ladies' shares a similar melodic and rhythmic profile with the opening chorus 'How Do You Do?' in *No, No Nanette* in the descending introduction and the syncopations of the opening phrase. The refrain finishes too with an echo in lyrics and musical shape when 'Just flippant young flappers are we' is refashioned by Wilson as 'For perfect young ladies are we'. The most lasting number of *No, No, Nanette* is 'Tea for Two', a description of blissful domesticity set in an easy soft-shoe style. Wilson's reinterpretation as 'A Room in Bloomsbury' describes a similar domesticity, to similar musical pacing and style. While Coward's song 'A Room with a View' (in *This Year of Grace!*, 1928) shares the imagery of 1920s couples 'yearning for the simple life', which Wilson identified and emulated (Wilson 1975a: 176–7), it also reveals just how much more specific the ties between 'A Room in Bloomsbury' and its American counterpart are. Wilson's title song draws on Richard Rodgers's melody for the title song of *The Girl Friend* (1926) and musically shadows the rising bass and resulting harmony of its refrain. But it is the acknowledgement in the title (from Hart's lyrics) and its rhythmic setting of the title phrase that make the connection jump out.

Musical modernity of the 1920s is signalled by the inclusion of a blues-styled and -titled number in the score, 'The "You-don't-want-to-play-with-me" Blues'. Such Blues songs were popular. Novello contributed the 'Old Acquaintance Blues' riffing off 'Auld Lang Syne' to the revue *Puppets* (1924), and *No, No, Nanette* in London (1925) included the 'Where Has My Hubby Gone Blues'.[7] Coward ends his national pageant *Cavalcade* (1931) with a scene in a nightclub in 1930, whose summary song is 'Twentieth Century Blues'. The blues element is conveyed through the downbeat attitude of the lyrics alongside the commonly found musical factors of a steady, insistent 4/4 pacing, a tendency towards the minor side of the harmony while keeping formally in the major key, and the introduction of a few strategically flattened 3rds and 7ths in the melody. In *Show Boat* (London 1928), 'Can't Help Lovin' Dat Man' fulfils this musical-emotional function while not stating 'blues' in the title.

Nothing shouts 1920s so much as a dance craze. The first of two in *The Boy Friend* is 'Won't You Charleston with Me'. The fingerprint, emphatic two-note syncopation that goes with the syllables of 'Charles-ton' gives Wilson his start for the refrain 'Won't-you / Charles-ton', then the refrain's midpoint '[together we'll] show-them', then bounces off again with 'How-the / Charles-ton'. The second dance song is 'The Riviera', modelled on 'The Varsity Drag' (from *Good News*, 1927). This song type describes the style and motion of the dance within the lyrics. The American song begins 'Down on the heels / Up on the toes . . . That's the way to do the Varsity Drag', which Wilson morphs into 'Wriggle your hips and kick up your heels . . . Everybody's doing the Riviera'. Moreover, the opening melodic contour of the refrain in both cases is the same: each opens with an assertive rise from the low tonic, followed by even crotchets that revolve around the upper tonic before descending on a final syncopation to the dominant.

The similarity of Wilson's version is sufficiently close to have prompted a rewrite of the refrain for the Broadway version to avoid copyright issues, although the newly altered opening phrases give more than a nod to Irving Berlin's 'Puttin' on the Ritz' (1927). A related copyright issue with the title song was surmounted with a programme acknowledgement of Rodgers as the inspiration (Wilson 1975a: 244–5). Yet recognition of these similarities is central to the concept: a knowing audience hears the source text ghosting the new one. The songs in the show collate 'classic' musical comedy numbers, situations and imagery. In addition to those already mentioned, Irving Berlin waltzes suggested 'Fancy Forgetting', 'It's Never Too Late' came from a similar cross-generational number in *Sally*, and Coward's 'Parisian Pierrot' prompted 'Poor Little Pierrette' (Wilson 1975a: 176–7). The impact of any 'tribute' song is strengthened at each point of recognition. In the late 1920s, Wilson would have been jumping on a bandwagon. By the 1950s he was pairing the active instance of memory with a simultaneous reinforcement of its temporal, generational distance. It is the same for gesture, staging, language, character type and plot: the show is packed with 1920s musical comedy references for anyone able to recognize them.

Divorce Me, Darling!

Recognition is baked hard into *Divorce Me, Darling!* (1964), a sequel to *The Boy Friend* in which many of the same characters return to Nice and the Villa Caprice a decade later. As the title implies, the comedy portrays adult experience, not youthful expectation. Its sequel status is signalled by the designation 'a new musical of the 1930s', set in 1936. Again, the show began with a production at the Players' Theatre. It had too the intention to include many of the original *Boy Friend* cast, but rehearsals and a transfer to the Globe Theatre necessitated changes. The ingredients are dictated as much by convention as those of *The Boy Friend*: misunderstandings, disguises and revelations among a narrow social group, but with many more of them. This is at its most extreme in the expansion of Madame Dubonnet from a French headmistress into the mysterious cabaret star 'Madame K' (name-checking 'Madame X'), who in the number 'Blondes for Danger' has the suggestive manner and cross-dressing appearance of Marlene Dietrich.

Wilson's song models from stage musicals of the 1930s acknowledge Cole Porter in particular. His 'You're Absolutely Me' is a classic Porter-style list song ghosted by 'You're the Top' (*Anything Goes*, 1934) with each new simile. The allusion is deliberate. Wilson acknowledges Porter as his source in his opening verse. In it, Hannah denies any knowledge of Mahatma Gandhi and Napoleon Brandy, to be countered with Sir Freddy's claim to ignorance of the Mona Lisa and the Leaning Tower of Pisa. Thus, they list the concluding similes of the second refrain of Porter's song. Wilson also captures elegantly the sublime–ridiculous juxtapositions of the Porter model, for example, with 'You're Westminster Abbey / You're the Empire State / You're a cat that's tabby / You're a Dane that's great' as well as the listing of contemporary cultural references slanted for a 1950s British audience to include HP Sauce, Yorkshire pudding, Claude Hulbert and a Baby Austin car. Hollywood film musicals of the decade influence the score too, with Bobby van Husen channelling Fred Astaire. His introductory number 'Someone to Dance With' sets a pattern of dance metaphors in the lyrics that the later 'Out of Step' reinforces – 'in step' signifies 'in love' – matched to the elegant balance of smooth melody with an assertive, syncopated ending. The features are reminiscent of Jerome Kern's 'I Won't Dance' in its lyric rewrite by Dorothy Fields for the Astaire film *Roberta* (1935).

The original cast recording illustrates the charm of the score, full of Wilson's exactitude as a lyricist and composer when working within well-defined, familiar boundaries. Yet the show itself failed to hit the mark with the public and ran for just eighty-seven performances. Philips identifies from correspondence in Wilson's archive that 'the production process was more than a little bumpy' (2021: 105), and the press response was unenthusiastic, even hostile. The genre palimpsest of *The Boy Friend* was already layered enough. With the sequel, not only is there similar ghosting, borrowing and allusion to create the 1930s-styled work, but there are reflexivities of plot and character and method with the 1920s parent work too. The first line of the opening chorus alerts the audience to this with its last word: 'Here we are in Nice again'. The show's genealogy blurs its focus:

> Possibly the Thirties do not so readily respond to parody and pastiche as the Twenties; possibly Mr. Wilson has missed the essence of them in their musical comedy manifestation in a deliberate effort to follow-up *The Boy Friend* with a similar type of production. It is difficult to tell, there being no really distinctive pattern or atmosphere in *Divorce Me, Darling!* It is certain, however, that with *The Boy Friend* Mr Wilson wrote a book and composed numbers that seemed to belong to the Twenties and to nowhere else, several of the songs being as good as the well-known originals which inspired Mr. Wilson. In *Divorce Me, Darling!*, nothing is quite good enough.[8]

If *Divorce Me, Darling!* had been presented in the same atmosphere and to the same audience as had seen *The Boy Friend* in 1955, then maybe it could have been different. Yet even as *The Boy Friend* still played in that long West End run, *Look Back in Anger* (1956) marked a shift in the *zeitgeist*, as did *Expresso Bongo* (1958) and the 'Soho musicals' explored in the next chapter. On stage, the elapse of ten years for Polly and Tony had changed little. During the actual decade beyond the stage, the mid-1960s audience had lived through the emergence of teen culture, the dominance of pop and the beginnings of rock. A tribute to pre-war musical comedy was now judged as dated rather than charmingly nostalgic. It would take a few more decades and a couple of generational shifts for 'old hat' to become 'retro escapism'. Maybe scale is tied into the reception too. The 1920s musical comedy came from the stage. By the 1930s, with the rise of the sound film, Hollywood's musical dramatizations had gained a wider reach: the big screen had big pictures for a big audience. Perhaps a stage show of the 1930s needed to involve that new sense of scale too, and that was not natural to Wilson's more compact vision – and Novello had got there first.

The Buccaneer

Wilson's show *The Buccaneer* overlapped with *The Boy Friend*. It was written and first staged in 1953 between the original short version of *The Boy Friend* and its expanded version. The contrast between the two shows challenges what has become the dominant perspective of Wilson as stuck in the past. By extension, with *The Boy Friend* as one of the only shows of that period to have sustained any recognition in the active repertory, the West End's new musicals of the time have been portrayed as stuck in the past too. *The Buccaneer* did not garner anything like the status and familiarity with the public as that 1920s 'valentine' of a hit, and it was only developed for a new production on a larger scale in 1955 because of the success of *The Boy Friend*.

The show does sit more easily within Wilson's output pre-*The Boy Friend* by virtue of its contemporary and satiric focus. The premise of the story is that an established, traditional 'Boy's Own' English comic is old-fashioned and failing. Its purchase by an American who will revamp and update its style offers one option to save it. The opposition of perspectives is summed up in the contrast between two numbers. On the one side is 'Captain Fairbrother', a description of the comic's long-established hero, the epitome of British Empire actions and values. On the other is 'It's Commercial', in which the prospective American purchaser extols what's modern and what sells, with Marilyn Monroe's tight sweaters and gory, murdered bodies among his examples. The intention is to replace Captain Fairbrother with 'Belinda Blast-Off, Space-Age Super-Girl', who 'threatens the British imperial past with modern femininity, technology and American power' (Philips 2021: 97).

At today's distance, it could be assumed that *The Buccaneer* was more of a Wilson warm-up to such later flights of fancy as his musical adaptations from Ronald Firbank's writings as *Valmouth* (1958) and of John Collier's bizarre story *His Monkey Wife* (1971), whose title is factually descriptive of the subject matter. Yet the idea for *The Buccaneer* arose from the national moral and social concerns over the effects of such imported American horror comics as *Tales from the Crypt* on the minds and behaviour of children. At the time, this was a hot topic across the country for a decade and beyond. The anxiety is possibly most widely known from an American perspective through Fredric Wertham's study *Seduction of the Innocent*, published in the United States in 1954 and in the UK in 1955. The book's thesis and documentation carries little weight now, but it did at the time. However, in the early 1950s the topic had already been well aired in the UK and was especially prominent at the time of *The Buccaneer*'s inception in 1953. For example, one regional newspaper that year editorialized that 'Many such publications have their origin in America. We suggest they should be kept in America. Their whole style is out of keeping with the day-to-day life of young British children, so much so that some these publications must be regarded being anything but "comic" – menace might be a better word.'[9] More sombre links that were made indicate the seriousness of the subject as when, in one Coroner's judgement, an unhealthy interest in sensational comics contributed to the untimely death of a thirteen-year-old boy.[10] The opposition of British and American styles of comics is one example of a wider concern over the effect transatlantic influences were having on the cultural and social values of Britain. It is this perception of a threat that underpins *The Buccaneer*.

Once more a theatre club, the New Watergate, played a significant part in the show's genesis: *The Buccaneer* was written for it and first performed at its Watergate Theatre home. Contemporary sharpness suitable for the proximity of a small audience went with the instigating venue and the central satire. The execution again shows Wilson's interest in detail more than an expansion of scale, albeit in part a practical consequence of its Watergate origins: a small cast of characters, ensembles within the cast rather than as a separately designated chorus, songs predominantly as solos and duets, limited changes of scene, action within a short period of time and geography. Wilson's brilliance in turning out a beautifully scanned, clear and surprisingly rhymed lyric sits well in *The Buccaneer*. His subversive wit runs throughout, as in the decidedly romantic song 'Unromantic Us' being parodied within the show in an alternative set of unromantic lyrics for cleaning ladies. Wilson's inspiration for this device arose during rehearsals from the need for a diversionary front-cloth interpolation to cover a scene change behind.[11]

Discussions of *The Boy Friend* often create a relationship with *Salad Days*, Julian Slade and Dorothy Reynolds's surprise hit, which ran even longer than Wilson's show but is mostly concurrent with it. *Salad Days* originated as a novelty piece for the company of the Bristol Old Vic. As a result, it utilizes the repertory company's varied skills, vocal restrictions and limited resource within what amounts to a set of revue sketches and diversionary numbers held together within the conceit of the pursuit of a piano that makes people dance involuntarily. Robert Gordon captures the seemingly random result of its bespoke nature in describing it as 'the most eccentric musical ever to achieve mainstream commercial success in the West End' (Gordon, Jubin and Taylor 2016: 16). What the two shows share mainly is the tight restrictions of scale derived from their site-specific, company-specific origins.

Philips reinforces this aspect in writing that the 'modesty of the scale and ambition' of *The Boy Friend* 'was itself a counterpoint to the string of blockbuster American musical which had filled London's largest theatres in the early 1950s' (Philips 2021: 76). That contrast of intention and aesthetic did help *The Boy Friend* stand out in 1955 as different, and in turn endowed the show with a certain freshness. And they helped *Salad Days* do the same too. But it was not an American–British contrast. There were large-scale, home-grown shows too that did well in large theatres in the early 1950s, such as *Gay's the Word* and *Love from Judy* at the Saville, and *Zip Goes a Million* at the Palace. We should also remember the commercial imperatives for uneasy producers. This led to them taking less risk through backing a proven foreign success rather than more risk by investing in a new, untested local project. Nowadays, the workshop and the low-budget test run are commonplace, but in 1950s they weren't, and a tryout was likely to be out of town but at full scale. *The Boy Friend* could run because it was small scale in a moderately sized theatre with moderate running costs (e.g. piano, bass and drums rather than a full theatre orchestra). Apart from any aesthetic difference, that alone gave it a commercial advantage.

The misleading link comes through making scale itself a national characteristic: bespoke shows of *The Boy Friend* and *Twenty Minutes South* (both from the Players') and *Salad Days* and *Follow that Girl* (both from Bristol's Old Vic) on the one hand, and such contemporaneous Broadway-to-West End imports as *West Side Story* and *My Fair Lady* on the other. In fact, there is only a short dip of a couple of years in which new, large-scale home-grown West End shows are scarce but with older shows still running. From late 1956, a new style of punchy and edgy British musical on a big stage emerges, for example, with *Grab Me a Gondola*, *Expresso Bongo* and *The Crooked Mile*. The following chapter will illustrate by comparison how *The Boy Friend* and *Salad Days* increasingly became charming oddities when a British musical mainstream reasserted itself strongly and swiftly. *The Boy Friend* may have acquired a place in the repeated narrative as one brief shining moment that was 'British', but the home-grown mainstream was heading in different, big and bold directions.

Transatlantic consequences

On Broadway, *The Boy Friend* opened in a new production at the Royale on 30 September 1954. It ran until 26 November 1955, then went on an extensive tour. It was the first post-war British musical to play on Broadway simultaneously with its West

End production and has become one of the most widely identifiable British musicals up to 1960. Through a lasting awareness of it in the United States that has not extended to the bulk of the other home-grown West End repertory of its day, it has influenced how British musicals in general are thought to relate to American musicals. The crucial sense of identity is distorted when the criteria and concerns of Broadway are assumed to be the natural and only ones and then applied to West End shows conceived for the home audience. A Broadway audience was not a West End audience, even less a Players' Theatre one, as John M. Clum shows in his recollections: 'My boyhood friend and I went to New York to see Julie Andrews in *The Boy Friend* the summer after eighth grade. We thought the show was hilarious. Already at age thirteen, I had an enormous love of camp and *The Boy Friend* was as camp as they came' (Clum 1999: 42). Clum responded to the show as he saw it at the time. Did he know that it had been tailored significantly for Broadway? It is not clear from what he writes fifty years later. The distinction matters.

In his autobiography, Wilson describes in detail the difficulties he had with changes to the show for Broadway, concluding that a 'dream come true' was 'transformed into a nightmare' (Wilson 1975a: 239–60), later calling the production a 'bowdlerized version' (quoted in Philips 2021: 77). Some alterations were simple and uncontentious – the reworked 'Rivera' number as described earlier, for example. Some were huge: listen to the difference between the original London cast recording and the original Broadway cast recording. The orchestration expands from the piano-bass-and-drums minimalism to pit orchestra at full blast, from demure to brash. That such scaling up was essential to meet Broadway expectations makes its own point about the different presentational contexts. Besides which, alterations to shows were the stock in trade of musical comedy, which is why *The Girl Friend* as first presented in New York was not *The Girl Friend* as it was first seen in London (altered story and songs). Paradoxically, in the light of Wilson's protestations, the changes made in the 1950s for *The Boy Friend* on Broadway were in line with the adaptive practices for musical comedy of the 1920s.

In America, the approach to the work and its resulting reception was subsumed by the local view of musical comedy heritage. The show's debt in the 1950s to American models of three decades earlier strengthened the perception of the musical's quintessential genre identity as American, to be treated accordingly. Could a West End import that acknowledged its sources so clearly have been perceived any other way? One consequence is that the American assessment of the show has lacked that essential formative ingredient of 'being in' the 1920s not 'looking at' the 1920s. The American understanding was cemented as 'an affectionate send-up' (Green 1994: 162), 'an affectionate spoof' (Suskin 1992: 589) and a 'British travesty' that 'ridiculed so accurately' (Bordman 1978: 565, 356) its source shows. What Wilson abhorred in the Broadway production was the lack of sympathetic stylistic recreation. He felt that Cy Feuer, who had taken over direction from Vida Hope, 'had kept [Hope's] physical production down to the last gesture and inflection, but he had removed the heart from it. What was left was a strident, graceless parody, without a trace of the truth and sincerity which Vida had gone to such pains to create from the moment of the very first reading at the Players' (Wilson 1975a: 258).

The essential elements for the West End had been happiness and genuine sentiment:

If you are young you will be somewhat surprised to discover that musical comedy in the twenties had a great deal more gaiety than the solemn musicals of today, and if you are not so young you will comfortably remember how banal you once thought the music, how preposterous the romance, and be pleasingly surprised that now in this extraordinarily happy pastiche they are both rather touching.[12]

A programme note in 1956 for the London production described the 'brilliant satirical picture of the manners and styles of the period' balanced by 'that essential component of the true musical – a feeling of nostalgia' (quoted in Philips 2021: 77). Wilson's summary of the tonal change for Broadway was 'There was no love in the laughter. They were laughing *at* the Twenties, and what we had intended as an affectionate lampoon had been transformed into a mocking burlesque' (Wilson 1975a: 257). His response to the start of the overture is as much about the whole production as the scoring: 'As I expected, it was too loud and brassy' (Wilson 1975a: 257). The variation is not between 'straight' and 'parody' within the show but rather between 'affectionate' and 'loveless' or 'graceless' attitudes towards presenting it. Green and Suskin mentioned earlier both find Wilson's treatment of the past in the show 'affectionate' from their Broadway perspective, which adds complexity through the varied receptive stances of those experiencing any performance.

Wilson felt powerless as he watched his creation transformed by others. To him, Julie Andrews sounded '"too terribly English for words" and her expressions and gestures mannered beyond all belief' (Wilson 1975a: 257). Andrews recalled the direction of Cy Feuer who had 'a wonderful penchant for dismissing everybody and getting in and directing it himself', as Wilson and Hope found to their cost. He told her just before the opening night: 'Forget what everybody else is doing, forget camp, be real.' Andrews 'made it as real as I could on opening night and it indeed made all the difference'. The inference here is that Andrews's 'real' would be thrown into relief by the other performer's 'camp'.[13] Wilson knew what he had conceived, Feuer knew Broadway and Andrews took professional direction. The contradictions between their perceptions – 'mocking' and 'mannered' set against 'camp' and 'real' – can't be squared by a single vision of *The Boy Friend*.

Generational perspectives bring in yet further considerations. The different responses of 'young' and 'not so young' are contrasted in the review quoted earlier, and a more precise view specific to London and 1954 hones such a comparison of attitudes: 'Every generation since time began has regarded its predecessor as supremely ridiculous and has cordially welcomed corroborative evidence. Such evidence is here amply provided for the new Elizabethans and therefore they, too, will flock to the Wyndham's box-office.'[14] In 1950s America, Clum's teenage impression of this show drawn from 1920s musical comedy led him to label it 'camp'. Further distinctions from an American perspective featured in critical responses to the 1970 revival on Broadway, when 'this kind of camp – replica rather than parody – has already become dated' in a production that was 'altogether too conscious that camp has come into being, and been analysed and devitalized, since *The Boy Friend* first plucked out its pleasant copycat tunes' (Suskin 1997: 99, 100).

A deferential production style presents the audience with a faithful immersion in the performative world. A deliberately parodic style gives the audience a conscious reinterpretation in which the meta-theatrical comes to the fore. When 'true sentiment' is removed there is a tonal space that the indulgent self-awareness of 'camp' can fill. Bluntly reduced, the 'affectionate' is a performance, and the 'loveless' is a performance of a performance. In practice, there is a continuum of responses that balances in different proportions what is the in-stage world (the show's own reality) and the onstage world (the show as a performance to an audience). What that balance is for any individual will arise from a nexus of reference points specific to them. Some points of recognition will come from the original text and an awareness of the context of the work, while others will arise from the show being performed in a different cultural context.

One perceptual layer has now disappeared. Wilson wrote a show with no recollection of an actual 1920s show in the 1920s. He may have been too young, but some of those in the first audiences for *The Boy Friend* were not. That authentic 1920s memory has gone, but it still exists as one temporal layer within the work. To borrow from an apt summary by Ethan Mordden (1997: 79) of the 1971 Broadway revival of *No, No, Nanette*, Wilson's *The Boy Friend* is part pastiche, part revival and part-time travel in how it revisits a conventional 1920s musical with a knowing spirit. This temporally layered quality explains why Ken Russell made the changes he did for his 1971 film adaptation. A striking film image for the dance routine to the song 'I Could be Happy with You' sets a sparkling chorus line of tap-dancing girls as tiny figures on a revolving phonograph 78rpm disc. Instead of 1920s stage musical comedy, the number now realizes 1930s Hollywood in Busby Berkeley style, which acknowledges the domination of mass entertainment by means of new technology. The imagery literally has the technological means of reproduction (the phonograph) shown big, which proportionally makes the people small. This encapsulates the perspective of a film director, and Russell's vision constantly prioritizes 1930s film filtered through his own idiosyncratic approach several decades later.

Russell subverts the very idea of live theatre by creating a contrast between the decaying world of the stage and the indulgent glamour of the burgeoning film industry. On the theatre side, the film follows the tribulations of a regional repertory company attempting to put on a tired musical comedy, *The Boy Friend*, in the face of declining audience interest. A Hollywood director catches the dismal show, during which he reimagines the stage song-and-dance sequences in the manner of big American film musicals. Cast members similarly project their own fantasies – they act on stage but dream on film. The reoriented storyline asserts genre hierarchy: opportunity lay with the silver screen in America, not on a wooden stage in Britain.

The backstage relationships of the troupe, the dodgy staging and the constant alterations from what had been rehearsed are juxtaposed throughout with the fantasy film sequences to assert a perceived superiority: film is a bigger, better, richer and more imaginative business than its old relation theatre. Big set pieces as though from film are staged by Russell to give a narrative of the medium's development, as with his inclusion of silent film pastiche (one is drawn from Greek myth in the manner of Daphnis and Chloe) as a contrast to 1930s high tech in a line-up of girls dancing on the wings of an aeroplane. While Russell's version is miles away from the narrative of

Wilson's original show, what does register is the past–present layering extended by Russell to assert his medium of choice when it exploded into popular culture. He stated as his three purposes 'A typical stage musical the '20s, an affectionate salute to the inventive musical fantasies of the 1930s, and a take-off on all the Hollywood backstage musicals of all time'.[15] Wilson and Russell were almost exact contemporaries. Wilson directly acknowledges this stage–screen tension through his pairing of *The Boy Friend*/stage/1920s with *Divorce Me, Darling!*/film/1930s. Russell makes the same 1920s–1930s associations direct in a single work, as when he turns 'A Room in Bloomsbury' into a 'Fred and Ginger' tribute.

Wilson disliked what Russell did to his original stage work. He described it as 'a mess: a wilful and at times incomprehensible confusion of Twenties and Thirties camp'. This crossed two lines: it was not consistent in period as the original had been, and camp was not respectful in tone. Yet he also conceded to Russell a principle for film adaptation in recalling the view of Vida Hope that *The Boy Friend* was a work rooted in 'a style of production and performance that relates totally to a live audience' (Wilson 1975a: 271). The interactions of stage and film with their respective audiences work differently. In reputational terms, the film has done the stage show an 'injustice' (Philips 2021: 135), not least through the dilution of its intended 1920s authenticity. In analytical terms, the film's juxtaposition of stage/1920s and film/1930s adds to an appreciation of the temporal complexity that underpins *The Boy Friend*.

In his autobiography, Wilson quotes Coward's responses to *The Buccaneer*. Coward thought 'Unromantic Us' as 'very Rodgers and Hart', which Wilson says is 'absolutely right'. Coward acknowledges Wilson's skill with words fulsomely: 'There are three good lyric writers today . . . Cole [Porter] – myself – and you' (Wilson 1975a: 213). There is no question that all three do indeed exhibit a shared verbal dexterity, and all three wrote consummately engaging and beautifully proportioned lyrics. Behind Wilson's selection of this memory is his desire to be included within a generation that preceded him. Wilson was only four by the time Coward had defined a 1920s spirit from first-hand knowledge in such songs as 'Poor Little Rich Girl' (1925) and 'Dance, Little Lady' (1928). In interview, Wilson expressed how he had 'hated' contemporary popular music from the 1950s on. His talent and his taste became all-too-swiftly out of step with his time: 'Since rock 'n' roll I've turned a deaf ear' (Philips 2021: 108). During the long run of *The Boy Friend* in the West End, *Expresso Bongo*, the subject of the next chapter, opened. Rock 'n' roll became part of the substance and well as the style of a new West End musical. The contrast between the two shows in so many ways, and especially the cultural associations that power them, couldn't be greater.

7

Expresso Bongo (1958)

Wolf Mankowitz and the More-Heneker-Norman trio

When *Expresso Bongo* opened in 1958, *The Stage* acclaimed it as 'the most important British musical of recent years'. It was 'by far the most successful attempt in this genre to take a section of contemporary life in an authentic idiom'. The show had 'an adult approach, a seriousness, which helps to give the best parts of the show something of the design and forcefulness to be found in a genuine work of art'.[1] Praise indeed, if we take on the chin that concluding, all-too-familiar slight that arises from entrenched cultural hierarchies. This wasn't an isolated view. The London Critics' poll for *Variety* – the American journal devoted to the entertainment industry – voted *Expresso Bongo* the best musical in the West End of 1957–8 with six out of eleven votes. The remaining five votes were split between the Broadway arrival *My Fair Lady* and the West End shows *Share My Lettuce* and *Free as Air*.[2]

Expresso Bongo is a musical dramatization of a short story by Wolf Mankowitz, whose authorial stamp is writ large through themes, locus, characterizations and language. It takes place for the most part in London's Soho contemporary with the musical's 1958 creation and offers a cynical slant on the fast-growing commercialization of youth culture. The show follows from behind the scenes the rise of a young dupe through the emerging world of rock 'n' roll, pop records and the entertainment industry. Herbert Rudge is none too bright, but he is an attractive teenager who loves to play the bongos and sing rock 'n' roll. While performing to his peers in one of Soho's new coffee bars, he is noticed by Johnnie, a low-level agent who spots the commercial potential of Rudge. Repackaged as 'Bongo Herbert', Johnnie's new client rises with television exposure to achieve a chart hit. He becomes the latest teenage pop fad, then is picked up as arm candy by an older, famous actress who uses the publicity to boost her flagging career. Johnnie's success as an agent is short-lived. Outwitted by the actress in collusion with a more powerful entertainment entrepreneur, he loses his control over Bongo Herbert's career and with it any profit. The show ends as Johnnie spots his next deal: to get his girlfriend Maisie – like Bongo Herbert, of limited talent – the lead role in a new stage musical.

Prior to London, the show opened in March 1958 in Nottingham. Its style and content immediately registered as new:

> Here is the first of the Angry Young Musicals – written, acted and produced by restive young talent, about young people of today – and aimed like a space-gun at the audience. It breaks all the rules. It even squeezes in the Bomb and packs a message – which, for a musical, has always been considered in the theatre to be box office suicide. But it is as fresh as this morning's paper, controversial, probing, astringent.[3]

After further performances in Birmingham, Newcastle and Leeds, *Expresso Bongo* moved into the Saville Theatre on London's Shaftesbury Avenue, next to the Soho streets where the musical is set. It ran there from 23 April 1958 to 24 January 1959.

Expresso Bongo has not been seen on stage since the early 1960s. Rights were not released for official amateur performance, later proposals for professional productions have not been of a scale to progress from intention to authorized staging, and the band materials would now require reconstruction. The speed of the transfer to film – 1959 – and its headline casting of a newly risen pop star of the time, Cliff Richard as Bongo Herbert, reinforce the musical's status in its day, but major changes in tone, plot and music for the film dilute significantly the bite of the stage original. In 2016 the British Film Institute released the original long cut (1959) and the reissued short cut (1962) on DVD and Blu-ray in remastered splendour. Today the film dominates the reputation of *Expresso Bongo*. This does not diminish the impact that the stage show had in 1958, when it demonstrated a new potential for home-grown approaches to the musical. That significance plays a part in how we understand the show and the period today. *Expresso Bongo* 'is much darker, more cynical, and Brechtian in its outlook than anything mainstream British audiences or – with the exception of *West Side Story* – American audiences had been used to' (Wells 2016: 276). That assessment alone invites an investigation of the show's qualities.

Challenges to convention

The director of *Expresso Bongo*, William Chappell, wrote an introduction to the published script (1960) that characterizes the edgy tone of the musical and its West End significance:

> It is now fashionable for [musicals] to be 'noir'; sleazy, shabby, dark and peopled by unpleasing and tough characters. *Expresso Bongo* was, I think the first of the really black English musicals (if you except *The Beggar's Opera*) and came a little before its time. But it began a whole cycle of low life pieces – what might be termed the S.S.S.S. Group, the Stratford-Soho-Sloane Square School of musicals. Unlike most of its progeny, *Expresso Bongo* has a good plot, a proper tale to tell, and believable characters who are not very nice: ruthless, cunning and fairly dishonest but human, and so acceptable. (Mankowitz and More 1960: 5)

Chappell acknowledges the two leading centres for a contemporary, urban style of theatre-making in the late 1950s. At the Theatre Royal, Stratford East, Joan Littlewood led the creation of works that experimented with reflecting the demotic qualities of East End life back to that theatre's own audience. This approach valued dramatic realism rooted in factual and empathic research, delivered in the idioms and accents of the streets. On the west side of London, in Sloane Square, the Royal Court theatre introduced experimental writing from a new group of writers, collectively to be labelled the 'Angry Young Men'. They presented a post-war critique of British society and the need for change, especially around class and privilege. The 'Angry Young Musical' manifests 'a perfect example of the typical Angry Young Man' (Wells 2020: 164). In less than two years, from the premiere of *Expresso Bongo* to the publication of its script, new British musicals were incorporating changes from the straight theatre revolution pinned around John Osborne's play at the Royal Court, *Look Back in Anger* (1956).

Expresso Bongo is set in London's Soho. The locality had long offered up a rich juxtaposition of immigrant communities, criminal activity and the sleazier side of metropolitan night life. The arrival of the first Italian coffee machines in Soho created for young people social meeting points where their music and dance fashions could flourish. Indeed, amateur performances in the small cellar of the 2i's Coffee Bar on Old Compton Street helped launch the career of several major British pop stars of the late 1950s–early 1960s. Soho was also a centre for the entertainment industry's agents and record, film and emerging television companies, which were well placed to spot that youth talent. With their shared locale, shows of this period and character have been labelled the 'Soho Musicals'. Although mostly geographically correct, the term also takes in some shows with similar interests in urban communities, liminal/criminal values and commercial transaction. *Expresso Bongo* was the first, followed by *Fings Ain't Wot They Used t'Be*, *The World of Paul Slickey*, *The Crooked Mile* and *Make Me an Offer* (all 1959), then *Johnny the Priest* and *The Lily White Boys* (1960). The recreation of a market street in Soho for the Act I finale of *The Crooked Mile* and of Fred's 'spieler' (down-market café and gambling joint) in *Fings Ain't Wot They Used t'Be* fixes these shows in time and place before even before considering character types, language, social interactions and the cultural resonances in the music.[4]

This group of shows encompasses hits and misses. *Fings Ain't Wot They Used t'Be* was first played in repertory at Stratford East's Theatre Royal as one of Littlewood's new works for her Theatre Workshop. In a revised version it transferred to the West End, where it ran until February 1962, a week over two years and just three short of 900 performances. Despite having a book written by John Osborne, *The World of Paul Slickey* lasted in the West End just short of six weeks, with 47 performances. Rather than such individual comparative success and failure, the importance lies in the grouping of these shows and how quickly they emerge. The collective resemblances register a new critical grittiness and an edgy challenge through dissections of the failure of contemporary urban society. When *West Side Story* arrived in the West End in 1958, an exploration of the same urban issues of the American show was already underway for London audiences, spurred by the first visit to London in 1956 of Bertolt Brecht's Berliner Ensemble. Straight theatre had responded first with the emergence of 'kitchen sink dramas', most notably *Look Back in Anger*, Arnold Wesker's *The Kitchen* – from which the description derives – and Shelagh Delaney's *A Taste of Honey* (Wells 2016: 273). Such plays reflected back to their audiences a world uneasily caught in the post-war tensions between reasserting pre-war norms and sweeping them away in the search for something meaningful to a changed Britain. Ineluctably, musicals began to embrace the same dramatic potential in the conflicts that had arisen during a decade of growing social and cultural rupture.

The creative team for *Expresso Bongo* was fresh to musical theatre. Wolf Mankowitz (born 1924) was the same age as Sandy Wilson. Any resemblance ends there. David Heneker (born 1906) was of a previous generation that included Vivian Ellis and was only five years older than Noël Coward, whose score to *Bitter Sweet* prompted Heneker into songwriting. Yet his approach is more up to date in the 1950s than either of those two contemporaries. Monty Norman and Julian More (both born 1928) followed only a little after Wilson and Mankowitz, but effectively they come of professional age as the 1950s begin. Everything about this grouping signals a new generation entering the sphere of British musical theatre. Within the creative team, Mankowitz brought recently achieved literary status and a distinctive, critical voice that had public recognition. The concept and impetus behind the musical was his – so much of his source short story down to small details finds its way into the script's dialogue and imagery.

Julian More brought the most prominent recent stage experience in musicals as the author (book and lyrics) of *Grab Me a Gondola* (1956, music by James Gilbert). When *Expresso Bongo* opened, *Grab Me a Gondola* was in the last few months of a long West End run. That show introduced contemporary themes and characterizations (stars and their shenanigans at the Venice Film Festival). With hindsight, it is more a work of brightly adapted convention than incisive innovation when compared to *Expresso Bongo*. But it played in a central West End theatre from November 1956 to July 1958 (the Lyric on Shaftesbury Avenue – not to be confused with the Lyric, Hammersmith, where the show had been tried out). At the time *The Boy Friend* and *Salad Days* were also playing to packed houses. By virtue of that juxtaposition, *Grab Me a Gondola* contributed to breaking home-grown musicals out of fantasy and/or the past towards the potential of clearer reflections on stage of the contemporary world offstage.

David Heneker started writing songs in parallel to his army career, then began working with More on an original musical. Monty Norman, a band singer, recorded some demonstration numbers for it, and although the project was abandoned, Mankowitz spotted them for a musicalized *Expresso Bongo*. The trio 'fitted the subject matter perfectly as they understood the seedy side of Soho and the cut-throat music business that the show inhabits' (Nicholls 2021: 117). Of course, it is farcical to imagine that writers must have the credentials and experiences of the characters they create: Coward's lovers weren't killed in duels before he wrote *Bitter Sweet*, and Novello never ruled a minor Balkan state so as to create *King's Rhapsody*. However, A. P. Herbert did write *Big Ben* with parliamentary experience – and insider knowledge adds to the bravura confidence of *Expresso Bongo*.

This new team, predominantly from outside musical theatre, was less constrained by conventions of the genre and more open to being led by the nature of the material. The story and setting employ music within a diegetic context that blurs the performance boundaries: a musical about a musician, a performance about performing, an entertainment about the processes that shape entertainment, a commercial production about commerce. The contexts that position the show in its time arise more from outside than inside the musical theatre repertory of the 1950s. The entertainment value was not intended to be predominantly diversionary and easy, and its score was wedded to its dramatic purpose such that numbers did not easily extract for the 'popular songbook' of show tunes. The concept was tightly bound to the means of its execution. Such holistic reflexivity produces a distinct tonal difference from other musicals playing when the show opened.

The best-known shows that immediately followed *Expresso Bongo* describe a commercial trajectory from initial experimentation and genre fusion towards more conventional, easily accepted shows. *Make Me an Offer* (1959), by Mankowitz, Heneker and Norman, continued the formal adventurousness of *Expresso Bongo*. It portrays with intensity another clearly defined world of business, the antiques trade. The familiar Mankowitz themes are there: the deal, high-low cultural divide, Jewish characters, the London street-market trade (Portobello Road, centre for antiques). All but three of the characters are described as 'dealers', qualified by age and gender ('young', 'lady'), status ('important', 'unimportant'), area of interest ('demolition'), nationality (American, Welsh, Irish) and ethnicity (Jewish, cockney). The only non-dealers are nonetheless related as a dealer's wife, a dealer's daughter and an auctioneer (Mankowitz, Norman and Heneker 1959: 3). The show advances the technical inventiveness of *Expresso Bongo* in its particularly fluid integration of song and dialogue, straight address to the audience, swiftly shifting scenes conveyed with minimal staging, and characterful use of styles of speech and vocabulary. *Make Me an Offer* was created at the Theatre Royal, Stratford East, alongside *Fings Ain't Wot They Used t'Be*. Both Soho musicals were developed and presented by Theatre Workshop during 1959 (*Fings* first) prior to West End transfers in December 1959 (*Make Me an Offer*) and February 1960 (*Fings*).

Heneker's scores for *Half a Sixpence* (1963) and *Charlie Girl* (1965, music with John Taylor) reach an accommodation of British popular styles with American show songs, building on the example of Lionel Bart's *Oliver!* (1960). Both *Oliver!* and *Half a Sixpence* had success on Broadway and were given large-scale film adaptations. Through that prominence, their perceived distinctiveness has been assimilated into a generalized historical narrative of musical theatre that covers both sides of the Atlantic, but is primarily led from a New York vantage point. Of Heneker's several later musicals, for most of which he was sole writer-composer, it is only *The Biograph Girl* (1980, with Warner Brown) that has retained any minimal traction among aficionados having achieved the qualifying *fan-fest* combination of critical approval and commercial failure. Heneker's work increasingly focussed on appealing, conventional show tunes – a skill not to be underrated or dismissed – within polished if also conventional dramatic approaches. He played to his strengths and interests, not contemporary fashion. Consequently, there is a progressive disengagement from the immediacy and innovation of the shows with which he was involved from 1958 to 1965.

After Norman's collaboration on *Make Me an Offer*, he wrote the songs to Mankowitz's book for *Belle, or the Ballad of Dr Crippen* – another short-lived musical with a long-lasting reputation among aficionados and also one of Mankowitz's co-producing projects. Its experimental nature as a musical about a famous convicted murderer, presented through a series of music hall acts, was a theatrical fusion too far at the time (Dunn 2013: 133–6). Given the changed theatrical sensitivities of a couple of decades later – witness Sondheim's *Sweeney Todd* (1979) – maybe its reception would have been different. Norman wrote and composed *Songbook* (1979), with More as co-lyricist, and composed the score for the highly inventive and genre-fusing *Poppy* (1982, book and lyrics by Peter Nicholls), which acts out the history of the First Opium War in the style of British pantomime. After *Belle*, Mankowitz wrote the script for *Pickwick* (1963, music by Cyril Ornadel, lyrics by Leslie Bricusse), a musical adapted from Charles Dickens's novel *The Posthumous Papers of the Pickwick Club* (aka *The Pickwick Papers*). It had a long West End run and a Broadway transfer, and is possibly best remembered for Harry Secombe in the title role and the now-classic song he introduced, 'If I Ruled the World'.

Mankowitz, Heneker, More and Norman do not cohere as a recognizable collaborative identity within the repertory in the manner of Novello and Hassall or Ellis and Herbert. They form a looser mix-and-match association. Illustrating this, Adrian Wright's discussion of this grouping is compartmentalized by multiple subheadings (mostly around Heneker and More) that differentiate the creative relationships and chronological groupings within their combined list of shows (Wright 2010: 169–94). The writing team that worked together for *Expresso Bongo* is prolific in British musical theatre across all their shifting creative combinations, but with only sporadic mainstream success and with differing degrees of individual prominence. Historical narratives of the musical often latch on to the dominance of long-lived writing teams who have gained widespread name recognition, from which a canon is inferred. This tendency diminishes the profile of *Expresso Bongo*. Serial mainstream success contributes to the bigger picture. So too does any single, innovative show.

Making a point

Wolf Mankowitz was 'not only the linkman between the 1930s generation of Jewish proletarian writers and the New Wave of the late 1950s, but was as committed as his near contemporaries to elucidating the opaque contours of post-war Britain' (Dunn 2013: 5). His unique voice successfully – unusually so – bridged the widening twentieth-century chasm between notions of high and low cultures. His experiences gave rise to thematic preoccupations that run through his prolific output of short stories, plays and film scripts. He was repeatedly inventive in how he wove new patterns from his pet tropes, and all are in *Expresso Bongo*.

Mankowitz's stories crossed the classes, acknowledged his East End Jewish heritage and revelled in the machinations of West End commercial entertainment. From the years immediately before *Expresso Bongo*, his novel *My Old Man's a Dustman* (1956) demonstrates a masterly combination of wit and compassion in unearthing the psychological scars of the recent war and takes sideswipes at the delusion and fakery within the film industry. Mankowitz was an authority on Wedgewood pottery and compiled two reference works on the topic (1952 and 1953). He used the subject of the first – *The Portland Vase and the Wedgewood Copies* – as the centre of his first novel, *Make Me an Offer* (1952), setting it around London's antique business, which he knew well. It fast became a success, and he adapted it as a television play (1952), then a film (1954), then a musical (1959). In fact, he adapted many of his novels or short stories from one narrative medium to another, including *A Kid for Two Farthings* (novel, 1953; award-winning film, 1955) and *The Bespoke Overcoat* (short story and stage play, 1953; television, 1954; film, 1955).

Especially in the second part of the decade, Mankowitz consolidated his 'ethnically inflected version of "the people" and their culture' (Dunn 2013: 29), to which end he embraced vernacular language and inflection along with distinctive vocabulary. Mankowitz believed in idiomatic language – place, social class or ethnic influence – as crucial to representing real people on stage or in print and for communicating that reality to his audience. He consistently demonstrated 'an extraordinary ability to fuse elite learning with new forms of popular culture in a far wider variety of media – fiction, film, theatre, television, journalism – than any of his contemporaries' (Dunn 2013: 67). With his interest in the developing media of the 1950s, he became a familiar figure through television and radio appearances in his own right: in the public's mind he became a personality with an attitude.

The ease with which Mankowitz's dramatizations come to life belies his mastery of creative complexity. This is repeatedly apparent in the characters of *Expresso Bongo*. Their actions and responses simultaneously draw together multiple themes, which gives them the depth and appeal of the real. Cumulative intensity is created by these cross-connections. However, such a degree of entwined purposes is difficult to dissect. Investigating each individual element risks losing the power of the bigger picture. Take one seemingly small detail: Johnnie's manner of speaking with an 'off-beat accent – not quite cockney – a sort of suburban cockney with a very faint American tinge creeping into it, now and then' (Mankowitz and More 1960: 7). This is like English Harry Fabian's fake American speech to bolster his business image in Gerald Kersh's classic novel of London's Soho, *Night and the City* (1938), adapted to film in 1951 (Kersh 2007: 13–14, 17). Laurence Harvey's hybrid accent for his portrayal of Johnnie in the film of *Expresso Bongo* was based on Mankowitz's own distinctive blend of accent and inflection as 'part Soho, part Jewish, and part middle class' (Dunn 2013: 105). The manner of speech is the iceberg tip for values, comparisons, expectations and motives resulting from geography, class and culture.

As with Johnnie's blended mode of speech, authenticity in Mankowitz's work is often achieved through hybridity. This extends to the show's mash-up of new wave theatre, musical theatre, show song and pop song, which results from the triple loci of area, activity and period. Mankowitz was not from a musical theatre background and drew from his experience with London's contemporary straight theatre. He kept the first-person narrator of his original short story at the centre of the stage drama. That role, Johnnie, was created by Paul Scofield, then an acclaimed classical actor on stage and considered since his 1948 interpretation the Hamlet of his generation. He matches Chappell's description of the role as 'an actor first and then a singer' (Mankowitz and More 1960: 7). Film status enhanced the lure for audiences of such star actor casting in the West End as Herbert Lom in *The King and I* and Rex Harrison in *My Fair Lady*. The esteem in which the theatre world held Scofield did similar and signalled an accommodation between straight play and musical.

Expresso Bongo adopted a new, confident, confrontational performance style. For a large-scale West End musical of its time, the show opens with a bold statement of theatrical intent. Couples enter the Deep South Jazz Club. Following them in is 'a gangly shock-haired youth from Hoxton, carrying a pair of bongos and a large yellow conga drum' (Mankowitz and More 1960: 9). Johnnie follows them on, then addresses the audience directly:

> This, my friends, is an historic occasion. You can tell from the full page spread in *The Pop Music Weekly*. [. . .] I come from a long line of small-capital big hopers, some of whom did not die bankrupt. Hope, unlike charity, costs nothing. With me, regardless of the facts, it's always hope in my heart. And for once in a while, it's justified. Down there, beating his tiny brains out, is my future meal ticket. The occasion is certainly historic. (Mankowitz and More 1960: 9)

There is no conventional opening chorus, and the fourth wall is broken with the first spoken line of the script. Three months after *Expresso Bongo* opened, a similar device began the West End version of the French musical by Marguerite Monnot and Alexandre Breffort, *Irma la Douce* (Paris, 1956). Its purpose is to introduce the slang terms in French retained in the English-language adaptation to convey the spirit of the original Parisian setting (Nicholls 2021: 118–19). More, Heneker and Norman translated and adapted *Irma la Douce*, and their approach to conveying the streets in which the eponymous prostitute lives echoes how they evoked the Soho milieu of *Expresso Bongo*. Also, *The World of Paul Slickey* begins with material directed to the audience, even more heavily mannered in presentation than the opening of *Expresso Bongo*: dancers, one of whom curtseys to the audience in acknowledgement, are followed by the quick interaction of news copy, orchestral interjection and photographic projection (Osborne 1996: 193–4). In these shows, a figurative curtain no longer goes up on a naturalistic scene.

The scene shifts to Herbert Rudge at a microphone in the Deep South Jazz Club. He sings, 'Don't Sell Me Down the River', which describes what Johnnie shortly intends to do to 'Bongo Herbert'. The ironic lyrics note, 'If you want to sell me, I can sell myself.' It's quite an opening for a musical in 1958, with the developing hallmarks of Littlewood, Theatre Workshop and the socialist agitprop of London's well-established Unity Theatre. Johnnie is observer, interpreter, MC and player in the drama. He pre-empts by several years two better-known MCs: that of Theatre Workshop's *Oh What a Lovely War* (London 1963, Broadway 1964) and of *Cabaret* (Broadway 1966).

The scene in which Johnnie visits Bongo Herbert's home – Bongo's age means that Johnnie requires parental agreement to be his agent – is cut short. There is no love lost between Bongo and his mother, and the encounter descends into 'family uproar'. Johnnie steps into a spotlight: 'Phew! I'm going to spare you that scene. When Bongo finished telling her, she looked like a pricked bladder of off-white lard. A tired, grey old char, who'd scrubbed millions of miles of floor – to find at the end the world is flat – the edge of it a precipice – complete with her only son to push her off' (Mankowitz and More 1960: 23). The speech revels in a certain ugliness of imagery and a nastiness of emotion. In the longer structural plan, the tone of the speech frames that central picture of the 'tired, grey old char', an unflattering maternal image that will be used in an unlikely way for one of the show's highlights, the song that ends the first act.

At the end of the next scene, Johnnie interprets the audience of a non-stop revue show within the musical for the actual audience of the musical in the theatre:

> People are always waiting. Outside the slummers are waiting to go in. Off-stage the girls are waiting to go on. The public in the back seats is waiting to get into the front seats. The public in the front seats is waiting till the last minute before going home to its wife. Five shows a day, non-stop, everybody waiting. Like I'm waiting now for Maisie to get off and get on. Well, that's life, we'll all wait together. (Mankowitz and More 1960: 27)

This is classic Mankowitz in its concatenation of the literal and the metaphorical through rhetorically structured, direct language. An act of theatre is analysed in existential terms while it happens. In Act II scene 4, his monologue switches in quick succession between interpretative updates spoken straight to the audience – outside the internal stage action – and him making a telephone call – within the stage action. By now, Johnnie's direct acknowledgement of the theatre audience is a feature of the show's style.

The structure is further animated with film-like cuts interjected into a scene between Johnnie, Maisie and then Bongo. It is a montage that takes stock of Bongo's 'big nation-wide build-up as a Teenage Rebel'. Spotlights direct the audience's attention to a lady columnist speaking to her editor, and then to Bongo's mother, to a psychiatrist and to a padre. After each new interviewee has made their point, the lights redirect attention back to Johnnie's, Maisie's and Bongo's reactions. The entire scene takes up just two pages of script. Its conclusion lands a punch. Johnnie's manipulation comes to the fore inspired by the padre's embracing of youth culture in stating, 'We have to reach people at their own level. I've started a Bongo Club in my crypt.' Johnnie ends the scene: 'Sex – we've got. Violence – we've got. Religion . . . (*There is a burst of organ music*) We've got to get religion' (Mankowitz and More 1960: 39). The result is Bongo Herbert's third diegetic song in the show's narrative, 'The Shrine on the Second Floor', the finale of Act I.

The song is double-edged with surface sincerity from performance and subtextual insincerity from the back story. The lyrics idealize and idolize a 'grey-haired madonna', parodying Bongo Herbert's self-centred and 'tired, grey-haired old char' of a mother whom he earlier called 'one of the Hoxton peasants' (Mankowitz and More 1960: 20). Bongo's introduction undermines any genuine emotion in the song or his performance. He declares that he is religious when we know he isn't. He dedicates the number to 'the lady who taught us that there's someone bigger than you and I. My mother' (Mankowitz and More 1960: 40). Yet in the build-up to that 'family uproar' a few scenes earlier, he rounded on her 'Call yourself a mother. I never had a mother. Just you' (Mankowitz and More 1960: 23). Thus announced, the song's sentimental style is heard by the musical's audience as exploitative mockery. One stage direction alerts us that even the connotations of the backing vocals are manipulative: 'As Bongo sings, the heavenly choir appears behind a gauze in the cloth and joins in the finale' (Mankowitz and More 1960: 40).

The scene is played as though the musical's audience in the auditorium is the actual audience to whom Bongo Herbert is performing from the stage of the Odium Palace Cinema. The musical's audience is once again both within the show's narrative (Bongo's 'genuine' performance) and simultaneously observing it by means of the distancing subtext to which in this second capacity they are privy. It's wonderfully theatrical. By the interval, the show's message is that entertainment industry creates value through the manufacturing process, not from its source content: the presentation of the song creates a simulacrum of genuine emotion where there is none. In such an exploitative enterprise, authenticity is not authentic, and the most polished example in the show of Bongo Herbert as a performer is also his least sincere.

The construction of the song is manipulative in a delightfully insidious way. The rhythm is slow-paced, animated by triplets to create a steady, insistent propulsion towards the climaxes. The brass pad of sound is warm and enveloping. The melody slowly climbs upwards as though striving heavenwards. There is the emotive, religious language of 'Shrine' and 'Madonna' with their connotations of devotion and love. The backing choir – and a 'heavenly' one at that – seals the deal. It's as though a satirist viciously crossed 'The Impossible Dream' with 'Climb Ev'ry Mountain'. The end of the song is not quite the end of the act. There is a brief but striking flash of Brechtian distancing from Johnnie to cue the interval. In five words, he directs the audience towards the opposing serious and cynical interpretations of the number at the same time: (*The stage blacks out. Johnnie comes on into spotlight*) 'That was lovely, wasn't it?' (Mankowitz and More 1960: 40).

Games and confrontations

Games are played continually through the interaction of the narrative drama, commentary on it and the resulting deconstruction of the genre for the audience. At a straightforward level, in Maisie's ballad 'Seriously' Johnnie's lines of dialogue are interpolated into Maisie's second sung refrain. This creates the simultaneous presentation of two vocal levels: song, which is natural in a musical, and speech, which is naturalistic for a play. Johnnie has two solos 'I've Never Had It so Good' (Act I, adapting Prime Minister Harold Macmillan's famous assertion on the state of Britain in 1957) and 'The Gravy Train' (Act II). Both switch from dialogue into music number unsignalled: no 'music under dialogue', no verbal exchange that cues a bell note. Moreover, the lyrics in both are part of Johnnie's conversational engagement with the audience. His confessional mode cuts through the fourth wall. This is not an audience eavesdropping on a musicalized inner voice. The approach exposes the theatrical devices rather than protects the stage as a self-contained, consistent reality.

The ensemble song 'He's Got' breaks the fourth wall in a celebratory manner, affirming Bongo's 'vim and vigour', 'pace', 'slinky figure' and 'face' just to start with. The lyrics identify Bongo's 'something special for the public', but also 'an extra special something' that has drawn the interest of each of the players in his career. Their ulterior motives are: toyboy sex and publicity for Dixie Collins (a screen star relaunching her career); scoops for Linda (a news reporter); status by association with the social circles

Bongo's fame opens up for Lady Rosemary Gorey-Platt (Dixie's upper-class publicist); the diversion of slumming it with a cockney for Cynthia von Ullenheim (Rosemary's daughter, an entitled debutante but none too bright). And for Johnnie, Bongo means a meal ticket, his 'Gravy Train' (Mankowitz and More 1960: 51). The accumulated juxtapositions of these individual motives express the show's late 1950s cynical world view: business, not love, makes the world go round. The same technique is used later in the song 'Nothing Is for Nothing', whose mood is pointedly cynical. This time, the ulterior motives of Dixie (sex), Johnnie (power) and the powerful record producer Mr Mayer (money) are juxtaposed within a common philosophy of competitive self-interest through the trade and the deal, in which 'Nothing is for nothing / That's the human plan. / Line up for the rat-race, / Man must live on man' (Mankowitz and More 1960: 59). These numbers state their agendas bluntly to the audience through parallel commentary by the characters rather than interaction between them. The songs stand adjacent to the chronological narrative of the story rather than in it. At this time *West Side Story* explores its themes through narrative integration, but *Expresso Bongo* questions what is performed and to whom it is addressed.

Blatant sexual references in *Expresso Bongo* taxed the prevailing tolerances of formal theatrical censorship, another sign of its innovative nature within musical theatre. It is clear from the depiction of its nude revue girls how far *Expresso Bongo* has moved from Coward's nightclub performers in *Ace of Clubs* (1950), the Hot Box Dolls in Loesser's *Guys and Dolls* (West End 1953) and the chorines in Rodgers and Hart's *Pal Joey* (West End 1954). The Reader's Report for the Lord Chamberlain considered that the entire scene needed 'almost line by line consideration, as it is *intended* to be dirty. First, what is Maisie [the stripper] wearing besides an academic gown and black satin shorts?'[5] The nightclub stage show features three historical tableaux in the manner of those famous through the Windmill Theatre's erotic revues, a famous/infamous Soho landmark.

> Are the girls to get the benefit of the nude rule because of their immobility? It seems to me that Mary Queen of Scots, in nothing but a short kilt and a crown, is more suggestive than the ordinary Windmill nude in a G string. The same applies to two girls as Ceasar and Brutus, each with one breast exposed; this could be very funny, but it is pure or impure Folies Bergères. Is it allowed? William I and Harold appear to be dressed.[6]

The application of the 'nude rule' to *Expresso Bongo* was summarized in later correspondence from the Lord Chamberlain's Office in respect of a production in 1963 at the ADC Theatre, Cambridge. It was directed by then student Stephen Frears (later film director, whose *Mrs Henderson Presents* relates the story of Soho's Windmill Theatre and its nude revues). In the production, Bongo Herbert was played by another student, Richard Eyre (later director of the National Theatre and director of an acclaimed staging of *Guys and Dolls*, with its pretend nightclub strip act 'Take Back Your Mink'). Under college pressure, five students withdrew from the nude female roles and local replacements were found. The nude tableaux was vetted by the University Proctor who responded, 'Frankly, I prefer Shakespeare.'[7] Frears obtained official reassurance for the theatre management of the legality of presenting the show with the nude scenes: 'The Lord Chamberlain has customarily allowed nude figures to appear on the stage provided that they assume their positions out of view of the audience and are completely motionless and expressionless whilst in view of the audience.'[8] There was an issue in the licensed script with a stage direction at the end of the strip club scene: 'Charlie, the stage-hand-cum-call-boy-cum-dresser, is chivvying the girls, who now cross half naked across the stage' (Mankowitz and More 1960: 25). This contravened the 'nude rule' that required completely still bodies, as the response to Frears explained: 'You will appreciate that the girls must not be chivvied off the stage if their breasts are visible.'

For its time, the show pushes the boundaries of heterosexual permissiveness in a large-scale West End musical through a clear challenge to society's conventions and taboos. The song 'Spoil the Child' within the nightclub scene caused difficulty for the censors, with the Reader's Report identifying it as 'salacious from beginning to end'.[9] The problem verses were heavily tamed for the resulting authorized version. 'Kiss me pretty / Stroke my fur / I'm your kitty / Make me purr' became 'Kiss me pretty / Kiss me now / I'm your kitty / Make me miaow'. The final couplet 'Don't don't spare the rod / Spoil the child' had one crucial word changed to become 'Spare, spare, spare the rod / Spoil the Child'.

Disingenuous defiance marks the replies of the show's manager, Oscar Lewenstein, to the Lord Chamberlain's instructions for changes to lyrics that relied on double entendres: 'Could you specify more exactly the words you object to? It appears to us that neither of these verses are objectionable.' This is bold, given that the Lord Chamberlain's office could refuse a licence and stop the show opening. At the time, musicals were associated with upholding rather than challenging the status quo. Behind the scenes, *Expresso Bongo* was preparing the way for stronger pushes to the legal boundaries of staged decency – or for many 'indecency' – by *Fings Ain't Wot They Used t'Be* (1960). That show critiques the Wolfenden Report (The Report of the Departmental Committee on Homosexual Offences and Prostitution, 1957) and the subsequent Sexual Offences Act (1957) in its accepting and positive presentation of female sex workers, its mockery of the police expected to enforce the new, punitive legislation against such activity and the inclusion of a gay character – an interior designer – at a time when homosexual activity was still criminalized. Times were certainly changing, musical theatre with them.

Promoting youth culture

On the evening of Thursday 11 December 1958, BBC Television broadcast forty-five minutes of *Expresso Bongo* direct from the Saville Theatre. The *Radio Times* promoted the broadcast through youth culture:

> Teenage idols, coffee-bar convulsions, the fabulous living to be made from a guitar string, and the exploitation of young and often untalented enthusiasts by the not so young but always talented publicity men and managers have become a part of

the show business pattern in the past few years. Sooner or later, it was bound to be taken up as a theme for a satire.[10]

More prominently promoted on the preceding spread of the *Radio Times*, the programme *Rebellious Youth* in the occasional series 'European Enquiry' tackled the same issue.

> Reports of youthful restlessness come today from many countries. Britain's Teddy Boys, who have made headlines not only in this country but also across the Channel, have their parallel in the adolescent 'Halbstarken' – the 'half-strong' – of Germany and Austria and similar groups of young people elsewhere. Newspapers have been writing in shocked tones about rock 'n' roll riots. In literature we have the phenomenon of the so-called 'Angry Young Men.' Behind the Iron Curtain where dissent is a grimmer business, it is largely the young generation who have been speaking out and in these countries the cult of Western jazz has become an actual symbol of youthful revolt. . . . What seems established is that in our present-day society young people tend to mature earlier. They have more money to spend on their leisure than their parents had and they demand sophisticated entertainment. Do these changes pose new social and moral youth problems?[11]

That final question had been recurring in British film through the 1950s. Tensions between the values and preoccupations of different generations in Britain post-war also found their way onto the stage. Petty (and sometimes not so petty) criminal activity, recidivism, sexual promiscuity and its consequences, drug use and disastrous interactions with the seamy side of adult experience proved ripe for dramatic exploration. With the prurient story lines came opportunities to assert decency and respectability through a dénouement of either retribution or a Prodigal return.

By 1958, an impressionable child who had been taken with American horror magazines – the inspiration of Sandy Wilson's *The Buccaneer* – had become a young adult experiencing new American subversive influences. These included the rebellious attitudes projected through rock 'n' roll, Elvis Presley and James Dean. James Kenney, the original stage Bongo Herbert, made his name in the lead role of Roy Walsh, a delinquent youth 'beyond parental control, cruel, thieving and selfish',[12] in the play *Cosh Boy* (1951) at the Comedy Theatre, then retitled as *Master Crook* at the Royal Court (1952) and then once more as *Cosh Boy* on film (1953). The 1950s is the decade in which the new 'X' film classification (restricted to sixteen years and older) came into effect with the purpose of allowing more adult topics to be addressed. *Cosh Boy* was one of the first British films to be given the new 'X' rating for its subject matter rather than any explicit images. For a few years, Kenney appeared in lesser roles in British films as 'clean limbed Englishmen or neurotic murderers'.[13] *Expresso Bongo* was his return to stage performance and also his first singing role. Kenney was again playing in the West End 'a character who belongs so typically to a section of life which is often in the news today'.[14]

Mankowitz's London voice is as redolent of a sense of time, place and community as Damon Runyon's for Broadway. In *Expresso Bongo* he literally shares ground with

Gerald Kersh, London's Runyon equivalent. Soho is as much a character in *Expresso Bongo* as the people we see inhabiting it. The East End, its Jewish culture and heritage dominate many of Mankowitz's stories, plays and scripts, such as *A Kid for Two Farthings*, *The Bespoke Overcoat* and *The Mendelman Fire*. The character who portrays this most clearly in *Expresso Bongo* is Mr Mayer, the record producer whom Johnnie hustles. Chappell describes the role: 'A Jewish actor is fairly essential for Mr. Mayer. A non-Jewish player, unless a highly skilled technician, will not give you the full flavour of this important character' (Mankowitz and More 1960: 7). The creator of the role on stage was Meier Tzelniker, also the only cast member to play the same role in the film adaptation. Mankowitz's admiration for him was such that he has an entry of his own (under 'Zelniker, Meier') in Mankowitz's witty *The ABC of Show Business*: '[He is] among the great Jewish comedians of the century and is one of the few players from the East End's Yiddish theatre who has been able to translate the ebullience and warmth of his native language into English' (Mankowitz n.d. [?1956]: 55).

Mayer embodies the perplexing contrasts between high and low cultural values and their relative rewards. He previously lost money producing opera with great singers he idolizes, but now makes money producing pop songs by awful singers he can't stand. His number 'Nausea' expresses his present business–art compromise in clever lines of crisply rhymed bathos, such as 'When I see this little bleeder, / And compare him with Aïda, / Nausea', wanting 'Meistersingers' but getting 'shystersingers', and imagining what to him would be the ultimate cultural crime Bongo Herbert could commit, 'Gott, why was this little swine born? / Next he'll want to sing at Glyn'bourne' (Mankowitz and More 1960: 17, 18). Mayer is a rounded and witty character who combines Jewish heritage and its East London locus with an astute sense for a business prospect. He best articulates in the show the late 1950s chasm between high culture/older generation and low culture/youth.

In the introduction to his *ABC of Showbusiness*, Mankowitz asks, 'What is Show Business? Is it an industry for the manufacture of synthetic laughs and tears? Is it the art of making money? Is it the science of packing theatres?' (Mankowitz n.d. [?1956]: 4) The alphabetically ordered definitions are often slanted to make a Mankowitz point that clearly comes from the perspective of an insider. Relevant to *Expresso Bongo*: Agents 'infest show business'; a Discovery is 'a hopeful anticipation of future business'; Musicals are 'as near as the theatre can get to a mass entertainment, and are consequently the most industrialized of products' (his entire entry for Ivor Novello lists only financial and business details); Publicity is 'what every starlet admittedly seeks and what every star professedly avoids'; Radio of the 1940s and 1950s was 'the most experimental of all show business media'; and Youth 'has always been at a premium in show business . . . It is therefore advisable to start in show business somewhat below the age of consent and never exceed 30'. Especially relevant to *Expresso Bongo*: Records allow 'anyone with a voice sufficiently undistinguished for teen-agers to be able to copy it in the bath may succeed in becoming the holder of a golden disc with sales running into millions and an income of thousands. Titles should contain references either to love or piety; atmosphere should be masochistic or frenetically excited'; Television 'pipes show business into the home like warm water from an atomic pile. [As it is] subject to mass approval for its success, it must necessarily accept and promote mass standards'; and Cinema is 'formerly said to be the death of the theatre and now said to be dying itself from television. Not as dependent upon acting as the theatre'.

The opening of the show enacts Bongo's rise from amateur live performance to professional pop recording entirely within the environs of Soho: a Soho club cellar (Act I Prologue); 'the Tom-Tom Coffee Bar, a typical Soho bar dominated by an enormous Gaggia machine and a mass of tropical trimmings' (Scene 1) into which enters Mr Mayer 'the hard to get Artiste and Repertoire man from Garrick Records' (Mankowitz and More 1960: 15); a recording studio for Bongo's first disc (Scene 2). We experience Bongo Herbert's first television appearance through Johnnie and Maisie's perspectives as they watch it on television in Johnnie's Soho flat (Scene 5). Johnnie gets the significance of this advance through levels of media as he watches 'my boy': 'Look at his lovely, contorted, teenage-rebellion face going out to five million tele-hugging imbeciles. He's singing our song, Maisie. It's our song that's going out to that great record-buying public.' Johnnie appreciates that 'Many a disc has started to roll on one T.V. plug' (Mankowitz and More 1960: 32, 33). Later (Scene 7) we hear the hit record 'Expresso Party' playing on a radio while Johnnie looks at newspaper reviews. The first act concludes with the performance of 'Shrine on the Second Floor' (scene 8). It is a live concert taking place on a cinema stage by Bongo Herbert, holding his microphone and giving us – finally – his fully formed pop singer act. With characteristic hybridity, Mankowitz sets all these different forms of technologically transmitted media within a live theatre performance of a musical. The one 'real' act is that of the live performance by actors on a stage in front of a physically present audience. This is the opposite of those radio, record and television performances within the diegesis. That form of theatrical comment is completely lost in the show's adaptation to film.

The film *The Golden Disc* came out three months after the stage musical *Expresso Bongo* opened. It is also set in the coffee bars and recording industry of Soho. The story also follows a pop singer who cuts his first record. The focus is on the business of entertainment . . . and how to set up a coffee bar. This makes for an intriguing contemporary comparison with *Expresso Bongo*. The central role is played by Terry Dene, an actual young idol of British pop (if briefly so). Ken Hollings pithily summarizes the film to highlight it as an alternate, contemporary pole to *Expresso Bongo*: 'A cheap piece of exploitation cinema, *The Golden Disc* subverts its fictionalized account of Terry Dene's rise to stardom by allowing it to take place in a world where failure is an absolute impossibility.'[15] The execution is naive and simplistic, staged in low-budget settings. Measured explanations of how that first disc and the coffee bar come about have the pedestrianism of a public information film more than a drama. The complexity and tension of *Expresso Bongo* is replaced with a sanitized, non-threatening version of new youth culture for the benefit of the film makers themselves and for the perplexed older generations.

Teen idols on screen

The entertainment industry was finding ways to accommodate teen culture's music, movement, image, popular icons and different values. The potential customer base was great, but as a new phenomenon it was unclear whether this was a temporary trend or would prove to be a more lasting realignment of cultural poles. The defiance by the younger generation of its elders made it a target for commercial exploitation, and British films of the 1950s reflected the changed focus of youth culture. With similar uncertainty, the practitioners looked to capitalize more long term on what could be (and often proved to be) short-lived personality success. As Hollings wryly portrays such late 1950s uncertainty, 'The kids in the coffee bars would soon be moving on to the next wild new craze. Might as well make a movie while you still have the opportunity. Show the world that you're not the novelty that rock 'n' roll will prove itself to be.'[16]

Putting pop talent, its fans and their values on the screen was big business, but unlike *Expresso Bongo* on stage any threat was to be tamed, as Tommy Steele's films show. The first, the *Tommy Steele Story* (1957), removes the generational threat of Steele as a rock 'n' roll teen idol. His character is shaped as a generous, lovably cheeky singer whose expression can be absorbed comfortably within the all-embracing atmosphere of light entertainment. His biography is denuded of sex and politics of the time, and his song repertory is inclusive of popular ballad and rock 'n' roll and thus attractive to a wide audience range (Mundy 2007: 175). Steele was the spur to Mankowitz's creation of Bongo Herbert, in which Steele's South-East London 'Bermondsey boy' is transmuted into an East London Hoxton lad. Both areas were implicit shorthand for low-class status and restricted access to social and financial mobility in the late 1950s (something in the late 1930s shared with Lambeth for Bill Snibson in *Me and My Girl*). The second of Steele's films, *The Duke Wore Jeans* (1958), concerns class too with the infiltration of royalty by a cockney rock 'n' roller (also reflecting a core trope of *Me and My Girl*).

By the time of Steele's third film, *Tommy the Toreador* (1959), he had been packaged as a song-and-dance light entertainer whose diversionary presence swamped any attempt at dramatic or thematic coherence. He advanced naturally into stage musicals as Kipps in *Half a Sixpence* in London and then on Broadway, and so into film musicals with *Half a Sixpence* (1967), *The Happiest Millionaire* (1967) and *Finian's Rainbow* (1968). Steele's professional evolution traces a productive marriage between the teen market and its pop performers and an entertainment machine that can reorientate its product/star as a lucrative all-round entertainer. The initial threat of teen rebellion was diffused to become acceptable to all the family and so maximize any commercial success. Steele's later career is defined by musical theatre and variety performance, not as a continuing pop star.

The image of late 1950s London is sustained in the film adaptation of *Expresso Bongo*, directed by Val Guest and released in 1959. There was a natural space for such a film in the developing British catalogue of 1950s works that interrogated concerns of post-war degeneracy among the younger generations, particularly teenagers. Notably, in 1959 the seminal film *Beat Girl* dramatized the corruption of wilful youth through sex, rock 'n' roll and the American beat aesthetic in Soho coffee bar culture. Among the design detail, the stage cast LP of *Expresso Bongo* tops the pile of records owned by wayward teen Jennifer, who is determined to go off the rails to spite her father and stepmother. In the same year, the film of *Expresso Bongo* undermined much of the dystopian bite of its source stage show by casting the recently successful young pop singer, Cliff Richard, as Bongo Herbert. Richard rose fast to prominence after his debut single 'Move It' in August 1958. His first film was *Serious Charge*, released in April 1959 a convenient three days before the release of his first album, *Cliff*. Although Richard played the younger brother of the central delinquent character, his character was given prominence in two ways. First, appearances by his character in front of a juvenile court open and close the drama. His potential delinquency is stemmed by the support of the local priest his elder brother viciously maligns in the central conflict of the drama. Second, Richard's rock 'n' roll singing is shoehorned in, if only briefly. Among these occasions, the song 'Living Doll' (written by Lionel Bart) is heard twice, first interwoven with dialogue and second as the main focus. In a slower interpretation, it became a chart hit for Richard and his backing group The Drifters (later renamed The Shadows) soon after the film's release.

In Steele's first film appearance the previous year, the B-movie crime feature *Kill Me Tomorrow* (1957), he is introduced playing the guitar and singing 'Rebel Rock' (also by Lionel Bart) while a group of young people jive in the El Rico coffee bar. There is no engagement between Steele and the film's narrative, and the camera's tight focus on Steele and his guitar obviates to some degree any diegetic need to show a drummer, bass player, electric guitarist and a saxophonist. The sound and image of youth culture to characterize a coffee bar is the sole reason for Steele's presence, reinforced by the visual inclusion of a jukebox as well as live performance. Steele is in the film credits as playing his pop self, not a fictional character. The assimilation of Richard within his film acting debut similarly sets him up to perform in the quasi-realistic locations of a coffee bar and a youth club and bestow contemporary street cred through the sounds and iconography of an age group and its oppositional culture as represented by an emerging pop star. In doing so, the second, long rendition of 'Living Doll' in the film creates a giveaway moment when it puts commercial audience appeal above dramatic consistency: how could an erstwhile juvenile offender be the singer on the commercially produced record the priest plays in his empty church hall?

Richard's elevation just six months later to a starring film role in *Expresso Bongo* (November 1959) provided an even stronger promotional window, yielding a silver disc in the singles charts for the newly added song 'Voice in the Wilderness'. Richard was the opposite in talent and business success to the character he played, but his quick rise up the pop ladder was similar to that of Tommy Steele. As a result, it is not the character of Bongo Herbert who comes to the fore in the film but Richard himself, assessed at the time as 'just a little too good to be "sent up" in this sort of way. He seems modest, unaffected by his rise to fame: he behaves, if not precisely acts, acceptably before the camera and even I can distinguish every other word of any "number" he puts over.'[17] The film falls between irreconcilable poles: 'The satire is still sharp enough to alienate a "pop" audience, but the sentiment will blunt its edge for the sophisticated.'[18] It was a sign for what came next. Richard followed the trajectory of Steele to a substantial degree in his subsequent film musicals *The Young Ones* (1961), *Summer Holiday* (1962) and *Wonderful Life* (1964). His image became that of the singing-dancing family entertainer, never straying too far from musical interpolations as set pieces only partly rationalized within plots that can't quite ditch entirely the diegetic convenience of 'putting on a show'. Despite these early film roles and those in the later, equivocally received stage musicals *Time* and *Heathcliff*, Richard's career – unlike Steele's – has first and foremost been in concert as a pop singer.

The ambivalence in these film representations of contemporary youth music was not a concern for *Expresso Bongo* on the West End stage. In a live stage musical you expect characters to sing and would be more than surprised if they didn't. Their fundamental rationale for doing so comes from the genre, not a diegetic pretext: the situation may influence the mode of musical delivery but not the fact of it.

Striking a new tone

Throughout the 1950s there was a growing sense of the stage musical needing to exceed its widely assumed diversionary purpose and, following straight theatre, have something significant to say about the here and now. The critic T. C. Worsley was in his mid-fifties at the time he reviewed *Expresso Bongo* and had grown into adulthood in the interwar years with values to suit. He noted the issue and the potential:

> They've been talking a long time in highbrow theatrical circles about the musical as 'the coming art form', as 'significant', as able better than any other form to 'reveal the contemporary situation' and so on and so on. And for a long time one had gone hopefully, expectantly, to the latest new musical, whether English or American, and so far from finding any of the quality promised, one has been very lucky not to be greatly bored. But the More-Mankowitz *Expresso Bongo* at the Saville really does justify all the chatter. It is a first-class musical play aimed right at the centre of life today, and it is, as they say, 'bang on'.[19]

Worsley continues that 'new' requires more than some visual indicators of the present day, such as costumes and locations. 'New' incorporates the attitudes of the time into the drama's core. The message has to be modern. To Worsley, *Expresso Bongo* took that essential extra step. Pointedly, Worsley makes reference to two recent American shows by way of comparison, *The Pajama Game* (Broadway 1954, London 1955, film 1957) and *Damn Yankees* (Broadway 1955, London 1957, film 1958).

> To be contemporary it isn't enough merely to pick the 'contemporary' subject, or those other musicals that are set in baseball dressing rooms, or garment factories would have got there already. What More and Mankowitz add to the choice of the contemporary subject is the choice of contemporary words in their sharp, astringent dialogue, and the lyric writers (Julian More, David Heneker and Monty Norman) have followed suit with songs that use wittily, bitterly and freshly the phrases of the moment. listen a moment to one of the numbers, sung in a menacing minor (with more than a touch of Brecht in the staging) by a crumpled-faced variety agent, a middle-ageing actress and a tin pan tycoon:
>
> > Nothing is for nothing, that's the human plan,
> > Line up for the rat-race, man must live on man.

Nothing is for nothing, nothing is for free.
I'll look after you, Jack, when [sic] you look after me.

With that song (modulating as it perfectly well can into reference to the 'mushroom cloud with the silver lining') the English musical grows up at last.

Expresso Bongo was similarly identified in the *Financial Times* as a turning point. Its reviewer, Derek Granger, writes, 'This is an exciting event in the history of the British musical theatre – and certainly the most startling outburst of original brightness since the war (and I almost mean the first!)'. This complements Worsley's identification of a new maturity within musical theatre by praising a level of presentation that stood out as 'something very special in English musical treatment – nothing less, in fact, than the integrity and strength of the full "legitimate" works'. The show did not reinforce the expectation of a musical as light and diversionary entertainment. Rather, it was purposeful, serious theatre in its own right and presented as such. There is too frustration in the review at the tone of other contemporary British musicals in that it took 'a stunning professionalism of assembly to make us realise that a London chorus-line and orchestra pit could spray us with something a little more stimulating than nostalgic charm.' Granger pushes this contrast further in summarizing *Expresso Bongo* as 'hard, brilliant, ruthless and – thank heaven – defiantly and jubilantly charmless.'[20]

Before *Expresso Bongo*, the bright inconsequentiality of *The Boy Friend* and *Salad Days* had been interpreted as nationally distinctive, even defining, in relation to a homogenized (if inaccurate) notion of the qualities of Broadway shows imported to the West End. *Expresso Bongo* brought that comparison starkly within the framing of British repertory alone. The small-scale freshness of *The Boy Friend* and *Salad Days* was revealed as a false dawn for any sustainable and meaningful new direction for the home-grown musical. The magic touch of Slade and Wilson was proved limited by their respective follow-on shows of *Free as Air* (1957) and *Valmouth* (1958).

Of itself, *Expresso Bongo* was a revitalizing force. It was also the vanguard of more fundamental change, with those other Soho musicals swiftly following on. They were part of a wider, dynamic change in British theatre. The post-war generation, angry or otherwise, were flexing their muscles. Looked at collectively, the repertory landscape of the West End in respect of home-grown musicals shifted by a generation in 1958–60. The shows of Novello and Ellis and Herbert as well as other pre-war show writers were growing old with their audiences in revivals and tours.

Previous chapters have interrogated the identities of shows that arise from the manner in which familiar elements are rebalanced and recombined in complementary ways. The usual pattern of change has been what could be thought of as respectful evolution from an inherited base: start with what's already reassuringly familiar, demonstrate due observance through the repetition of tropes and conventions, but rework them with a few new twists. Change registers in small increments. There is a crucial change through the 1950s with a growing, conscious questioning of that pattern culturally, sociologically, politically and morally. Among those entering adulthood post-war, there is a growth in the deliberate creation of ruptures with accepted past values. Change of itself becomes the focus, making it abrupt and prominent. Inevitably, the upheaval hit musical theatre too.

The adoption of musical style in *Expresso Bongo* is like nothing in *Bitter Sweet*, *Me and My Girl*, *The Dancing Years*, *Bless the Bride*, *The Boy Friend* or even *My Fair Lady*, all of which integrate retrospective qualities. Musical styles and techniques were gathered around Mankowitz's central story to encapsulate the immediacy of its here-and-now setting. The overture blasts into action with brass and saxophones leading the repetitive, simple patterns of the song 'Expresso Party', which is to launch Bongo Herbert to public attention. Walking bass, drum rhythms, rock 'n' roll-style high piano interjections establish the tone. Musically, the song is as basic as you can get. The melody, such as it is, consists of a repeating three-note cell extended into pentatonic phrases. The basic material is an even simpler version of the opening phrases of 'Don't Sell Me Down the River'. The riff repetitions of rock 'n' roll characterize both songs. In 'Expresso Party' the harmony sticks almost entirely to the tonic chord with occasional decorations by a dominant before the bar line (a series of transpositional slides upwards disguises, but does not alter, the static harmonic base). Such simple and simplistic melodic and musical material is effective in representing the attractive surface and empty substance of Bongo's world – even his name characterizes him by rhythm not melody.

James Kenney was not a singer, but he developed his voice for the role.[21] Bongo Herbert's music guys current pop styles, and Kenney talks full advantage of this in his vocal delivery. The original cast recording captures his exaggerated pop mannerisms of smudged pronunciation and an energetically raucous tone in the establishing 'Don't Sell Me Down the River' and to an even more pronounced degree in 'Expresso Party'. For the relative sophistication of his ballad 'The Shrine on the Second Floor', Kenney captures the 'sob' emotionalism characteristic of popular singer Johnnie Ray throughout the 1950s in the sustained vocal lines and mock-sincere lyrics. 'Expresso Party' and 'The Shrine on the Second Floor', the two songs from Bongo under contract, encapsulate complementary poles of commercial pop and its cynical packaging up of raw talent: the visceral, unrefined and uptempo in contrast to the manipulative and manufactured.

The solo numbers of Maisie and Dixie Collins are from a different branch of popular song. They are attractive, emotionally expressive ballads characterized by long melodic lines that contribute a more conventional musical-theatre element to the breadth of the score. Maisie's 'I Am' is the most conventional, a 1940s/1950s romantic ballad in its flow and swell, underpinned by a slowly shifting, lightly rhythmic accompaniment over which the long phrases soar. The musical approach in the first phrases complements the pattern in the lyric, which conveys growing insight by the cumulative expansion through 'I . . . I think I am . . . I feel I am, in fact I'm almost sure I am in love'. It charms – as does Maisie, 'the only thoroughly nice character in the play' (Mankowitz and More 1960: 7). Style articulates Maisie's changing performance registers too. The sincerity of the character evoked in her numbers 'Seriously' and 'I Am' is paralleled by an obligatory vocal charm required of the real actress (in this case Millicent Martin making an early West End mark in creating the role). For Maisie's onstage act in the Soho club act 'Spoil the Child', her character performs in a tacky revue act. The song's perky upbeat nature is a direct match with the showgirl songs in *Pal Joey*, *Ace of Clubs* and *Guys and Dolls*. The simplicity of its construction allows the risqué lyrics to register and invites choreography appropriate for such nightclub entertainment. Primarily it is a display of energy, not melody. This is a parallel to what we first see of Bongo Herbert's talent in another type of Soho performance space.

Dixie Collins represents an alternative path within the entertainment industry: the international, glamorous star. We don't see her perform in a professional capacity, as we do with Maisie and Bongo Herbert. Rather, Dixie's two main numbers amplify different aspects of her rich, sophisticated lifestyle. Her first number, a duet with Lady Rosemary, is defined by sharp and comic verbal play as they list the hedonistic indulgence that wealth has afforded them. Their credo provides the first line: 'Whatever we saw, we liked, we bought' (Mankowitz and More 1960: 65). With the need to get the wordplay across, the melody is secondary, and the punch of the number is more in the brittle rhythms of the short lines and multiple rhymes. The scene takes place at Dixie's villa in Majorca, where Bongo is staying. The blatant implication is that Dixie has bought Bongo. As he concedes, 'Anything you say, Dixie. You're the boss' (Mankowitz and More 1960: 67). But Dixie's acquisitions, including Bongo, don't bring her happiness.

Dixie's second number follows the first almost immediately. In 'Time', she soliloquizes, wistfully voicing her private thoughts to the show's audience while she rubs suntan lotion onto the young, attractive, recumbent, shallow and unsatisfying Bongo. The song is a beguine, well-suited to the 1950s, when Latin American rhythms had become increasingly fashionable in American popular song but not so much yet in Britain. The 1950s resonance is increased in the song with the added sophistication of jazz-inflected chromatic harmonization and melodic major 7ths and 9ths. Dixie is just back from living in America, and the song shades in some backstory atmosphere, distinguishes her in song style from Maisie and widens the score's range of contemporary popular music genres.

In the refrain of 'I Never Had It So Good', Johnnie conveys more the style of a swing band singer, with something of the music-hall entertainer in his emphatic three-bar tags that conclude each series of lists in 'He's Got Something for the Public'. For example, the three stressed first beats (underlined) melodically hammer home the 5th ready to land on the tonic conclusion on 'bread': 'And me because his dough is making my daily bread'. His blues number 'Gravy Train' is one for a popular singer of the day. As a character, Johnnie lives behind the scenes, not on stage. Yet in his songs as well as his direct addresses to the audience, his role is conspicuously performative such that it marks him simultaneously as a participant in the action and an observer of it. The melodic phrases in the main verses droop towards the lower tonic, grounding the number as an opposite to the rising contours that convey aspiration in 'Shrine on the Second Floor'. The steady pace matches the moody flattened-note inflections of the melody, firmly in blues territory. The words confirm that Johnnie's failed dream leaves him 'back where I started' and 'a million miles from Shangri-la'. It is one of the few numbers from the show that can work out of context, being a self-contained journey through the building of the dream and the final shattering of it, told in beautifully phrased lyrics with a well-matched setting.

For the penultimate scene of the show, Johnnie is centre stage, for once seeming honest as he is knocked down. The show could well have ended there. But Mankowitz is consistent in Johnnie's irrepressible optimism. The little flash of hope that concluded the original novel makes it into the stage script when a chance conversation suddenly provides an opening for Johnnie's next opportunity to make it rich. In response to the casting of a new musical, Johnnie starts his next hard sell: 'That's what this kid of mine is – an absolutely brand new all British Judy Garland, the entirely gorgeous, real sex-sational, Maisie King' (*Maisie is heard singing 'Don't Sell Me Down the River'*) (Mankowitz and More 1960: 75–6).

Making history

The Saville Theatre on Shaftesbury Avenue is on the edge of Soho. It would have taken an audience member just a couple of minutes to reach the 2i's Coffee Bar on Old Compton Street and be immersed in the world they had just witnessed on stage. Tommy Steele, Cliff Richard and Terry Dene had all been talent spotted when they performed on its basement's tiny stage, which reinforces *Expresso Bongo* as a distorted reflection of a genuine slice of Soho life as it was happening. The date of the premiere was 23 April, so the show added its own timely national self-reflection to St George's Day and putatively William Shakespeare's birthday.

Exactly one week later, on 30 April, *My Fair Lady* opened at the Theatre Royal, Drury Lane, a few minutes' walk south through Seven Dials and Covent Garden. The Theatre Royal itself is just round the corner from Covent Garden's Bow Street, on which the Royal Opera House façade stands. The market piazza is behind the Royal Opera House. The set for the show's opening scene features both the Bow Street facade and the pillars of the market building. In reality, you can see one or the other, but not both. But, when peopled with the first scene's society opera goers and market tradespeople, such artistic licence creates an apt, visual encapsulation of the opposition that propels the show's London-specific, class-focussed story.

My Fair Lady arrived with the advance publicity of a major Broadway success, knowledge of its story through the source play of George Bernard Shaw's *Pygmalion* and familiarity with its music. The line-up of leading performers was particularly British and of high profile, with a conspicuous reflexivity between their professional personas and the characters they played. Julie Andrews – a child singing star in variety in Britain before Broadway discovered her through *The Boy Friend* – now mirrored the transition from youthful potential to star in the guise of Eliza Doolittle and the acquisition of a cut-glass English accent. As Henry Higgins, Rex Harrison, one of most distinctive of British actors on stage and in film, could exhibit his familiar superiority and irascibility tempered with innate charm. Stanley Holloway, a household name through his music hall and acting careers, brought to Alfred P. Doolittle all the wordsmith storytelling quality of his famous monologues. Further, Mrs Higgins was played by Zena Dare, a leading lady of Edwardian musical comedy and a regular of Novello's unofficial repertory for his plays and musicals, and famous to generations of the West End audience. The settings were by the leading American stage designer

Oliver Smith, but the costumes were by Cecil Beaton, an internationally renowned British photographer and designer associated with fashion, celebrity and glamour. Together they made for quite a line-up of talent even before we add the names of lyricist Alan Jay Lerner and composer Frederick Loewe, whose *Brigadoon* (1949) and *Paint Your Wagon* (1953) were among the more recent American imports into the West End. By the time *My Fair Lady* reached Drury Lane it had been polished until it sparkled and generated huge anticipation. London saw a wonderful show in a great production with a star-studded cast that resonated in one way or another with every generation in the audience.

Expresso Bongo makes for a stark contrast. That show's writer and literary source signalled contemporaneity. The musical itself was new and barely tested, fresh from pre-London development during its provincial tour. True, Paul Scofield essaying a musical was a theatrical event, and James Kenney as Bongo Herbert brought a small profile from recent British film. Neither brought a Broadway gloss (*de rigeur* for some at this point) to the musical. Hy Hazell was known to the West End audience from variety, pantomime and film, although her more noted roles followed *Expresso Bongo*. Millicent Martin was just starting what would become hugely successful transatlantic career in main roles on stage and in television. Wolf Mankowitz as originator and writer ensured that the show never lost sight of its distinctive London roots, but David Heneker and Julian More had at this point nothing like Mankowitz's public profile, while Monty Norman was better known as a broadcaster and singer. On a tick list of promotional points for any producer, *My Fair Lady* was way ahead. Given all this, it is impressive that *Expresso Bongo* was referred to by some as 'the other musical' to distinguish it from *My Fair Lady*.[22]

The London premiere productions total 2,281 performances for *My Fair Lady* and 316 for *Expresso Bongo*. But then *The Boy Friend* ran for 2,084 performances and *Salad Days* for 2,289. In the same period, *West Side Story* achieved 1,039 performances. Between the end of April 1958 and early February 1959, all five shows played concurrently in the West End. What they represent are overlapping, complementary approaches under an all-embracing genre term 'musical' that means multiple things to audiences who bring multiple preferences and expectations into the auditorium before a performance has even begun. All these shows garnered praise and all sustained audiences, albeit to varying degrees. But *Expresso Bongo* loses out in respect of the public awareness created by the sheer longevity of a run that can turn a theatrical residency into a tourist landmark.

Such quantitative thinking goes some way to explaining how, in November 1958, Leslie Mallory's article entitled 'Out with Picture Hats – Up with Realism' could seem so assured in its view: 'The British musical is distinguished by a callow undergraduate amateurism known as "charm". [. . .] Whimsy and fairy fantasy are the squirm-making ingredients of the domestic brew.'[23] The article focussed on the perceived up-to-date qualities of American musicals, which crushed the feeble British ones as exemplified by those of *The Boy Friend* and *Salad Days*. The author's inflexible perspective in the face of events in progress mirrors Frances Stephens's for *Theatre World* through the 1950s (see Chapter 1). While *Expresso Bongo* was acknowledged as having the potential to be a corrective – note that by this point it was into its seventh month – the article heading is doubly unfortunate in its unintended irony: realism was at the core of *Expresso Bongo*, while picture hats were a memorable feature of the Ascot costumes in *My Fair Lady*.

As with the earlier close juxtaposition in 1947 of *Bless the Bride* and *Oklahoma!*, a different way to assess *Expresso Bongo* alongside *My Fair Lady* is to consider them literally in situ for London in how a British audience related to them. In the case of 1947, an American reflection of home and its continuation of Broadway culture was transmuted by crossing the Atlantic and being represented to another country and a different society. It became for that new audience an exotic escape to a different time and land. We can be more specific in 1958 in how *Expresso Bongo* and *My Fair Lady* reflected London back to a London audience. What emerges is a reversal of that usual depiction of the oft-repeated narrative of American musicals always providing the lead – and a superior one, to boot – for British ones.

This time, the American import was based on a tried-and-tested popular play set in Edwardian London, glamourized and stylized in its design, and focussed on the contrast of upper and lower classes by means of journeying through Covent Garden, Belgravia, an embassy ball, a visit to the races and afternoon tea. Could it be more stereotypically English? The script annexed the sophisticated ear of the original author George Bernard Shaw and highlighted a triumphant rise achieved through the ability to alter a class-defining accent and superficial behaviour. The ending – note that Puccini-esque final, bold orchestral statement of a theme associated with Eliza's success at the Embassy Ball – is warm and uplifting, a seal on the romantic/romanticized aura of the show. Its score is the product of European operetta fused with the ballad style of the American songbook of the 1930s and 1940s with a little bit of the American marching band for Doolittle.

However, *Expresso Bongo* was contemporaneous with the Saville Theatre's locale in story, setting, fashion, music and language. The show's reference points were not primarily those of musical theatre. Instead, the dramatic lead came from contemporary British drama, youth culture, the commercial music business and the melting-pot language of Soho and the East End. Its upper-class characters were introduced for ridicule not as a focus for aspiration, and social comment was both challenging to and unavoidable by its audiences. Criticism of contemporary society revolved around commercial mobility, self-interest, greed and all the capitalistic opportunities, vices and crushed dreams that late 1950s London could offer. The show flaunted sex rather than love, while romance was portrayed merely as a technique through which to gain personal advantage. The sound blared into action with electric guitars, trumpets, saxophones and drum kit, hitting the rhythms of skiffle and rock 'n' roll, and with the messages fired straight out into the audience, the fourth wall having been broken as the curtain went up. That opening line of Mankowitz's script now reads as not so much an enticement into a story but a statement about the show itself: 'This, my friends, is an historic occasion.'

8

Oliver! (1960)

Lionel Bart

Of all of the case studies in this book *Oliver!*, from 1960, has the most successfully sustained profile. A quotation from *Expresso Bongo* would have provided an apt title for this book – 'We saw it, we liked it, we bought it' – but very few people would have recognized that song. In contrast, the majority of the song titles, lyrics and significant lines from *Oliver!* are engraved on the memories of several generations. From *Oliver!*'s premiere on 30 June 1960 at London's New Theatre (renamed the Albery in 1973 and again in 2006 as the Noël Coward), it ran for 2,618 performances until 10 September 1966. Overlapping London, it opened on Broadway on 6 January 1963, where it played for a year and eight months. In 1968, it was adapted lavishly and relatively faithfully for film, directed by Carol Reed, and became a classic for family audiences. Professional stage revivals and amateur community performances at all levels have cemented its place in the repertory, especially in Britain.

Few of the case-study musicals in this book have been subject to investigation beyond descriptive chronicling. Philips (2021) provides one exception in using *The Boy Friend* as the hub for the contextualization of Sandy Wilson within gay and theatrical culture. However, only *Oliver!* is the sole focus of an authoritative academic monograph. In the opening sentence for *Oliver!: A Dickensian Musical*, Marc Napolitano describes his study as a 'biography' of the musical (Napolitano 2014: 1), not a study of Lionel Bart and his works. Napolitano's investigation stems from a specialist interest in Charles Dickens, the author of the source novel *Oliver Twist, or The Parish Boy's Progress* (serialized 1837–9; published in novel form 1838).

Taken together, the widespread familiarity with *Oliver!*, availability of performance material and Napolitano's detailed narrative on its creation allow this chapter to sidestep much of the exposition and description required for the less remembered works of the previous ones. Such familiarity implies a significant division in British musical theatre repertory: unperformed/neglected pre-*Oliver!* and performed/considered post-*Oliver!*. Taking into account later hit shows, it has seemed 'the most successful British musical before *Cats*' (Steyn 1997: 171). However, when viewed in relation to its predecessors it appears as 'the biggest international smash to come out of Britain since *Floradora*' (Suskin 1992: 592). Approached this way, *Oliver!* becomes what Robert Gordon has described as 'the crowning achievement of all the experiments and explorations in the creation of new types of musical theatre after the war' (Gordon, Jubin and Taylor 2016: 44). For the first time, the home-grown modern musical in the West End also overlaps sufficiently with Broadway values to work successfully for both repertoires and their audiences, and beyond too. *Oliver!* is a musical of inspired consolidation across the boundaries of play, musical, film and geography.

The rise of Lionel Bart

On 2 December 1959, the *Daily Mirror* pop column 'Spinning Disc' drew attention to the release of an LP of Bart performing his own songs.

> Three years ago Lionel Bart was just a caveman. With chisel and club he hammered out the first crude songs that brought fame to a cabin boy called Tommy Steele.... Back in the rock age, you could find Bart in a cellar hewn out under Soho – surrounded by coke-sipping teenagers.... Today you ring his office and a secretary says: 'Mr. Bart is not available this afternoon. He will be giving a Press conference next week.'[1]

Bart rose to celebrity status fast, which the article links to the world of the previous chapter through rock 'n' roll with a raw London tone, not an American accent. He inhabited the emerging bohemian coffee bars, with their mixture of skiffle, left-wing politics and philosophical angst. Tommy Hicks – to become Tommy Steele – was on the same scene, ready to perform at any opportunity. Both got their big break most directly through the 2i's Coffee Bar in Soho, when Steele caught the attention of Decca Records. The result for performer Steele was his first chart hit 'Rock with the Caveman' (1956), which was also Bart's first songwriting hit (Stafford and Stafford 2011: 39–46). Bart wrote many songs for Steele during the three years the article mentions, including for his first two films *The Tommy Steele Story* (1957) and *The Duke Wore Jeans* (1958). In late 1950s London, Bart helped define its youth culture scene and brought young pop talent to commercial notice, as he did for chart successes Marty Wilde and Georgie Fame (Stafford and Stafford 2011: 55–6).

On 6 July 1960, only six months after the 'Spinning Disc' article and six days after the opening night of *Oliver!*, Bart's publishers placed a half-page advertisement in *The Stage*: 'We Offer Our Congratulations to LIONEL BART' (original emphasis). It highlighted three shows: from 1959 both *Lock Up Your Daughters*, with lyrics by Lionel Bart and music by Laurie Johnson, and *Fings Ain't Wot They Used t'Be*, with music and lyrics by Lionel Bart and book by Frank Norman; and new for 1960, *Oliver!*, book, lyrics and music by Lionel Bart. *Oliver!* was 'Unanimously acclaimed by the Press A SMASH HIT', and in support of the boast, the *Daily Mail* (1 July 1960) is quoted: 'A joyous evening ... A British Musical at last, that will and must charm audiences all over the world.'[2] Bart – versatile, successful and prodigious – was now also at the centre of the musical theatre world, working across the three creative levels of lyrics (*Lock Up Your Daughters*), music and lyrics (*Fings*) and a triumvirate of book, music and lyrics (*Oliver!*). In practice, the order of creation was a draft of *Oliver!*, then *Fings*, then *Lock Up Your Daughters*, then the completion of *Oliver!*. The press endorsement chosen for the advertisement specifies a 'British' identity for *Oliver!* and includes an imperative 'must' in relation to what was prejudged to be an inevitable response to it beyond Britain.

Bart's music theatre involvement had grown during the 1950s alongside his pop music presence. He had been part of the socialist Unity Theatre productions early in the decade, notably writing songs for and playing an Ugly Sister in the pantomime *Cinderella* (1953). He made his last contribution with *Wally Pone, King of the Underworld* (1958), Ben Jonson's Jacobean play *Volpone* (1606) updated to London's contemporary East End. It failed to attract audiences, but characterized elements found throughout Bart's shows: East End London, lower-class characters, oppositions of the entitled–disadvantaged and of the legal–illegal, street language, Jewish representation and empathy for society's underdogs. They match elements within Wolf Mankowitz's work of the same time. *Wally Pone* was 'a musical version of our own colourful crime belt in Soho' with 'a cast of tarts, thugs, pimps and policemen', so falls within that Soho grouping of contemporary London musicals explored in Chapter 7.³

The same characteristics carried through to Bart's first songwriting contributions to Joan Littlewood's Theatre Workshop company at the Theatre Royal, Stratford East. This was *Fings Ain't Wot They Used t'Be*, the second of the three shows highlighted in *The Stage* (West End 1960) but the first to be staged (Stratford East 1959). It was pulled together in less than three weeks from a forty-eight-page script by Frank Norman, who would write 'a few more pages of bad language' to keep up with the moving-target rehearsals of Littlewood's improvisation-led directorial process (Norman 1975: 36, 50). Bart similarly wrote songs in the moment, which Littlewood judged 'the best' of his numbers for that score. 'In the middle of the scene, he'd shout "Hold on! I've got an idea." And the song would happen, then and there.' She concluded, 'it was the Frank/Lionel/workshop combo which made *Fings* so successful' (Littlewood 1995: 541, 545). Norman was less positive about the process, which he satirized bitterly at length in his novel *Much Ado about Nuffink*. In it, the director of a new play tells his cast in front of a first-time playwright: 'The printed text is no more than a starting point in the theatre process; words are simply not enough. Building up the action until it becomes a dramatic truth is what theatre is all about. The acceptance of a script is therefore, very often the moment of departure from it' (Norman 1974: 123).

The same speed of creation followed when Bart became the lyric writer for composer Laurie Johnson on *Lock Up Your Daughters*, a musical version of Henry Fielding's Restoration comedy *Rape upon Rape* (1730). The musical opened the new Mermaid Theatre at Blackfriars (emblematically halfway between the West End and the East End). It was critically hailed ('rousing, bawdy entertainment, fresh and amusing, and very well played'⁴), and the audience response extended the musical's planned six weeks to six months (28 May–5 December 1959). A revival transferred to the West End for a year and half (16 August 1962–30 November 1963), running concurrently for the most part with Bart's later show *Blitz!* (book by Joan Maitland, music and lyrics by Bart) at the Adelphi (8 May 1962–14 September 1963), with 553 and 568 performances, respectively. With the six-year run of *Oliver!* providing a steady backdrop to all this, *Maggie May* (book by Alun Owen, music and lyrics by Bart) followed *Blitz!* into the

Adelphi for a run of more than a year (22 September 1964–4 December 1965). These listings show how prominent Bart was in West End musical theatre for seven years through overlapping, successful runs – his name continually visible on the posters, in reviews and interviews and on the cast LPs. Bart was visible too through his continuing flow of pop songs in the charts and in films.[5]

Lock Up Your Daughters takes a mainstream approach with discrete songs punctuating a script that keeps to period. This brought out Bart's sophisticated dexterity with a style of language inappropriate for the characters in *Fings*. Lines that provide song titles demonstrate the Restoration mood in their interpolation of what was for 1959 more rarified vocabulary in a musical: 'When Does the *Ravishing* Begin?', 'Red Wine and a *Wench*' and 'There's a Plot *Afoot*'. Bart uses many internal rhymes, as when the title song instructs in exuberant waltz style 'Go round and knock up the locksmith to lock up your daughters now!' (Johnson and Bart 1960: 38). Bart's range of vocabulary, register and technical brilliance here is in a different lyric world from his hit song for Steele, 'Rock with the caveman / Roll with the Caveman / Shake with the caveman / Make with the caveman'. Laurie Johnson's music is so well integrated with the lyrics that the sophisticated and witty score remains a holistic joy.

Frank Norman described his impetus to write the draft script that evolved into the musical *Fings*:

> The notion of writing a play came to me almost by accident and was in no way connected with the revolution that John Osborne had set in motion. Indeed, if there was one thing that characterized the new wave of playwrights of the fifties and sixties more than anything else, it was their individuality ... Osborne's rivals, not disciples. (Norman 1975: 34)

Bart's individuality suited the time. He responded to the environments of Unity Theatre and Theatre Workshop, but though he was in them he was not absorbed by them. Bart is a chameleon in these early works as he plays with music and text to integrate with who and what is around him while drawing on the mercurial inspiration driven by his character and background. As his sphere of activity moved away from the Theatre Workshop world, his ideas grew bigger – so did the shows and the theatres that hosted them.

With *Oliver!*, the process of creation was not improvisatory. There were lengthy stages of drafting from the initial *Oliver!* script to a reworking as *Oh, Oliver!* and to the final version, again as *Oliver!*. The script and score were formalized before rehearsals began. At each step the subject and apportioning of musical numbers was considered in relation to the whole structure by Bart and, in the later stages of development, by the show's director Peter Coe, with whom Bart had already worked on *Lock Up Your Daughters* (Napolitano 2014: 51–78). There was a crucial balance of styles between them: 'The combination of both their approaches was vital to the overall success of the show: Bart's emphasis on glamorous spectacle ensured that the adaptation would resonate with a mainstream audience, while Coe's devotion to the Dickensian component ensured that style never eclipsed substance' (Napolitano 2014: 78). That dual identity within the show becomes polyvalent when the score and the staging are taken into account. This quality expands the potential within *Oliver!* for the same material to resonate in different ways with different audiences, which has been a major factor in the show's wide appeal when new and in sustaining that success, as we will see.

Oliver! has become the flagship work of its time. Not so Bart's subsequent musicals. Few today know *Blitz!* (1962) and *Maggie May* (1964), which expand impressively one's appreciation of Bart's originality and skill. *Twang!!*, Bart's self-financed Robin Hood romp of a musical, is remembered for chaotic creation, a disastrous, brief run and for triggering Bart's bankruptcy. In 1968, the acclaim for the film of *Oliver!* renewed interest in Bart's work. His unstaged adaptation from 1967 of Federico Fellini's film *La Strada* was taken up in America for production. Bart was not present for rehearsals, during which the changes were so sweeping that almost none of Bart's show, songs included, survived to the New York opening. It was a Lionel Bart musical by name, not in how it was executed: the pun is deliberate – it lasted just one night, 14 December 1969.

Impressions of the past

Historical sensibilities within *Oliver!* are layered. Dickens set his novel in the 1830s, contemporary with its publication, as a social critique, not an objective chronicle. He dramatized his themes to elicit humane judgements from his readers on the values of their society. Beyond the page, Dickens brought his own writings to life as a performative storyteller, an 'audio-visual Dickens, in a series of performances of quite remarkable virtuosity as he crowded his red-draped, gas-lit Reading platform with his own noisy characters. It was like watching the man create his fictions – become his fictions – in a furnace of energy' (Andrews 2006: viii). The blurring of the boundaries between the author, the actor and the characters was especially powerful in Dickens's own reading of the death of Nancy from *Oliver Twist*, as recreated from contemporary reports:

> [Bill Sikes] swaggers backwards, puts his own hand up to his face in horror, gropes for his heavy club, and smashes it on the upturned face. Dickens, in evening dress, sweat pouring down, is battering the air and the desk with ferocious energy. Again and again and again. It is over. There is an appalled silence and stillness in the hall. Slowly faces being to steal out from behind the hands, eyes towards the platform, half-expecting to see a bloodbath. What they see is a man behind the red desk leaning on it, head bent and breathing heavily. (Andrews 2006: 223)

The acting out of that scene by Dickens has become a part of the identity of the novel. As now with so many of Dickens's novels, *Oliver!* arrives with a whole cultural backstory in place, which includes knowledge of the central elements of its plot and attitudes towards its characters to the extent that they overshadow or replace the original text.

Although the novel is updated to 'about 1850' for the musical, the show maps itself to general mid-twentieth-century assumptions of the Victorian world and the fiction of 'Dickensian' London. Richard Watts Jr reviewed the opening of *Oliver!* in New York and admired 'the resourceful maintenance of the Dickensian mood' not least through Sean Kenny's set whose 'pictorial excitement' captured 'the dramatic quality of the raffish slums of Victorian London' (quoted in Suskin 1990: 510). The show is not concerned with faithfulness to Dickens or history. Instead, it harnesses the widely embedded constituents of a latter-day mythology: 'The Artful Dodger was now the singer of "Consider Yourself" instead of the snub-nosed pickpocket who is ultimately transported for life. Fagin was now the roguish song-man who deserved a second chance as opposed to the devilish corruptor who warranted a trip to the gallows' (Napolitano 2014: 106). Bart's *Oliver!* is neither accurate history nor faithful Dickens, yet it stands for both. In fact, David Lean's now-classic British film adaptation (1948) exerted a more direct influence on the stage musical than did Dickens's novel. The film provided for Bart 'a point of reference for the story, along with an effective outline for the plot' (Napolitano 2014: 47). To a widely shared cultural artefact of Anglophone literature with a century of accreted interpretations, Bart adds another layer in a musical that has the sights and sounds of multiple historical periods fusing into a composite image of London's sociology and geography as well a familiar generic idea of the Dickensian world. This is central to its success.

Frank Norman described his play *A Kayf Up West* (1964) as 'a great rambling panoramic documentary of Soho's lower depths during the post war years', but the results was 'as big a flop as *Fings* had been a success' (Norman 1975: 81, 82). He pinned *Fings* success on its timing in benefiting from the rise of the anti-Establishment 'Angry Young Men' of the late 1950s. As they became in the 1960s Establishment middle-class, grumpy, older men their cutting edge was no longer sharp (Norman 1975: 90). *Oliver!* presages that swift change of tone by 're-imagining the dark (though sometimes comic) world of Dickens as a happy, melodious world which both children and adults could appreciate', and – in the opposite direction of travel to the Soho musicals – leading towards what has been seen in the filmed version as 'a sanitized portrayal of the brutal society depicted in Dickens's novel' (Napolitano 2009: 80). The West End hit musicals that landed in the immediate wake of *Oliver!* and that have retained some repertory presence ameliorate any social comment around work, money and class. They are upbeat, romanticized adaptations that incorporate big-scale song and dance and inhabit the centre ground of modern musical theatre styles. *Half a Sixpence* and *Pickwick* (both 1963) and *Charlie Girl* (1965) come to mind as the first-generation heirs of *Oliver!* The last of these is set in its present day of the mid-1960s, but retains a historical dimension in employing the contrasting values and imagery of lower class and upper class. This goes back most directly to *Me and My Girl*, but also to the shop girl-aristocrat Cinderella trope of Edwardian musical comedy (Macpherson 2018: 63–90) inverted and updated through the motorbike, jazz-singing modernism of a titled young woman who lives in a stately home, and a tongue-tied, money-averse (but football-pools-winning) lower-class suitor.

Half a Sixpence was adapted by Beverley Cross (book) and David Heneker (music and lyrics) from H. G. Wells's novel *Kipps: The Story of a Simple Soul* (1905). Like *Oliver*

Twist, the book was among the film adaptations of British literary classics from the 1940s, as *The Remarkable Mr. Kipps* (1941). The musical eschews the contemporary, gritty approach of the Soho musicals, and indulges its Edwardian setting and class-based story through a light, romanticized adaptation. The title role suits a showman, and Tommy Steele as Arthur Kipps contributed to the publicity around the show and to its performance success in the West End, on Broadway (1965) and on film (1967). Four months later, *Pickwick* (after Dickens's *The Posthumous Papers of the Pickwick Club*, 1836–7) consolidated the success of such English literary adaptations in bringing a third musical to the West End. The British celebrity Harry Secombe took the title role. The novel had also been the subject of a noted British film adaptation (1952), with a roll-call cast of British character actors headed by James Hayter in the title role. Several of the London cast of the musical, including Secombe, briefly toured in America before opening on Broadway (1965), although without achieving the same success as *Oliver!* and *Half a Sixpence*. However, it did mean that for most of 1965 there were two such new British 'heritage' musicals on the Broadway stage. The significance is not that all three shows played on Broadway, two with long runs, but that it was these particular shows that crossed the Atlantic rather than the Soho musicals or Bart's two post-*Oliver!* West End successes, *Blitz!* (1962) and *Maggie May* (1964).

Blitz! and *Maggie May*

Bart's shows from *Lock Up Your Daughters* through *Fings Ain't Wot They Used t'Be*, *Oliver!* and *Blitz!* to *Maggie May* take new approaches. He believed, 'It's a fatal thing when an artist does what's expected of him. To me, art is a search, and if you start repeating yourself you perhaps believe that you have found yourself, and then surely there's nothing more to say and little more to do.'[6] Yet Bart's serial success in the late 1950s–early 1960s is reduced to a single hit in the current repertory. Understanding the creative contrasts Bart pursued after *Oliver!* throws light on what has made it the one show to have continual major success.

Blitz! was personal in motivation, long in gestation and on a vast scale of production unique at the time in the West End. As the title indicates, it is a drama around the sustained bombing raids on London by the German air force from September 1940 to May 1941. The Blitz is part of the wartime identity of London and by extension the whole country – many other cities experienced such bombing – and the phrase 'spirit of the Blitz' still defines a British character trait of communal bonding and stoic endurance in the face of adversity. In 1962, that spirit was not an abstraction, but real to anyone in their mid-twenties and older who had lived through wartime life. Joan Maitland, Bart's personal assistant of several years and a co-creator of the show, described how its themes 'galvanised both of us, but sometimes the remembering was painful. We both have personal recollections of the horror of those days.' The formidable Jewish matriarch of the story, Mrs Blitzstein, embodied 'so much of the spirit and courage' of Bart's mother and became 'so real to him that during our writing sessions it was almost as if Mrs. Blitzstein "wrote" her own lines'.[7] The stage set was technically the most advanced for the West End at the time. Three-storey, motorized towers and a large flying gantry changed position to present naturalistically the streets of East London. Following *Lock Up Your Daughters* and *Oliver!*, the design was again by Sean Kenny:

> The blitz on London had fantastic visual possibilities, and we would try to get the same effects on the stage – buildings burning, toppling, falling across the streets, firemen ascending and descending ladders and a great chaos over everything . . . We showed in this musical show that the stage could produce technical and enormously exciting effects that were far better than anything that the cinema or television could do. It was there before the audience's eyes; something to revive memories and bring people back to the live theatre to see great, moving and realistic spectacle.[8]

The plot is involved. Mrs Blitzstein does not get on with Alfred Locke, who has the market stall in Petticoat Lane next to hers and they don't speak to each other. Mrs Blitzstein's daughter Carol and Locke's son George fall in love as they relay messages between their respective parents. Wartime disrupts everything: Carol is blinded during an air raid, Mrs Blitzstein's eldest son Harry deserts the army, George returns from the Front disillusioned, and Mrs Blitzstein is rescued from the bombed-out wreckage of a kosher restaurant just after hosting the wedding celebrations of Carol and George. Scenes are dominated by communal activity on the East London streets around Petticoat Lane, Bank Underground Station (used as a bomb shelter) and a school playground. Bart promoted the piece as symbolic, with 'three human stories inside an epic canvas; the major human conflict – the major plot – personifies the spirit of London and how that spirit developed during the period of the piece [September 1940]'.[9]

The songs are styled as contemporary/dramatic or from the recent past/pastiche. The distinction is Bart's: 'There is period pastiche to create the atmosphere of those days, but the dramatic statement is my own, and timeless. I may use something which has the feeling of "We'll Hang Out the Washing on the Siegfried Line" to convey atmosphere, but the lovers' duet relating to a dramatic mood is musically 1962 because that's as far advanced as I go.'[10] These period styles were familiar to the Adelphi audience: 'The Day After Tomorrow' is a convincing 1940s ballad; 'Who's This Geezer Hitler?' is a comic music-hall chorus; 'Leave It to the Ladies' is a 1940s big-band swing number. On the contemporary side, 'I Want to Whisper Something' and 'Who Wants to Settle Down?' include syncopations characteristic of the late 1950s in their melodies and would fit into a contemporary Tommy Steele film. The romantic solo ballad 'Far Away' could slip effortlessly into a 1960s cabaret set alongside 'As Long as He Needs Me' from *Oliver!*.

The soundscape is that of the Second World War, which in 1962 was still alive in the collective memory. The show starts with the undulating wail of an air raid siren, while its concluding company reprise of 'Who's This Geezer Hitler?' is announced with the sustained tone of an 'all clear' siren. The drumbeats of the 'V for Victory' morse code used on radio in Europe during the war as a signal for the Resistance movements recur throughout the score. Bart wrote the song 'The Day After Tomorrow' to suit the style of singer Vera Lynn, 'the Forces Sweetheart', whose songs 'The White Cliffs of Dover' (1942) and 'We'll Meet Again' (1943) remain potent 'national anthems' that evoke Britain in wartime. Lynn recorded Bart's song to be used as a broadcast within a scene in which the characters sing along to the radio. Winston Churchill gave permission for extracts from his own broadcasts to be used within radio broadcasts too. 'Underground shelters with lights wincing at distant detonations – anti-aircraft beams sweeping the savaged sky – sirens, smoke and splintering glass – all twang half-forgotten strings in the hearts of Londoners who lived through it, and presented a vivid picture of to the generations young enough to have escaped it.'[11] Aurally, visually and thematically, *Blitz!* was a national pageant.

Next, Bart created the concept, lyrics and music for *Maggie May*. He had known the folk song of the title since childhood and drew on its sketch of a sex worker on Liverpool's dockside for a musical 'loosely based on the characteristics of this time-honoured sailor's heroine'.[12] The book was by Alun Owen, a playwright native to Liverpool and familiar with its folklore and distinctive dialect (Bart was 'lost on the chat' when it came to the authentic speech of the city).[13] The setting was contemporary, the 1960s, and distinctive to the waterfront life of Liverpool: the dock gates, a dock warehouse, the Liverpool–New Brighton ferry and the Pierhead by the Liver Building. It concerns the two young lovers Patrick Casey, who goes to sea, and Maggie May, who is left yearning for Casey and gets by as a sex worker around the docks. When Casey returns to Liverpool, Maggie is waiting for him. However, the dockers see in his return a sign that he is to lead them, as his father had done, in union action against capitalist forces in control of the docks. Against Casey's leanings, he ends up leading strike action, during which he is killed. Maggie is left once more alone to make her living on the dockside.

The characters are lower-class workers associated with the docks who speak in the local dialect and with a Liverpudlian accent (aka Scouse), parodied in the song 'Dey Don't Do Dat T'dy'. The show includes influences from traditional culture, not least in the title song. 'Right of Way' is in essence a sea shanty, complete with call and response, while 'Stroll On' alternates between spiritual and jig. Other traditional influences can be heard in modal melody, as with the refrain of 'Love a Man' and the subtle flattened 7th-tonic inflection introduced into 'I Told You So', which is otherwise a standard show tune of the time. Jazz plays a significant part in the score's atmosphere too, as in the kinetic 'Casey' song and scene. Character cameos, as with the milkman's 'Shine, You Swine', prompt associations with *Porgy and Bess* and *Street Scene* in the fluidity of the vocal lines within an evocation of community. Contemporary culture is given a particular Liverpool 1960s voice in 'Carryin' On', a Merseybeat number in line with Bart's pop-song skill such that the term pastiche is inappropriate. It is performed diegetically in the 'Catacomb Club', a reference to Liverpool's landmark Cavern Club and its association with many local groups including The Beatles. The Flanagan-and-Alan, soft-shoe 1940s-style variety number 'Away from Home' and the lyrical ballad 'The Land of Promises' supply the tuneful approach of conventional musical theatre too. Owen characterized his home town as 'a sly wink from a fancy woman', and the show as 'an attempt to put a town on the stage, to see it working and playing, loving and going on strike but always living'.[14] Taking all these dramatic and musical elements together, the show is as defined by Liverpool, its docks and working community and the mid-1960s as *Blitz!* is by the East End of London in 1939–40.

Bart's shows after *Oliver!* adopt the 'slice of life' approach of the Soho musicals. The audiences were expected to identify the resonances of wartime London in *Blitz!* and 1960s union activity in *Maggie May* along with music that related to precise times and places. How readily and viscerally an audience relates to this material has changed through the generations with the progressive loss of exact associations and first-hand knowledge. In contrast, *Oliver!* began as a created, escapist world, nominally set outside living memory at a century's distance from its audiences. It was not a historicized commentary but instead used clichés – albeit engagingly employed – of 'Dickensian' London. Since then, the myth of that Dickensian world (especially in adaptations to film and television) has grown evermore familiar internationally.

Music hall and musical

The score of *Oliver!* encodes similarly layered recognition as does its pseudo-Victorian setting. Robert Gordon notes how Bart's shows 'combine a genuine feeling for the forms and styles of working-class entertainment with a flair for histrionic effect' (Gordon, Jubin and Taylor 2016: 45). In *Oliver!* Nancy's songs provides examples of both qualities. The singalong waltz 'Oom-Pah-Pah' that opens Act II shows its music-hall origins in the solo verses, each a little story with a punch line, that prompt a communal 'all together now' response. The type of waltz matters: it is not the gravity-defying whirl of the Viennese waltz but a weighty, on-the-beat, version with roots in the Ländler and the German beer garden. American song composer Harry Von Tilzer annexed this down-to-earth form for 'Under the Anheuser Bush' (1903). It was written as a promotional song for the Anheuser-Busch brewing company, and its lyrics by Andrew B. Stirling refer to hearing 'the old German band' and drinking 'a stein or two'. The song was popularized in Britain with the lyrics adapted to name a pub in London's Hampstead, becoming 'Down at the Old Bull and Bush'. The reference to a German band – and thus too the implied reference point for the music – was kept (with 'old' replaced by 'little'), but 'a stein or two' became a 'dance or two'.

The Anglicized version became a signature number of music-hall singer Florrie Ford, who recorded it in 1903. At the time of *Oliver!*, it was known as staple of the music-hall repertory and gained renewed attention as the regular closing number for the cast and audience on British television's music-hall recreation *The Good Old Days* (1953–83, see Chapter 6 in relation to the Players' Theatre). The style relates too to those waltzes for less socially polished characters in Edwardian musical comedy, as with 'The Girl with the Brogue' in *The Arcadians* (1909). This Irish folk-tinged song is a musical relative of the American 'Bowery' waltz, after the song 'The Bowery' in the New York musical comedy *A Trip to Chinatown* (1891) (Banfield 2016: 128). Directly before *Oliver!*, the gangsters who can help you 'Brush Up Your Shakespeare' in *Kiss Me, Kate* (New York 1948, London 1951) gave the Bowery waltz (marked as such in the score) its most widely recognized version in a post-war musical.

Bart's opening lyrics establish the street and the ordinary people – 'There's a little ditty they're singing in the city' – and the public house environment – 'Espeshly when they've been on the gin or the beer'. The text is reflexive as a song performed in The

Three Cripples public house to open Act II. The crowd sing the chorus, then Nancy is introduced to formalize the rendition as a diegetic performance. Reinforcing this, a Chairman uses a gavel to attract attention then introduces Nancy in florid terms: 'Ladies and gentlemen, brethren, sinners all, I call upon our goddess of the virtues to give us her well[-]known rendition of the old School Song – OOM-PAH-PAH!' (Bart 1960: 81). This introduction copies the style of the Chairman of the Victorian supper rooms, revived by the Players' Theatre. Nancy's performance becomes a formal part of the entertainment, not improvisatory (as it becomes in the film adaptation). The song and its placing encourage the audience to view it as of 1850s London, even though musically it fits better half a century later, where it is independently identifiable from American, British and German perspectives. The result is that a generic effect can be interpreted specifically by audiences in different locations according to their points of reference: American as a Bowery waltz, British as a music-hall classic (with its American origins unfamiliar or irrelevant to the British home audience), with European roots too even signalled in the term 'Oom-pah', which derives from the onomatopoeic description of a 'little German band'.

'Histrionic' Bart comes with 'As Long as He Needs Me'. Nancy's cathartic solo is presented within her self-contained world, a soliloquy heard by the theatre audience. It has the sentimentality of the Victorian parlour ballad. The context overlays the 1850s with a torch song of the 1960s – 'dramatic statement' is musically 'timeless', as Bart described in relation to *Blitz!*. The arrangement defines the period further in its light use of contemporary jazz inflections in the chromaticism of the inner harmonic lines. Even the introduction as directed in the score presents an abrupt change of musical register from past to present: 'The hurdy-gurdy can still be heard outside and is interrupted by the first chord of the song.' The sound of the Victorian street is negated by that single chord of introduction, a spread chord of F major (F–A–C) enriched with added 6th (D) and 9th (G) characteristic of soft jazz (Bart 1960: 94).

For Georgia Brown in the original cast this was her big number, finishing on the thrill of her voice at the top of its belt range. It is about Nancy's predicament, and it becomes histrionic – about the theatricality of portraying emotion – made visceral in sound and dramatic symbolism. Until this scene, Nancy's codependent relationship with her violent partner Bill Sikes has only been implied through oblique references: 'the occasional black eye' ('It's a Fine Life') and 'not for me the happy home' and 'Even fight my Bill?' ('I'd Do Anything'). Now, brief defiance of Bill by Nancy results in him striking her, and the song immediately follows. The dramatic power comes from the abruptness of the violence and Nancy's counter-intuitive response. We can see here how the use of such well-known characters in a famous story – reinforced by the embedded cultural memory of Dickens's own readings – contributes to the song's ability to generate an emotional extreme for the audience with the minimum of onstage detail.

Outside the show, 'As Long As He Needs Me' is a free-standing torch song. Shirley Bassey recorded it for promotional release a couple of weeks before the musical opened in London. The record's success was such that it became a signature song of Bassey's repertory. For her first appearance in a Royal Variety Performance (6 November 1961), it provided the powerful climax of her three numbers – dressed as unlike Nancy as possible, 'glamorous in skin-hugging white gown'.[15] Many popular singers have covered it since, and it is a repertory standard. Cumulatively, there is the expression of the character's inner voice in the show, the performance of the song by the actor/singer in the part, and the song as hit number sung live in cabaret. Each way of appreciating it widens its ability to work simultaneously with different constituencies within the theatre audience, and a history of associations increases with further decades of performances.

Coexisting connotations in the score of *Oliver!* extend beyond solo numbers. Bart's description of composing 'Consider Yourself' connects it to a Sousa march and Meredith Willson's 'Seventy-Six Trombones' from *The Music Man* (Broadway, 1957, West End 1961, film 1962) (Stafford and Stafford 2011: 99). Willson played in Sousa's band early in his career and had absorbed the characteristic march style first-hand. The melodic outline of Bart's song shares several similarities of motif, pitch profile and harmonic pacing with Sousa's march *Liberty Bell* – but the commonality illustrates Sousa's compositional style rather than a specific reference by Bart. The scene's power derives from the nature of the lyrics, the city location and its communal spirit of ordinary workers, which forms a package of visual, verbal and kinetic London tropes.

British musical theatre marches have tended to adopt a firm duple time from the predominant military march style as, for example, with the vigorous 2/4 march 'All Down Piccadilly' (*The Arcadians*, 1909) and the stately, ceremonial 'Rose of England' (*Crest of the Wave*, 1938). A lively, compound 6/8 tends to carry in British repertory associations with country dance forms and the jig, an off-the-ground thrust rather than a grounded one. However, one exception would have been familiar to many of those in the 1960s, but not today. A classic moment in early British film shows Gracie Fields leading a march of mill workers back to their reopening factory. The song 'Sing as We Go', also the title of the film, is by Harry Parr Davies, who later became Fields's regular accompanist. It is a march in 6/8, with a celebratory communal infectiousness that matches that of 'Consider Yourself' as it evolves into a community number. The way in which anyone hears 'Consider Yourself' – American Sousa march and/or British working-class outpouring – will be influenced by the references brought into the theatre by each audience member. The score of *Oliver!* continues the melodic style of Bart of the 1950s. The songs employ ubiquitous verse-chorus structuring in even multiples of 4-bar units. Melodies consist of main hooks and releases, all using standard time signatures (two, three and four beats in toe-tapping regularity). Versification matches technically precise rhythm, stress and rhyme. Bart's musical characterization and dramaturgy build on the recognition of such familiar musical structures which are then individualized through the inflections in the detail and the contexts in which they are deployed.

The theatrical ethos of Theatre Workshop described earlier required the reality of contemporary East London. Street vocabulary, contractions and distinctive phrase structure are hardwired into *Fings Ain't Wot They Used t'Be*. Phonetic indications smother the text, for example, 'I do me fair stint / I'm coinin' a fair mint', 'So even if yo're skint / I'm laying abaht' and 'The ceiling's comin' dahn / Ter fink I could have been / An housewife / A bungalow wivout no stairs' (Norman and Bart 1960: 18, 23). Frank Norman's initial inspiration came from his writing an article on London slang for *Encounter* magazine in 1958 (Norman 1975: 36), and the linguistic tone chimed with

Bart's own East London background. *Oliver!* was created with a view towards the West End, as a commercial musical with the evocation of loose literary-historical character, not as the fortuitous transfer from a theatre company with a social agenda and with a political message predicated on contemporary, gritty urban reality. Consequently, Bart streamlines language for place, atmosphere and social level, so that the text of *Oliver!* has a veneer of cockney and class-defining colour, which also echoes its literary source. The manner of performance – accent and dramatic setting – conveys the demotic quality more than a precisely scripted text.

The portrayal of Bill Sikes is one of the more exaggerated in its scripting to establish him quickly as the hard man the audience can love to hate: 'Wiv me / Jemmy in me hand / Lemme see the man who dares / Stop Me / Taking what I may / He can start to say his prayers!' (Bart 1977: 2-1-4) The script drops its logging of speech characteristics where the performer will almost certainly present 'e can start to say 'is prayers!' *Oliver!* has enough linguistic colour to convey the social level, but not so much as to be anthropologically driven. *Fings, Blitz!* and *Maggie May* revolve around the well-defined communities of a Soho 'spieler', London's streetmarket East End and the Liverpool docks. *Oliver!* includes a wider range of society's levels and locations because a contrast of high and low class is a central to the plot – from Mr Brownlow at the top, through the aspiring middle of Mr Bumble and Widow Corney, to the street urchins at the bottom. Its various 'voices' are there to colour the differences between those layers, not to unite them within a single, self-supporting community. Oliver's journey is to leave the environment of his upbringing, not to assert it.

Bart was sensitive to stylistic range in his music and described this in relation to *Blitz!*:

> I've gone back to English folk groups and based things on English street cries and English nursery rhymes. And I'm a Jew, so there are Jewish things in it, too. I use jazz where it comes in. Jazz is unavoidable, it means today, 1962; it means civilization or decadence, whichever is the right word. I'm not a musical scholar but I have a good ear and I've gone into musical origins. Jazz, real African jazz, isn't far from Jewish music, which is quite close to Gregorian, and leads on to Celtic music and then to English folk songs and Cockney street chants.[16]

We can see Bart's interest in selecting particular musical styles within a whole score. These musical articulations occur in *Oliver!*. With their street cries, 'Boy for Sale' and 'Who Will Buy?' are precursors to 'Petticoat Lane' in *Blitz!*. The Jewish elements that define Fagin's songs 'Pick a Pocket or Two' and 'Reviewing the Situation' carry through to Mrs Blitzstein's 'Bake a Cake'. The nursery rhyme qualities – short refrain, limited harmonic change, diatonic simplicity and motivic repetition – of 'Be Back Soon', which uses in counterpoint the refrains of Fagin and his urchins, become the threefold melodic layering of 'Mums and Dads' in *Blitz!*. There are similar features in *Maggie May* too, adapted to suit the adults-only, Liverpudlian setting. For example, the street cry element is glimpsed in the milkman of 'Shine you Swine' as well as the repeated sex worker-to-client calls on the street of 'Casey'. The street cries morph into the community-based, call-and-response elements of the sea shanties.

There is a crucial difference between the song score for *Oliver!* and the song scores of *Blitz!* and *Maggie May*. The music for the two latter shows had to relate in some way directly to the audiences in conveying 1940–1 and the mid-1960s, respectively. The audiences would know first-hand whether the sound was sufficiently accurate to be convincing within the theatrical context. The Dickensian world of *Oliver!* is not concerned with accuracy, and the sound world needs only to be convincing within musical theatre convention. Anything that can be misconstrued as accurately evoking mid-nineteenth-century London is an atmospheric bonus.

Genre fusions

In impact, Cameron Mackintosh, the producer of the major London Palladium revival in 1994, considers *Oliver!* a musical theatre version of *Look Back in Anger*. He recalls that the preceding British hit musicals 'in the 1950s were *Salad Days*, *The Boy Friend*, *Irma La Douce*, and suddenly, this piece came, which then was considered very dark and different'. For Mackintosh, 'From the moment [*Oliver!*] came on, the musical theatre was literally never the same in this country' (Napolitano 2014: 21). Unlike almost all the previous shows discussed in this book, in its flow and music *Oliver!* fits the expectations for a mainstream, 'modern' post-war twentieth-century model. Hybridity has helped. Forces coalesced to hit multiple targets to great effect: the familiar story, literary tropes and connections were readily recognizable in the 1960s and remain so today. The music too allows multiple points of cultural compatibility across generations, not least in catchy verse-chorus songs. The production in 1960 added to the cross-genre identity in the way it was structured and staged to draw on theatre and especially film in the flow of the show and the pace of its delivery.

Two years before *Oliver!*, *Expresso Bongo* was darker in theme than its predecessors and was directed with an evocative rather than fully literal staging, with the mechanics of theatrical presentation and performance crucial to its identity. The previous chapter quoted its description in 1958 as 'the first of the Angry Young Musicals'[17] and as 'the first of the really black English musicals . . . what might be termed the S.S.S.S. Group, the Stratford-Soho-Sloane Square School of musicals' (Mankowitz and More 1960: 5). It opened the door too for the overtly allegorical, social and political themes that emerged through the 1960s, for example, with *The Roar of the Greasepaint – the Smell of the Crowd* (a success on Broadway after its failure in Britain) and through to *Hair*. *Oliver!* is not the sole instigator of such developments but is the best remembered of the West End shows of the period and has come to stand for them.

The directness of style and experimentation with form encouraged through Theatre Workshop contributed in *Oliver!* to Bart's focus on the essentials of plot, character and dialogue. In parallel, the paring down of a big story into a musical, with the example of film, influenced the rapid changes of scene and focus on stage. Sean Kenny's innovative set design made this approach work in practice. Kenny already had experience of using a wooden skeleton set from *Lock Up Your Daughters*, and extended the openness and fluidity of this for *Oliver!*. A revolve allowed a two-storey structure to be moved at speed to create different figurations with the adjacent static tower. Specific places were suggested with the minimal addition of quickly added and removed props and furniture. The character of Victorian London came through in the rough wooden form, such details as small-paned windows, a backdrop that showed the cluttered London skyline and the nineteenth-century costume designs.

With transitions between locations possible at speed, aspects of film technique were adaptable. Attention could be focussed by the configuration of the mobile aspects of the set, including when in motion, and by lighting and stage positioning within different areas to signal transitions of space and mood. The huge, detailed, literal but static sets of *My Fair Lady* playing the other side of Covent Garden at the Theatre Royal, Drury Lane, illustrate by comparison the impressionistic design of *Oliver!*. With the ability in *Oliver!* to move people around locations so swiftly on a visibly altering set, other aspects of the show could be pared down. The dialogue is minimal, and the action flows with the barest exposition and explanation, sometimes none. Nearly the whole of Act I scene 2 is devoted to the comic diversion of Mr Bumble wooing Widow Corney in the duet 'I Shall Scream'. The central plot development of Oliver's removal from the workhouse is signalled with one line from Mr Bumble at the start of the scene ('We must get rid of this canker in our midst') and one line at the end from Widow Corney ('Get a good price for him, Mr Bumble'). That's it.

'Boy for Sale' follows immediately, with the song alone acting as the transition from workhouse to street to undertakers. Oliver sings 'Where Is Love?' with no framing monologue – he is left alone . . . and he starts singing. He flees the undertaker's parlour and immediately arrives at Paddington Green to be found by the Artful Dodger. There is barely a minute of dialogue between 'It's a Fine Life' and 'I'd Do Anything', after which just eight lines from Fagin cue 'Be Back Soon'. There is no dialogue between 'Oom-Pah-Pah' and 'My Name'. 'As Long as He Needs Me', sung by Nancy in the Three Cripples pub, runs musically into 'Who Will Buy?', with only the barest of mime over the introduction to establish Oliver being cared for in Mr Brownlow's house in Bloomsbury.

Changes of location and contractions of time go with the storytelling of musical theatre, but the degree to which they are used in *Oliver!* – with transitions in full view of the audience as part of the spectacle – is distinctive for when it was first staged. Today, such kinetic stage design is standard to musical theatre expectations. In 1960 it was not, which invites an association with film in the manner of these brief transitions or direct cuts that take jumps in narrative and place for granted. Bart learnt from David Lean's film adaptation. There is too something of the music-hall or cabaret approach in the way that many scenes are presented entirely through song: the immediate progression to a contrasting number heightens the audience's performative awareness. The clearest example is Nancy's comic singalong 'Oom-Pah-Pah', explicitly introduced by a Chairman as within the formalities of tavern performance, which changes in a moment to Sikes's character number 'My Name' as if the next act on the bill.

Some songs in the stage show emulate the self-contained numbers of a music-hall bill, characterful but incidental. The two comic turns of 'I Shall Scream' and 'That's Your Funeral' follow a similar structure in the use of a recurring line that interjects into the build-up towards a witticism that ends each verse. Both songs were cut for the film. The first is the substance of the diversionary scene between Widow Corney and Mr Bumble.

On stage, this seems a vestige of comic romance associated with a secondary couple in a musical comedy in a show without any of the conventional romantic relationships. Losing it hardens an audience's perception of the couple. There is more room for the interpolation of a short comic scene in a live theatre performance, where the whole event is framed as knowing performance, and 'That's Your Funeral' states its performance artifice in Mr Bumble's line 'I don't think this song is funny'. 'My Name' was also cut for the film, with Sikes's violent temper easily conveyed on screen with costume and physicality and close-ups of Oliver Reed's face. In the case of 'Oom-Pah-Pah', the quality of the music-hall turn in the stage show is redirected into a clear dramatic purpose in the film. The tavern singalong is not for atmosphere, but to generate the distraction of a boisterous crowd so that Nancy can rescue Oliver from Sikes.

The show sets the music as a dominating feature from the start. While an opening chorus is as conventional a genre feature as you can get, 'Food, Glorious Food' runs straight into a whole musicalized scene that alternates registers and purposes. There are different types of vocalization, from straight speech (minimally present) to full song (dominant): speech ('Please sir, I want some more'); intoning (the very opening line from the boys 'Is it worth the waiting for?'); formal chant (Mr Bumble's 'For what we are about to receive'); recitative ('Before we put the lad to task'); arioso (between speech and full melody, 'Catch him!'); and lastly melody ('Food, Glorious Food' and 'Oliver!'). Musical passages maintain a flow from section to section, establish atmosphere and reflect the physicality of the stage action. Music, and especially tuneful music too, is at the core of this particular Dickensian world-turned-theatre.

The end of the show is fast and furious. It stages: Sikes's murder of Nancy; Brownlow seeing Sikes drag Oliver away; Brownlow discovering Nancy's corpse; Sikes and Oliver arriving at Fagin's den, simultaneous with a crowd gathering around Nancy's body on London Bridge; Fagin in the doorway of his den as the crowd on the Bridge hear what Mr Brownlow saw; the crowd identifying Sikes as the culprit; the crowd following Sikes's dog to the den; Sikes dragging Oliver onto a roof; a policeman shooting Sikes, who falls to certain death; Oliver being rescued; the crowd breaking into the den; the Bow Street runners arresting the Artful Dodger and finding Fagin's money but not Fagin; racing after him wrongly to the Three Cripples; Oliver reuniting with Brownlow; everyone leaving; Fagin appearing from where he has been hiding, under London Bridge; Fagin finishing the show with just a few lines of the verse of 'Reviewing the Situation', which hint that he could change his ways: 'I'll turn a leaf over and who can tell what I may find?' (Bart 1960: 126–34).

Throughout the sequence, music – not speech – underpins the action and the atmosphere. There are familiar effects from melodrama to heighten suspense, such as tremolos, trills and steady drumbeats juxtaposed with abrupt alternations of silence and sound. Thematic motifs are drawn from throughout the show. The menacing introductory section combines the first phrase of 'My Name' for Sikes and the opening notes of 'As Long as He Needs Me' for Nancy. Nancy's theme is played in an extended and chromatically harmonized version quietly as Sikes slowly realizes he has killed her and draws back from the body. Pairs of punching quavers sound as the crowd gather round Nancy's body. This motif was heard in Act I first as Widow Corney and Mr Bumble's 'Catch him! Snatch him!', which was also used to kick off the crowd's chase after Oliver from the bookshop. In Act II it appends the 'chase' association to Sikes, who now has Oliver with him. When the dramatic focus turns to Fagin's kitchen, the phrase from 'My Name' is replaced with the opening phrase of 'Be Back Soon'. 'Where Is Love' accompanies Oliver's return to Mr Brownlow after which a solo violin cadenza provides the aural cue for the focus to turn back to Fagin as he ends the whole drama with a striking image: '*Alone and friendless, Fagin walks over the bridge off into the dawn.*' 'Fagin exits stage right' would be the more expected type of instruction in the script to end the show with an empty set. Instead, the direction maintains the novelistic descriptive attitude of the final section.

This complex conclusion, predominantly achieved through melodrama – action to music, not dialogue – requires a set with levels, corners and spaces to imply a range of places while being simultaneously visible for the audience within the single frame of the performing area. Alongside this, the description of action, shifting focuses and underscoring absorb the techniques of film and the film script. Stage and screen methods become complementary. This allows audience members to connect with the show beyond the context of theatre performance alone. The process is far from unique to *Oliver!*. Later shows – *Cabaret, Sweeney Todd, The Phantom of the Opera* and *Rent*, for example – come to mind for the same reason. It is a welcoming and inclusive approach, not one bound by a single-minded prescriptive observance of the conventions of musical theatre. What is distinctive is how effective *Oliver!* was in enabling it for the time at which it was first staged.

Oliver! expanded

The scale of *Oliver!*'s success troubled Bart, as a draft letter from 1966 shows: 'I am very much involved in trying to forget that I was ever responsible for [*Oliver!*]. . . . I avoid walking or driving down Saint Martin's Lane in London where the posters outside the New Theatre say "OLIVER! LONGEST RUNNING MUSICAL IN HISTORY". Who wants to feel eighty-four when you're only thirty-six?' (Napolitano 2014: 210). He continued that he felt such success pinned him in his past, with no room to experiment and fail. He was 'pigeon-holed as a successful pro.[*sic*]' when he thought himself 'still an amateur'. To understand fully Bart's talent, the issue is not one of diminishing *Oliver!* – its 'classic' status is deserved – but of appreciating it within broader contexts.

The 'singularity' of the show in the narrative of the British musical has become familiar through repetition. In 1963, the majority of Broadway reviews for *Oliver!* praised the show. One summary claimed it as 'a breakthrough for the British in a field which has so long been dominated by Americans' (John McClain, quoted in Suskin 1990: 510). This assessment is problematic within West End history, the locus within which the show arose. Behind it is an acknowledgement that the show is sufficiently identifiable with an American set of values to count as effective musical theatre: it fits on Broadway. A surface comparison with the leading Broadway standard provides one point of reference – *Hello, Dolly!* opened in New York in December 1964, which overlaps the Broadway run of *Oliver!*. The music and lyrics by Jerry Herman provoke points of recognition in the mixture of ballads, marches (4/4 and 6/8), character numbers and choruses delivered with an accomplished tunefulness and lyric elegance. For the time of its arrival in New York, *Oliver!* dovetails with the sound of such mainstream Broadway shows. From later perspectives, it also fits a model of a 'musical' in which the adjective 'American' is assumed.

It is easy to take for granted the ethnic background of Dolly Levi, marriage broker and widow of Ephraim. The strong Jewish influence that runs through New York musical theatre is a given, but not so for British shows. It becomes unavoidable with Fagin. His speech and character are written to convey his ethnicity, which in turn is composed into his music, most famously in the klezmer-influenced 'Reviewing the Situation' (Taylor 2016: 489). Bart was an East End Jew who understood the context and the difficulties of adverse stereotyping, but the nature of the character requires some consideration in performance of the balance between his unique individuality and his acquired ethnic heritage. Ron Moody created the role in 1960. Before rehearsals he 'became very depressed, feeling no man could do what Fagin did and not seem to be a monster'. Bart and director Peter Coe put to him a 'modern interpretation' as 'a mischievous crook who one need not necessarily hate'. Reassured, Moody went ahead with his research:

> Would Fagin speak with a Yiddish or a Cockney accent? That question had to be faced and answered at the outset. Mr Moody decided that he would be Cockney because the large-scale invasion of Middle European Jews did not occur until about 1890, which was after Fagin's time. Fagin would therefore be Hebrew rather than Yiddish and speak with something of a Cockney accent.[18]

Dickens's Fagin could antagonize audiences, if left unmediated through performance in America too. Norman Nadel's review of the Broadway opening describes the 'transformation' through the writing and Clive Revill's performance from a 'cruel conniving character who has so often been used to stir up anti-Semitism' into 'the kind of lovable old codger you'd invite to a Hadassah tea'.[19] The Jewish diaspora provides another example of how a central element of *Oliver!* can resonate beyond its London home and beyond musical theatre. While there can be no automatic assumption of a universal and equal familiarity with Dickens or the Jewish influence, such points of cultural contact contribute at least to the potential for widening an audience base beyond the home audience for whom the show was conceived.

Producer Cameron Mackintosh revived *Oliver!* on a grand scale in 1994 at the London Palladium, with Sam Mendes (director), Anthony Ward (designer) and Matthew Bourne (choreographer). The longevity of the production – four years in that theatre – boosted the musical's profile with new generations of family audiences. The Palladium, one of the largest West End theatres, has a seating capacity almost three times that of the New Theatre, and a revival of the production in 2009 ran for two years at the similarly large Theatre Royal, Drury Lane. The new production expanded to fill the larger spaces and to bring the show more in line with expectations of what musical theatre had become in the intervening three decades since the show's premiere. This was not a case of reinventing the nature of the show to suit a new time, as the revival of *Me and My Girl* had been in the 1980s: excepting a few localized changes (such as an added chorus of Workhouse Governors in the title song) the general form, dialogue and song list of *Oliver!* remained intact.

What had changed since 1960 were methods of presentation. Shows of the 1980s had increasingly defined musical theatre through elaborate production and climactic spectacle. With the long-running examples of such shows as *Cats*, *The Phantom of the Opera* and *Les Misérables*, the big new musicals had become 'events' whose impact and profile spread well beyond the nightly performances. Moreover, any show at the London Palladium or the Theatre Royal, Drury Lane, continued a history of indulgent stagecraft. Sean Kenny's original set design for *Oliver!* used a revolving framework to evoke spatial change and differentiation. Using the technology of a large, modern stage, Kenny's evocation was expanded by Anthony Ward into a travelling design that was geographically specific and detailed. For example, when Oliver meets the Artful Dodger, their 'Consider Yourself' journey through London is conveyed with a travelling backdrop of naturalistic elements of the London streets. Where the dome of St Paul's cathedral was just visible in the skyline at the top of the rear of the 1960 set, in 1994 a lifelike view up Ludgate Hill had as its focal point the cathedral shown from ground level to the top of the dome. That concerted number concluded by signalling the London location and its mid-nineteenth-century period with the detail of architectural imagery. Similarly, 'Who Will Buy?' was backed by a near photographic image of a crescent in Bloomsbury, just as it had appeared in the film. Which was the purpose.

The set, costume design (shape, accessories and colour) and even gesture in the 1994 stage show echoed the 1968 film. Increasingly through the 1990s and especially into the new century, the stage musical has taken its cue in content and presentation from film musicals. Many of the audience experience the theatrical performance as a comparative re-enactment running alongside the familiar film version in their minds, especially where this overlaps with the growth of a distinct category of family musicals swelled by film-to-stage adaptations. Disney led the way with adaptations from such animated films as *Beauty and the Beast* or, as with *Mary Poppins*, from mainly live action. The family audience brings a dominant familiarity with the film experience to the stage experience. Capturing that audience base has been commercially crucial in mounting costly stage productions. The interplay between a stage original and its film adaptation also has a longer track record: witness how stage productions of *The Sound of Music* routinely interpolate the film songs 'I Have Confidence' and 'Something Good', and productions of *Cabaret* replace 'Sitting Pretty' with 'Money Makes the World Go Around'. Film has increasingly influenced the staging of musicals, which has impacted *Oliver!* in a way that needs at the very least active consideration by any commercial producer now. Of all the case studies in this book, only *Oliver!* – the most recent – raises the need to take any filmed version into account in considering the relationship of the audience to a new stage production.

The aural experience of *Oliver!* in 1994 was different from that of 1960. The original orchestrations by Eric Rogers kept within the sounds of a small pit orchestra appropriate to music hall and to a more intimate theatre in which amplification was not dominant. The tonal palette was expanded for the new production by new orchestrations from William David Brohn, which feature faster and more extreme shifts of instrumental texture both between and within numbers. Formal dance sequences were added to the set chorus numbers of 'Consider Yourself' and 'Who Will Buy?' that previously combined singing and movement, but which did not have those spaces for dance sequences alone in which the dancers present themselves face front to the audience, acknowledging the transience of the fourth wall in a large-scale stage musical. New dance breaks interpolated between sung sections not only fulfilled the conventional expectation of some dance element in a musical but also emulated the massed choreography of the set-piece moments of the 1968 film.

A new Prologue staged during the brief instrumental introduction showed the birth of Oliver at the workhouse during a storm, which provides a little context for the premise of the story that had been taken for granted in the 1960 script. The music is essentially the same as 1960 but grown in Gothic stature through the orchestration and the addition of a music-box fragment of 'Where Is Love?'. This new version could easily work as an alternative musical opening to *The Phantom of the Opera*, with the descending arpeggios of the 'Food, Glorious Food' refrain paralleling the descending chord motif of Christine's regression to the world of the Phantom, and the music-box echoing the auction's 'Masquerade' quotation. The heavy thuds of accompaniment as the boys enter could also work for the chain-gang prisoners at the start of *Les Misérables*. These adaptations made the opening typical of the mid-1990s.

The physical scale and the shadow of film was addressed through the complex amplification of multiple individual voices, instruments and sound effects. This replicates cinema in that the sound of the live performance is heard by most of the audience from speakers, not acoustically from the stage or pit. Amplification levels are set well beyond anything possible by unmediated acoustic means, which had been the natural state for the first runs of the central musicals of previous chapters up to *Expresso Bongo*. In that show, conspicuous amplification was easily subsumed into the onstage world through virtue of its locus in pop music with its usual mechanics to deliver sound in live performance. While front float microphones had been in use in the West End for some musicals since the 1940s, they could only supplement some vocal projection. The balance with instrumental accompaniment still had to be achieved by means other than a sound desk alone.

A review for *Variety* in 1994 of the Palladium production captures the tension between a moderately scaled work of 1960 and the expanded nature of the 1994 production. In 1960 the work was innovative, but more than three decades later its continued success could be considered in the review 'amazing . . . given its skimpy book, lack of characterization and its peculiar mixture of the sentimental and (in the Bill Sikes-Nancy story) the lurid'. More damningly, 'There's very little in *Oliver!* to engage an adult mind.'[20] This assessment does not accord with the overwhelming one of the show in the 1960s in the West End and on Broadway. What stands out here is how the ground rules for assessing what a musical is about and how it should relate to its audience have changed in the thirty-four years the review specifies.

The single assessment of a work for a specific time, place and audience is different from an evolving assessment that reflects a plurality of times and places and audiences. Each of those adverse features listed in the *Variety* review have appeared in some form in the discussion earlier, although the context within which to read them has varied. The minimal nature of the book in *Oliver!* makes a fast-paced production possible, with the narrative and interpretational gaps filled from prior knowledge of Dickens directly from the novel, or from film and television adaptations including the 1968 film musical. The 'peculiar mixture' stems from the eclecticism of its theatrical and musical sources, which arises from Bart's spheres of activity in the 1950s. The outline characterizations allow room for individual star performances. The juxtaposition of the sentimental and the lurid encompasses Nancy's big ballad, Oliver's happy-ever-after family reunion as well as two villains, one we can love to hate and one who proves more sympathetic than he has any right to. This inclusive tonal palette creates a drama of contrast, as the abrupt shifts from one performance register to another compound in a celebratory carnival of modes of music theatre performance. This is all of a part with the experimentation within West End theatre from the mid-1950s on. To look for what counts today as integration and consistent dramaturgy within *Oliver!* is to look for something that was not written into the piece. A simple comparison with the praise heaped on the show in the 1960s demonstrates that. It illustrates too that the show's almost skeleton-like structure – like Kenny's original set – is solid enough to be functional, yet impressionistic enough to become the backdrop to the fuller animation generated by performance.

The success of the 1994 production (with tour and revival) acknowledges the continuing power *Oliver!* has to engage and entertain a broad audience. The way the production was adapted acknowledges a changing relationship with the audience too. The sources that fed into the original *Oliver!*, of 1960, have become less immediate, unclear or non-existent to an audience today. Here is the power of time to reframe what is significant to common cultural memory. A work may stay essentially the same in its book, lyrics and music, but the understanding of it adapts in response to the fluidity of cultural memory in time and place. However well we think we know any musical, each time we revisit it we have to think it out again.

9

'I know what I am'

The bigger picture

Each of the case-study musicals in this book is a West End success. Each is significant within the body of work of the people who created it, and each has appealed to audiences whether as meaningful, diversionary or both. They represent snapshots of shared success and striking differences, yet one does not ineluctably lead to the next. The limitations of a train-track chronological progression through musical theatre history become self-evident as soon as we compare the shows in terms of genre, contemporary reference, repertory reference, musical reference, performer style, performance tradition, interaction with other dramatic and narrative art forms, processes of creation, the level of active challenge to convention and inherent qualities that help or hinder a sustained repertory existence.

The shows here commended themselves because of their initial hit status. The respective lines of enquiry arose from their individuality. An appreciation of the purposes and effects of any show is enhanced by the fullest awareness possible of the environment out of which it was created, so any assessment made solely from the perspective of a later time or removed entirely from the surroundings of history will be different. One assessment may also be differently balanced from another too according to the extent the direction of enquiry has been set by historical discovery and to what extent it takes its lead from the active performance repertory at a given moment. Yet whatever the purpose, any assessment should complement the one made in the light of the time and place for which the show was devised, not become a replacement for it that consequently writes off any original significance. That a show does not have wide, or even any, immediate appeal now does not negate it having been a valid, understandable success then.

The 3D view

The context of the time of creation directly affects the content – obvious maybe, but easily taken for granted. For example, the reputation of the serial musical successes of Ivor Novello is heavily slanted towards nostalgia. It is a second-hand impression. The shows themselves are rich in a marriage of contemporary references and fantasy. Many of the perceived nostalgic elements – such as the romantic ballads and waltzes – were common currency across the musical stage of the time, not traits of Novello alone: the exceptionality lay in their quality rather than their presence. These shows have not been in the active repertory for some considerable time, so the actual detail has become hidden, its corrective significance has gone unrecognized and the cliché-driven reduction of Novello's shows to 'waltz songs and Ruritania' persists. Compounding the distortion, the casual summary of one theatre history reference work is too easily replicated as the accepted fact across subsequent ones.

At least Novello still figures somewhere. The Ellis-Herbert-Cochran shows seldom figure at all in today's bigger picture. They clearly deserve a place, yet their cross-genre nature makes them hard to insert into the narrative of the 'integrated' musicals of the post-war years. *Bless the Bride* is indeed wonderfully integrated, but not in the accepted format for a musical now, and certainly not for 1947 if the benchmark for all shows of the time in the West End is led by contemporary Broadway imports. Importantly, the three Ellis-Herbert-Cochran shows arise from the specific situations of the Second World War and its immediate aftermath – both the general experiences of the time and the specific ones of A. P. Herbert. Viewing the creative personnel too, the age range from Wendy Toye to C. B. Cochran demonstrates a wide cross-generational input.

Expresso Bongo is at another extreme: absolutely of its day in terms of its music, theatrical style and subject. Knowing about the show does not solve the problem of its lack of performance visibility in the present. However, it does raise questions that distinguish a different trajectory for home-grown shows in the West End from those originating in other places with their own distinctiveness. This injection of youth culture into the onstage world of the musical has a boldness that deserves acknowledgement. It is a watershed moment of generational change rather than generational fusion. Just as *Bless the Bride* reads completely differently given a wartime context, so *Expresso Bongo* emerges as a different show if placed alongside the broad picture of youth culture and 1950s challenges to a pre-war/post-war consensus. The context makes a difference in the detail too, as the preceding chapters have demonstrated. Look at the show in isolation and you get some of its impact. Look at it in a 3D context of stage, culture and social upheaval, and it becomes that much more vivid and impressive.

Popular theatre is designed for a time and a place to be – unsurprisingly – 'popular'. Whether that aim is achieved is another matter, but it is nonetheless one which all the shows addressed in this book have done. Longevity in the repertory is an incidental bonus somewhere down the line but not an imperative at the outset. This is even more the case when we consider how a long initial run pre-1960 is of a much shorter order than one post-1970. Even at the extreme for this early period, the performance record of *The Boy Friend* in London in the 1950s pales against that of *Les Misérables* or *The Phantom of the Opera* from the 1980s on . . . and on. The selection of successful shows and the endorsement of what are perceived to be their commonalities create 'the canon'. That process of selection – a de facto effect more than a consistent, conscious evaluation – is valuable. It provides one type of framework for understanding the natural selection of the musical stage. However, such a selection is not useful when replicated down the decades, a reinforcement that in turn promotes evolutionary selection into literal historical writ. Creating shows with an eye on posterity seldom works: posterity makes its own choices.

Here there is a vital tension between what we have collectively and passively chosen to remember and value, and the way in which we may project our judgements of today back on any work created for a different time and place and audience.

We can see this in action in what matters to us now in enjoying *Me and My Girl* and what mattered when the work was presented in 1937. Its originality came in the detail and in a performance incarnation substantially moulded by its star, Lupino Lane. Changes made for the revival were in large part pragmatic, for different performers at a different time, of songs that are no longer of a current age, of social interactions that are differently loaded (but still present) in the twenty-first century. Yet that distinctive grounding in the physical nature of performance and the impetus of fast comedy remained vital to the bigger nature of the show. Translate that core and the show travels through time; lose that core – as with the 1999 attempt to reframe *Bless the Bride* – and the connection between the identity of the show and the audience collapses. The revision in 1985 of *Me and My Girl* as a 1930s period piece of itself makes the point that audiences at any given moment respond to many types of musical theatre, not to a single-minded embodiment. Multiplicity and individuality are vital. Distinguishing the ways in which shows are uniquely distinctive can be as revealing, if not more so, as pinning down their commonalities.

Active consideration of the 'integration' concept in musical theatre came to the fore in the later years of the period from *Bitter Sweet* to *Oliver!* It arises as the result of the amalgamation of a variety of forms – operetta, musical comedy, farce and so on – described in relation to the shows explored here. However problematic to apply in practice, that more specialized 'musical theatre' identity represents a new selectivity of criteria that have now become baked into the territory. Reading the works explored here from a future position as though they were part of a conscious search for an integrated form is misleading. It runs the risk, and so often achieves it, of denying exactly those features that made the shows work for their first audiences: better to take the story off the security of the train tracks and allow the freedom to explore in many directions.

The musical as memory

In *Half a Sixpence*, Ann soliloquizes in song that 'I know what I am'. It is a poignant rebuke to Arthur Kipps who is trying to replace the traits of his lower-class background with the alien values and behaviours of the upper class. He fails. Ann does not fool herself. She does not accept passively the status given her. Rather, she embraces it as a strength in its own right, as the foundation of her honesty and integrity. The term 'knowing your place' is double-edged. The phrase is usually employed to suggest an inferior rank ordering, as Kipps would interpret it. Yet the meaning can also be redirected to describe a self-contained honesty and integrity, as Ann sees it. The same switch of focus runs through this investigation. Rather than viewing this repertory through a fundamentally comparative lens, the stance has been to discover its initial integrity in the sense of what holds each show together in its own right.

One way to achieve this is to get as close as possible to understanding each show as though actually there in its opening weeks. It is an act of close reading, research and imagination. The questions raised in doing this are legion and the availability of resources and the time to digest them impose significant constraints. However, the value comes with the questions that arise and the new standpoints they promote, especially in relation to the variety of perspectives among the audiences. For example, the resonances of *The Boy Friend* take on a different view when acknowledging that some people at the 1950s performances could make direct comparison with their experiences of new shows in the 1920s. The historically distanced main part of Coward's *Bitter Sweet* is in crucial contrast to its contemporary framing, similar to that of *The Dancing Years*. The recognition of those temporal points would stem from entirely different places in today's audience's varied frames of reference from what they were in 1929 and 1939, respectively.

The restoration of memory is central. Through it, we can discover what has been retained as shared cultural memory, what has been distorted or replaced, what has been ignored and what has been lost. The physical presence of a particular star on stage is fragile in its transience. Its significance can be too easily overlooked given the difficulty – often the impossibility – of establishing its nature through primary sources. Some sort of script and score are most likely to have survived, and a textual reading offers a more dependable and consistent route of enquiry. Yet Lupino Lane has been shown as central to *Me and My Girl* at the level of both conception and performance iterations. Similarly, all but two of the shows of Novello were designed around him in the leading male role (the exceptions are *Arc de Triompe* and *Gay's the Word*). The criteria for judging the resulting works have to take that specific star's presence into account. Within the period studied here, such personality performers for whom shows were intended as overt expressions of their own performing selves include Cicely Courtneidge (*Under Your Hat, Under the Counter, Her Excellency* and *Gay's the Word*), Arthur Askey (*The Kid from Stratford* and *Bet Your Life*) and, as extensions onto the stage of their significantly more prominent film identities, George Formby (*Zip Goes a Million*) and Anna Neagle (*The Glorious Years*) (Snelson 2003: 161–204; J. Snelson 2016). The star appeal that generates this strand of celebrity-centred musical comedy directs the nature of the shows through the introduction of cross-genre and cross-media elements: the personality already established across stage, film, recordings, broadcasting and news media is the very essence of the show. The signature characteristics of these performers fade from memory during the following decades, and with them the vital undercurrents that each star brings to the show's text do too. The resulting loss of meaning can easily lead to a loss of recognition of that seminal significance.

By way of example, Courtneidge was famous for her seemingly inexhaustible energy. When linked to shows that included themes that captured a national spirit, she became symbolic of British pluck and determination in the face of any adversity. In *Under Your Hat* (1938) she played a spy, scoring a triumph with the lampooning number 'The Empire Depends on You', while *Under the Counter* (1945) and *Her Excellency* (1949) drew comedy from the effects of wartime rationing. In *Gay's the Word*, Courtneidge embodied a revivifying force of nature for the British musical stage, encapsulated in the long Act I finale 'Vitality'. Film director Herbert Wilcox took an American producer of musicals to see the show. After watching her in 'Vitality', the producer asked Wilcox, "'How often does she do that?" I told him eight times a week. "They can't do that to her. They can't do it", was all he could mutter. He was too astonished even to applaud' (Courtneidge 1953: 208). The power of a specific theatrical presence in the theatrical moment is vital here to the recreation of the show's impact on its first audience.

Music too is susceptible to the effects of memory loss. Tastes and styles change not with a single show and a single year but with decades and generations: the familiar music of one's parents becomes the forgotten repertory of one's grandparents. Audiences don't forget everything they have seen before when they enter a theatre to see a new show, or indeed any show for the first time. Yet the repertory in this study is now sufficiently distant to make shared memory of the cultural character of the time of creation absent in large part from any audience today. The longevity of *The Boy Friend* and *Me and My Girl* has been helped by the clarity of their music being within a single, identifiable style period. The choice for the first was deliberate, the second sufficiently distinctive in its 1930s contemporaneity to be packaged up as a period work later. The relationship is self-evident: the audience remains in their present looking back at something that actively presents the past. It is a different matter with the cross-genre, cross-era musical reflections in the shows that make a feature of stylistic hybridity. Contrasts of past and present musical styles are composed into the scores of *Bitter Sweet*, *The Dancing Years* and *Bless the Bride* as part of the way in which the core dramas are articulated. How do those contrasts read today when the references are 'past' and 'even further past', and an easy familiarity with the range of styles cannot be taken for granted? The contemporary significance of the musical style and the cross-genre links it provokes require active reconstruction in the analytical unpacking, not only for the sake of the sound but also to bring out layers of dramatic meaning apparent 'then' and forgotten 'now'.

To the significance of performers, synopses and songs we can add all the references in storylines and text to events, attitudes and the whole range of day-to-day life which the original audiences would have seen mirrored on the stage. Consider how in 1958 *Expresso Bongo* stridently dramatizes the contemporary, the only show of this book's selection that seems to exclude the past in a polemic about its present. It reflected the world back to its original audience with attitude. However, in 1929 *Bitter Sweet* provided an 1880s image of swirling, waltzing colour, in 1947 *Bless the Bride* revelled in mid-Victorian fashion, and in 1953/4 *The Boy Friend* demanded cloche hats, dorothy bags and the full gamut of 1920s elegance. In contrast, the wardrobe directions in *Expresso Bongo* for the young jazz club ensemble acknowledge an essential contemporaneity that even goes beyond the originating period of the late 1950s: 'Take a look around you and see what they are wearing at the time you are doing the play, for styles in their world change more than most people realize.... The more *beatnik* or modern, or whatever the title for the type is by the time you go into production, the better' (Mankowitz and More 1960: 6). Could there be a punk updating of *Expresso Bongo* that slants Johnnie towards a Malcolm McLaren figure promoting a Bongo Herbert who channels Johnny Rotten? That the thought occurs signals a core contemporaneity within the show's concept, which makes it fundamentally different from the other case study shows, in which retrospective elements are prominent.

The national/international musical

It is a given today that a musical can be understood as much more than just a diversionary entertainment. This has not always been the case. As the interrogation here of press reviews and summaries of the day has shown, the expectations of the professional commentators were shaped by the values and the mood of their time. Plus ça change. Any show summarized in its day as inconsequential may well not present the full or balanced story. *The Dancing Years* and *Bless the Bride* make this especially clear: the significance of their crucial wartime aspects was not prominent in reviews of the day, the shows' texts were later changed, and thus the theme is so easily overlooked. We can miss the point when looking at close range as well as from a distance.

What mattered in the day and how it mattered – the *zeitgeist* – has been especially impactful on a genre that deals so visibly with the transience of popular entertainment in a period when the hierarchy of high and low culture was particularly strong. We can register it, for example, in the comments of Coward, Ellis and Wilson on the low value ascribed to popular music in Britain compared to the respect afforded it in America. It comes through too in the inconsequence and ephemerality registered in judgements made in the Lord Chamberlain's Department when faced with a script such as that of *Me and My Girl*. Reputations are made through pronouncements on cultural worth, and that early influence can persist unquestioned and reinforced. A fundamental point returns: if something was a success in its day it did something right, it made a connection with its audience and its time. The formal sources we may be drawn to for contemporary assessment are reliable for what they are. But we need more to generate that more holistic, imaginative, informative recreation of what the audience experience was and how that vital connection in live theatre was made.

The investigations here tend towards teasing out the relationship of a work with its setting more than homing in on the work's internal self-referencing. Pinning down formal designations of genre has not been a prime focus, but it has played some part. Analysing lyrics and music for their contemporary resonances contributes to this part of the bigger picture, less so in this study when tackled from a technical perspective. For example, there is a place in music analysis for teasing out such unifying factors in Lionel Bart's music for *Oliver!* as its recurring melodic motifs (a scale descent from the tonic, often with flattened 7th, and a chromatic pattern used both rising and descending are prominent). It is not significant to this strand of investigation into the broader context of the show and hence not a priority for this study. A parallel study of Bart's musical style would intersect with the *Oliver!* chapter here, not least in understanding further the interplay and distinctions between the styles of popular music as Bart deployed them. Such a complementary study can only add to the breadth of understanding of the work, but any single research perspective will not comprehensively convey the rounded significance.

Thematic aspects often provide a way to compare and contrast across the repertory. This could be, for example, by way of class, sexuality and gender, national identity or race. Themes create focus, which any workable investigation needs. For example, discussions of sexuality in relation to Novello and Wilson can provide important insights into contexts and readings of the time of creation of the works and reveal changes in the social recognition of gay identity after. Yet we should also note that a thematic approach can end up dominating the perceived character of a work: 'gay culture' (*The Boy Friend*), 'class structure' (*Me and My Girl*), 'regional identity' (*Zip Goes a Million*) and so on. Complementary planes of investigation can build up that picture of 'gay culture *and* performance culture *and* genre memory', and 'class structure *and* physical comedy *and* star identity'. The more '*and*'s that can be added, the better the 3D image comes into focus.

This type of investigation does encompass an awareness of national specificity. It is unquestionable that core points have local resonance: witness *Bless the Bride*, which is intrinsically of the Cochran-Herbert-Ellis team, with all the associations they have in British popular culture, as well as being influenced by lives grounded in wider British culture. If they had been from another country they would have created different shows. Coward came to embody a certain clichéd view of the English to foreigners and to his compatriots. The national dimension cannot be avoided, nor should it be. As Chapter 1 outlined, national identity has created tensions in the assessment of musicals in the West End from their first outings on the stage. The constricting effect has been especially formative in respect of West End–Broadway comparisons. What comes to the fore here in approaching the historically rooted investigations in this study is not the necessity of an insider view – nationality does not bestow all-encompassing knowledge of one's fellow citizens in all and any periods. Rather, there needs to be a keen sensitivity to the potential that more is going on than seems immediately apparent to the observer of whatever origin: those contemporary reference points do not spring out automatically as they used to, if at all. The responses to particular works of theatre are not fixed because they reflect a relationship at a given moment between work, stage and the variety of perspectives contained with an audience. There is always the potential for misinterpretation and thus misrepresentation unless the local values are the starting point, even for a comparative study. How an approach or value is understood in Germany, or France or the United States will be different from the UK. This is not nationalistic so much as geographically and culturally specific. The genre may be expressed in a national context, but the genre itself is not nationally owned.

The curiosity of both the inside and outside investigator can pick up what seems strange now but wasn't then, provided that the focus is on the work in its home context rather than being constrained by an externally imposed, pre-existing narrative. This is true of any geographically focussed repertory. There may be an identity in a musical-theatre work which dovetails with facets of local cultural identity at a given time and in a given context and so reflects an element of national pageant. That does not mean the work is exclusively a work of national identity, as we can see through the intercontextual resonances of *Oliver!*. The musicals discussed here are 'British' in the sense that they originate within the national theatre system from people brought up within its culture. One line of enquiry pushes that further to link approaches to class, sex, subversion of convention, awareness of heritage, presentational experimentation and genre fluidity as instances of Britishness: the manner of presentation is specific and the approach to the values is specific. But these are universal themes of drama too and thus open to different but effective alternative resonances when experienced in other places and other times. If they were not, there would be no productions beyond the home territory and no revivals beyond an initial run.

The end of the beginning

The variety expressed by the shows here is fascinating, confusing, revealing and challenging. Other shows within the same period amplify the themes and issues raised here, although with less easy access to materials. Four shows fuse operetta with popular song, two are variations on musical comedy and two read as closer to the book-song model of a modern post-war musical. There is a visible change through different traditions towards new forms. *Expresso Bongo* and *Oliver!* come the closest to the archetypes of the modern post-war musicals in a way that none of the others in their original forms do. The works have not changed, but in reading back – the hindsight of knowing what followed them – we notice in them first what is familiar to us. We gain an immediacy in relating to them, and we lose the novelty of what made them stand out so much in their own times. As happens with the very creation of canonic works, they start as rebels and end up as the Establishment: what made them different at the start is superseded by what makes them the same in retrospect.

There has been a need to pull the repertory of the British musical away from value judgements and criteria of other places and times, not to isolate it, but to rediscover what in it is especially distinctive yet has been buried through loss of memory, performance and interest. The repertory is large, the variations within it many. I hope that reviewing these seven case-study shows will contribute to a reassessment of these fine examples of West End shows. In bringing to wider attention the range of sources and types of approaches they invite, I hope as well to contribute to an ever-growing release of the fascinating individuality of this repertory as characterful expressions of particular times, places and people. Through this, the musical can be increasingly revealed as more than diversionary and transient entertainment. It is also a valuable and subtle multilayered record of its time and, by implication, a measure of change from the past through to each new today.

Shows

Outline chronology for the core British musicals discussed (West End and related London premieres)

Title/theatre/premiere date. Creatives (music, lyrics, book)

1929
Mr. Cinders, Adelphi, 11 February 1929. Vivian Ellis (m), Clifford Grey and Greatrex Newman (lyr, bk), Leo Robin (lyr).
Bitter Sweet, His Majesty's, 18 July 1929. Noël Coward (m, lyr, bk).

1930–9
Conversation Piece, His Majesty's, 16 February 1934. Noël Coward (m, lyr, bk).
Glamorous Night, Theatre Royal, Drury Lane, 2 May 1935. Ivor Novello (m, bk), Christopher Hassall (lyr).
Twenty to One, London Coliseum, 12 November 1935. Billy Mayerl (m), Frank Eyton (lyr), L. Arthur Rose (bk).
Careless Rapture, Theatre Royal, Drury Lane, 11 September 1936. Ivor Novello (m, bk), Christopher Hassall (lyr).
Crest of the Wave, Theatre Royal, Drury Lane, 1 September 1937. Ivor Novello (m, bk), Christopher Hassall (lyr).
Me and My Girl, Victoria Palace, 16 December 1937. Noel Gay (m), Arthur Rose and Douglas L. Furber (bk, lyr). Revised version: Adelphi Theatre, 12 February 1985.
Operette, His Majesty's, 16 March 1938. Noël Coward (m, lyr, bk).
The Dancing Years, Theatre Royal, Drury Lane, 23 March 1939. Ivor Novello (m, bk), Christopher Hassall (lyr).

1940–9
Arc de Triomphe, Phoenix, 9 November 1943. Ivor Novello (m, lyr, bk), Christopher Hassall (lyr).
Perchance to Dream, London Hippodrome, 21 April 1945. Ivor Novello (m, lyr, bk).
Big Ben, Adelphi, 17 July 1946. Vivian Ellis (m), A. P. Herbert (lyr, bk).
Pacific 1860, Theatre Royal, Drury Lane, 19 December 1946. Noël Coward (m, lyr, bk).
Bless the Bride, Adelphi, 26 April 1947. Vivian Ellis (m), A. P. Herbert (lyr, bk).
Tough at the Top, Adelphi, 15 July 1949. Vivian Ellis (m), A. P. Herbert (lyr, bk).
King's Rhapsody, Palace, 15 September 1949. Ivor Novello (m, lyr, bk), Christopher Hassall (lyr).

1950–9

Ace of Clubs, Cambridge, 7 July 1950. Noël Coward (m, lyr, bk).
Gay's the Word, Saville, 16 February 1951. Ivor Novello (m, bk), Alan Melville (lyr).
And So to Bed, New Theatre, 17 October 1951. Vivian Ellis (m, lyr), J. B. Fagan (bk).
The Boy Friend, Players', 14 April 1953. Sandy Wilson (m, lyr, bk). Revised version: Players', 13 October 1953; Embassy, 1 December 1953; Wyndham's, 14 January 1954.
The Buccaneer, New Watergate, 8 September 1953. Sandy Wilson (m, lyr, bk). Revised version: Lyric Hammersmith 8 September 1955; Apollo, 22 February 1956.
After the Ball, Globe, 10 June 1954. Noël Coward (m, lyr, bk).
Salad Days, Vaudeville 5 August 1954. Julian Slade (m, lyr, bk), Dorothy Reynolds (lyr, bk).
The Water Gipsies, Winter Garden, 31 August 1955. Vivian Ellis (m), A. P. Herbert (lyr, bk).
Expresso Bongo, Saville, 23 April 1958. David Heneker (m, lyr), Monty Norman (m, lyr), Julian More (lyr, bk) and Wolf Mankowitz (bk).
Fings Ain't Wot They Used t'Be, Theatre Royal, Stratford East, 17 February 1959. Lionel Bart (m, lyr), Frank Norman (bk). Revised version: Theatre Royal, Stratford East, 22 December 1959; Garrick, 11 February 1960.
Lock Up Your Daughters, Mermaid, 28 May 1959. Laurie Johnson (m), Lionel Bart (lyr), Bernard Miles (bk).
Make Me an Offer, Theatre Royal, Stratford East, 19 October 1959. David Heneker (m, lyr), Monty Norman (m, lyr), Wolf Mankowitz (bk).

1960–

Oliver!, New Theatre, 30 June 1960. Lionel Bart (m, lyr, bk).
Blitz!, Adelphi, 8 May 1962. Lionel Bart (m, lyr), Joan Maitland (bk).
Half a Sixpence, Cambridge, 21 March 1963. David Heneker (m, lyr), Beverley Cross (bk).
Maggie May, Adelphi, 22 September 1964. Lionel Bart (m, lyr), Alun Owen (bk).
Divorce Me, Darling!, Players', 15 December 1964; Globe, 1 February 1965. Sandy Wilson (m, lyr, bk).

Notes

Chapter 1

1. On the cover and title page of the programme booklet that accompanied the premiere production, the title is hyphenated: *Bitter-Sweet*. In the back cover programme advertisement for the 78rpm discs of songs from the show, the title is not hyphenated. The former appears to be deliberate typesetting, the latter a convenience of the graphic design, in which the title has been split over two lines. Contemporary reviews used hyphenated and unhyphenated forms, sometimes in the same copy. The published vocal score and scripts (both Coward's *Play Parade* and French's acting edition) do not hyphenate the title. I prefer the sense of the hyphenated title and its use solely in the context of the 1929 production; some reference sources still include it in all occurrences. Coward very occasionally used the form *Bittersweet* in later diary entries, suggesting a preference for a single word form rather than two separate words. In practice, the hyphen quickly dropped from general use, and this book follows that convention. The dieresis in Noël Coward's name is similarly often dropped. He used it, and the name is presented throughout to reflect that even where any source quoted does not include it. Other names are similarly standardized throughout, for example, that of Franz Lehár.
2. James M. Glover: 'The Music Box', *The Stage* (25 July 1929), 15.
3. R. B. Marriott: 'Oliver! – the Best British Musical', *The Stage and Television Today* (7 July 1960), 17.
4. In respect of one of the musical's forerunners, operetta, an understanding of the routes of cultural transfer and the consequent effects on the iterations of the shows particularly in the centres of Berlin, London and New York has been richly opened up. See, for example, Scott (2014), Platt, Becker and Linton (2014) and Scott (2019).
5. For example: Beverley Baxter: [review], *Evening Standard* (2 November 1951): 'But I would not place *South Pacific* in the same street as *Oklahoma[!]*. It is contrived – skilfully but laboriously – whereas *Oklahoma[!]* just came busting out.' Anthony Cookman: 'At the Theatre', *Tatler and Bystander* (1 November 1951), 408: '[T]his is a play with musical interpolations and not a show like *Oklahoma!* Between the songs we are apt to look for dancing, but get instead slabs of narrative.'
6. 'Film Payment', *The Stage* (Thursday 25 July 1929), 14.
7. Respectively in *Charley's (Big-Hearted) Aunt* (1940), *I Thank You* (1941), *Back-Room Boy* and *King Arthur Was a Gentleman* (1942), *Miss London Ltd.* (1943), *Bees in Paradise* (1944), *Make Mine a Million* (1959) and *Bet Your Life* (1953).
8. Lord Chamberlain's Collection, British Library. Playscript LCP 1948/36, 24.
9. Ibid.
10. The study *An Inconvenient Black History of British Musical Theatre* (Mayes and Whitlock, 2022) provides one such perspective, where the repertory complements but only rarely touches this investigation. The broad collection of perspectives to be

gained from *The Oxford Handbook of the British Musical* (Gordon and Jubin, 2016) interacts and augments with those here in a different, extensive and vital way.

Chapter 2

1. 'News Flashes', *Daily Herald* (Friday 19 July 1929), 5.
2. Morton Eustis: 'High Jinks at the Music Box', *Theatre Arts Monthly* (February 1939), 115–20.
3. *Bitter Sweet*, 'The Railroad Hour' [radio broadcast, USA], 31 March 1949. https://www.youtube.com/watch?v=ehcgTbBgtz4, accessed 2 February 2023.

Chapter 3

1. [unsigned]: 'Me and My Girl' [review], *The Stage* (23 December 1937), 10.
2. Lord Chamberlain's Collection, LCP Correspondence 1937/68, Reader's Report 27 September 1937.
3. Lord Chamberlain's Collection, British Library. Playscript LCP 1937/43, 98.
4. The variants Arthur L. Rose and Arthur Rose do occasionally appear, especially in typescripts (e.g. on the title page of *Twenty to One* as submitted for licensing in 1935). The most consistent form of credit is L. Arthur Rose, which is adopted throughout here as indeed on the printed programme credits of *Me and My Girl* in 1937.
5. *Twenty to One*, Lord Chamberlain's Collection, Playscript LCC 1935/35, 1–21.
6. Ibid., 1–40.
7. Ibid., 1–56.
8. Ibid., 1–34.
9. Ibid., 2–20.
10. Ibid., 1–61.
11. Lupino Lane (*League of Nations*, revue, Oxford Theatre), Barry and Wallace Lupino (*Round in Fifty*, Hippodrome Theatre), Stanley Lupino and brother Mark Lupino (*Phi Phi*, London Pavilion) and Cissy Lupino (Alhambra).
12. See for example *The Return of Lupino Lane*, 'Arena' [BBC Television]: https://www.youtube.com/watch?v=fDb_9CU49y0. Accessed 2 February 2023.
13. [unsigned]: 'Me and My Girl' [review], *The Stage* (23 December 1937), 10.
14. HMV BD 596, recorded 27 February 1938.
15. Lord Chamberlain's Collection, British Library. Playscript LCP 1937/57, 79.
16. Television listings, *Radio Times*, 7 January 1938, vol. 58, issue 745, 15.
17. Television listings, *Radio Times*, 28 April 1939, vol. 63, issue 813, 14. In respect of the claim of a 'first' for televising of a musical 'in its entirety' from its theatre, the accompanying texts to the listing of *Me and My Girl* clarify that the recent '*Magyar Melody* [27 March 1939] did not quite fall into this category'. For a detailed explanation of the context for the BBC broadcasts, technical arrangement and significance see Napper (2014: 155–66).
18. Lord Chamberlain's Collection, British Library. Playscript LCP 1937/43, 14.
19. Ibid., 49–50.
20. Ibid., 108.

21 Ibid., 118–21.
22 Lord Chamberlain's Collection, British Library. Playscript LCP 1937/57, 92.
23 Ibid., 93–4.
24 Lord Chamberlain's Collection, British Library. Playscript LCP 1937/43, 94.
25 Lord Chamberlain's Collection, British Library. Playscript LCP 1949/37, II-1-6–II-1-12.
26 *The Lambeth Walk* (dir. Albert de Courville, 1939) Timecode 00:57:15–01:04:08.
27 The September version LCP 1937/43 included the word 'Pansy' (102), which was duly censored. It was replaced in the December version LCP 1937/57 by the newly offending 'Cissy' (76).
28 Lord Chamberlain's Collection, British Library. LCP Correspondence 1937/928. Internal memo 'D', H. C. Game, 5 April 1938.
29 Lord Chamberlain's Collection, British Library. Playscript LCP 1949/37, title page.
30 Lord Chamberlain's Collection, British Library. Playscripts LCP 1937/43, 128 and 1937/57, 101–2.
31 Lord Chamberlain's Collection, British Library. Playscript LCP 1937/43, 87. In the playscript 1957/57, 72, the direction has been reduced to '(Enter COSTERS)', but the filmed stage extract confirms that formal evening dress in whatever state is the dress code.

Chapter 4

1 Ivor Novello: 'Ivor Novello tells his story of . . . *The Dancing Years*', *Radio Times*, no. 1366 (16 December 1949), 5; also reproduced in Noble (1951: 227–30).
2 Ibid.
3 News footage of Novello's funeral: Gaumont British (Reuters) film ID VLVA2MVNZPBRTZPNTF4P7CI5USG69, also https://www.youtube.com/watch?v=xiOuMWJRLHw. Accessed 4 February 2023; and British Pathé film ID 1443.12 (also on https://www.youtube.com/watch?v=zHH1U8wWSAA. Accessed 4 February 2023). Radio broadcast 'Ivor Novello – Man of the Theatre' (8 March 1951) on https://www.youtube.com/watch?v=etB7t_ETqSI. Accessed 4 February 2023.
4 For a justification of the portrayal of Novello in the film, see Slattery-Christy (2008: 117–19).
5 Barry Sinclair [interview] 'Today', Thames TV (6 December 1975).
6 For a considered comparison of contemporaries Novello and Coward, see Webb (2005: 85–95).
7 In addition to the long biographies by Noble and Macqueen-Pope already cited, there is a later one by James Harding (1987). Those of Richard Rose (1974) and Sandy Wilson (1975b) provide copious illustrations alongside shorter biographical summaries and work details. The short, reflective biography by Webb (1999, 2005) has the stated intention of countering the decline in the understanding of Novello's significance. David Slattery-Christy (2008) takes a more individual approach. None of these books include detailed citation of sources, which is a practical response to the interest in Novello having long been generated by residual popular appeal rather than exploration within the academy. That the two most recent biographies originated as self-published works is indicative of the mismatch between Novello's cultural influence and his commercial significance. A comprehensive, critical study of Novello's life and a contextual analysis of his works is well overdue.

8   See for example Slattery-Christy (2008: 148). For an extensive consideration of Ruritania as a political and literary construct see Goldworthy (1998).
9   For details see the song listings in Wilson (1975b: 167–270).
10 Ivor Novello: 'Ivor Novello tells his story of . . . *The Dancing Years*', *Radio Times*, no. 1366 (16 December 1949), 5.
11 For chronological lists of Novello's films and stage plays as actor and/or author, see the appendices in Wilson (1975b: 270–4).
12 *The Dancing Years* Lord Chamberlain's Collection, British Library, Lord Chamberlain's Playscript LCP 1945/1, 59–62.
13 This Novello-Lehár fusion can be heard very briefly as transitional music to introduce the onstage presentation of *Lorelei* in the film of *The Dancing Years* (1950) and in full on the CD recording *The Dancing Years*, Jay Records CDJAY2 1452, 'War music' disc 1 track 22.
14 'The Leap Year Waltz', *The Dancing Years* No. 21 (Novello and Hassall 1949: 100–5). Introduction, bars 1–22; principal waltz (C major), bars 23–55; second waltz (C major), bars 56–87; third waltz (F major), bars 120–159. Bar counts begin on the first main beat, not the anacrusis bars. The recording of the 1939 version adopted slightly different repetitions and modulations, but the sectional contrasts remain the same.
15 Alan Bott: 'Entertainments à la Carte: Mr. Novello Does it Again' [review], *Tatler and Bystander* (19 April 1939), 22.
16 Ibid., 23.
17 Lionel Hale: 'Novello's Caprice Viennois "The Dancing Years"', *Daily News* (London edition; 24 March 1939), 8.
18 Unsigned: 'The Adelphi: *The Dancing Years*' [review], *The Stage* (19 March 1942), 1.
19 Ivor Novello: 'Ivor Novello tells his story of . . . *The Dancing Years*', *Radio Times*, no. 1366 (16 December 1949), 5.
20 *The Dancing Years* Lord Chamberlain's Collection, British Library, Lord Chamberlain's Playscript LCP 1939/14, Prologue, 1.
21 Ibid., Prologue, 3.
22 Ibid.
23 Ibid.
24 *The Dancing Years*: Reader's Report, 12 February 1939, Lord Chamberlain's Collection, British Library, LCP correspondence 1939/2468.
25 *The Dancing Years*: N. W. Gwatkin to the Management, Theatre Royal, Drury Lane, 15 February 1939, Lord Chamberlain's Collection, British Library, LCP correspondence 1939/2468.
26 *The Dancing Years* Lord Chamberlain's Collection, British Library, Lord Chamberlain's Playscript LCP 1939/14, inserted loose typescript letter.
27 Included in the vocal score as No. 27 'Incidental music' (Novello and Hassall 1949: 119). It can be heard as 'War Music' on the CD recording *The Dancing Years*, Jay Records CDJAY2 1452, 'War music' disc 2 track 20.
28 *The Dancing Years* Lord Chamberlain's Collection, British Library, Lord Chamberlain's Playscript LCP 1939/14, 4.
29 Ibid., 6.
30 Versions are included in the published vocal score. However, the music is shorter and substantially different in detail if not character from the 1939 version, which can be heard on CD recording *The Dancing Years*, Jay Records CDJAY2 1452: disc 1 track 13; disc 2 track 5, track 12.

31 By the time of the 1945 tour version, Part II had disappeared from the list of numbers, and Part III was renumbered Part II (*The Dancing Years* Lord Chamberlain's Collection, British Library, Lord Chamberlain's Playscript LCP 1945/1, iii). This renumbering carries through to French's acting edition (Novello and Hassall 1953: 2). The vocal score (Novello and Hassall 1949) retains the tripartite designation along with other mismatches with the published libretto that show it as a mixture of original production, touring production and further amendments to suit amateur production. Notably for casting in the acting edition libretto, Ceruti's presence becomes a near-voiceless 'Lover' in the 'Lorelei' sequence, which removes the need to cast a strong solo operatic tenor. The first of his associated solo renditions of 'My Life Belongs to You' has been cut from the libretto on what should be the first occurrence marked in the vocal score as No. 10 (Novello and Hassall 1949: 32–4). The second (vocal score No. 12: Novello and Hassall 1949: 63–4; libretto no.14: Novello and Hassall 1953: 30) is easy to cut as a reprise in front of the tabs (to cover a scene change) at the end of *Lorelei* sequence. Indeed, in the author's copy used for amateur performance in the 1960s it has been marked for such deletion.
32 'The Dancing Year', BBC Radio broadcast 24 December 1949, British Library, Sound and Image Archive 1LL0014118–1LL0014129, Part 18.
33 'Our London Film Critic' in 'The Dancing Years: Screen Version of Ivor Novello's Play', *The Scotsman* (6 April 1950), 9.
34 In this author's copy of the libretto used in the 1960s by a regional amateur operatic company, the masques and the final interrogation scene are marked as cuts. The planned broadcast on 27 August 1979 was postponed by long-running strike action by the television company technicians and rescheduled to Sunday 30 December.
35 See, for example Nicholls (2016: 210); Snelson (2017: 260–2); and Macpherson (2018: 196).
36 Our Dramatic Critic: 'And Now "Televariety"', *Daily Mirror* (7 March 1935), 2.
37 For a detailed analysis, see Snelson (2003: 192–230).

Chapter 5

1 Anthony Cookman: 'At the Theatre: *Bless the Bride*' [review], *Tatler and Bystander* (14 May 1947), 6.
2 Interview by the author with Wendy Toye (25 August 1998).
3 Ibid.
4 John Courtenay: '*Bless the Bride*' [review], *The Sketch* (11 June 1947), 308.
5 Anthony Cookman: 'At the Theatre: *Bless the Bride*' [review], *The Tatler and Bystander* (14 May 1947), 197.
6 Interview by the author with Wendy Toye (25 August 1998).
7 See production photographs reproduced in *Theatre World*, vol. xliii, no. 270 (July 1947), 11–18. The bridal scene is reproduced among the set design references in Herbert (1948).
8 Henry Adler: 'Music by Vivian Ellis', *Everybody's* (21 June 1947), 6–7.
9 Ibid.
10 Interview by the author with Wendy Toye (25 August 1998).
11 Columbia DX1396.
12 Reprinted in the collection Herbert (1977).

13 Anthony Cookman: 'The Theatre: *Big Ben*' [review], *Tatler and Bystander* (31 July 1946), 134.
14 John Russell: 'Stage Cameos', *The Sketch* (7 August 1946), 64.
15 [unsigned]: 'Chit Chat', *The Stage* (25 July 1946): 4.
16 Anthony Cookman: 'At the Theatre: *Bless the Bride*' [review], *Tatler and Bystander* (14 May 1947), 6.
17 Vivian Ellis: 'Give Us a Chance!', *Plays and Players*, vol. 3 (1956, January 1956), 17.
18 Interview by the author with Wendy Toye (25 August 1998).
19 John Courtenay: '*Bless the Bride*' [review], *The Sketch* (11 June 1947), 308.
20 Maureen Paton: [review] *Daily Express* (12 August 1987); reprinted in *Theatre Record* vol. vii, no. 16 (30 July–12 August), 983.
21 Laura Cotton: [review] *City Limits* (20 August 1987); reproduced in *Theatre Record* vol. vii, no. 16 (30 July–12 August), 983.
22 Charles Osborne: [review] *Daily Telegraph* (13 August 1987); reproduced in *Theatre Record* vol. vii, no. 16 (30 July–12 August), 984.
23 Mark Steyn: [review] *The Independent* (13 August 1987); reproduced in *Theatre Record* vol. vii, no. 16 (30 July–12 August), 985.
24 William Russell: [review] *The Herald* (15 June 1999); reproduced in *Theatre Record* vol. xix, no. 12 (4–17 June), 745. The tonal mismatch Russell describes accords with this author's memory of the production.
25 Michael Billington: [review] *The Guardian* (9 June 1999); reproduced in *Theatre Record* vol. xix, no. 12 (4–17 June), 742.
26 Roger Foss: [review] *What's On* (16 June 1999); reproduced in *Theatre Record* vol. xix, no. 12 (4–17 June), 745.

Chapter 6

1 Even the title signals generational difference. Wilson was insistent on the two words 'boy friend', as used throughout the script, not the more modern form 'boyfriend'. This chapter adopts the 1920s form for citations and quotations and the single-word form for generic use.
2 Anthony Cookman: 'At the Theatre: The Boy Friend', *Tatler and Bystander* (27 January 1954), 132.
3 [unsigned]: 'Wyndham's: *The Boy Friend*' [review], *The Stage* (21 January 1954), 9.
4 Wilson uses burlesque in the English sense of ridiculing or sending up, not as though in the manner of an American burlesque show.
5 A dorothy bag (sometimes capitalized) in the 1920s was an adaptation of the Victorian reticule and had a long cross-body strap. It was usually highly decorated with tassels, beads and embroidery.
6 The acting edition (Wilson 1960b) is cited here for its detailed instructions on the staging. The earlier script published by Deutsch (Wilson 1955) has minimal staging instructions throughout.
7 The song was included in the London stage show but not printed in Chappell's London version of the vocal score. It was recorded (18 March 1925; Columbia 3631) by Irene Browne from the London cast.
8 R. B. Marriott: 'Polly Browne and her Friends in "Divorce Me, Darling!"' [review], *The Stage* (4 February 1965), 15.

9. [Editorial]: 'These Horror Comics Must Be Boycotted', *Bucks Herald* (4 September 1953), 10.
10. [unsigned]: 'Boy's Tragic Death: Coroner's Reference to Comics', *New Ross Standard* (10 April 1953), 2.
11. Interview by the author with Sandy Wilson (1999).
12. Anthony Cookman: 'At the Theatre: *The Boy Friend*' [review], *Tatler and Bystander* (27 January 1954), 132.
13. Alec Baldwin: 'Here's the Thing: Interview with Julie Andrews', *WYNC Radio* (2015); broadcast on BBC Radio 4extra, 12 May 2018.
14. [unsigned]: 'Wyndham's: *The Boy Friend*' [review], *The Stage* (21 January 1954), 9.
15. Promotional trailer included with *The Boy Friend*, DVD (Warner Home Video, 2011).

Chapter 7

1. R.B.M.: 'London Theatres: The Importance of *Expresso Bongo*' [review], *The Stage* (1 May 1958), 11.
2. [unsigned]: '"Bongo" Top of British Poll', *The Stage* (3 July 1958), 1.
3. Noel Whitcombe [sic]: 'Bongo! The Angry Young Musical', *Daily Mirror* (26 March 1958).
4. See, for example, production photographs in *Theatre World Annual*, no. 11 (1 June 1959–31 May 1960), 56, 109.
5. Reader's Report, *Expresso Bongo* (22 November 1957), Lord Chamberlain's Correspondence.
6. Ibid.
7. [Unsigned]: 'Five New Nudes for Varsity *Bongo*', *Daily Mirror* (Saturday 16 January 1963), 2; [Unsigned]: 'Undress Rehearsal', *Daily Mirror* (Wednesday 13 February 1963), 32.
8. Letter from Sir Eric Penn, Assistant Comptroller, *Expressso Bongo*, Lord Chamberlain's Correspondence (8 February 1963).
9. Reader's Report, *Expresso Bongo* (22 November 1957), Lord Chamberlain's Correspondence.
10. [unsigned]: 'Round and About: Expresso Bongo', *Radio Times*, vol. 141, no. 1830 (3 December 1958), 4.
11. [unsigned]: 'European Enquiry: Rebellious Youth', *Radio Times*, vol. 141, no. 1830 (3 December 1958), 2.
12. [unsigned]: 'A Name in a Night: James Kenney in Master Crook', *The Stage* (24 January 1952), 10.
13. R. B. Marriott: 'James Kenney Returns – as a Potential Star of Musicals', *The Stage* (1 May 1958), 10.
14. Ibid.
15. Ken Hollings: 'On the Concept of Brexit, Covid & Exceptional Success: A Fable in Eighteen Parts with Two Addenda and Seven Supporting Quotations', *Die Aktion 4.0*, no. 19 (2021), https://olaf.bbm.de/nummer-19-ken-hollings-on-the-concept-of-brexit-covid-exceptional-success. Accessed 2 April 2021.
16. Ibid.
17. Elspeth Grant: 'Cinema: Mr. Richard, You've Got a Grievance' [review], *Tatler and Bystander* (9 December 1959), 45.

18 Brenda Davies: [film review] *Monthly Film Bulletin* (January 1960); reproduced in *Expresso Bongo*, British Film Institute (BFIB1241), disc booklet, 8.
19 T. C. Worsley: 'Growing Up at Last', *New Statesman*, vol. 55, no. 1416 (3 May 1958), 565–6.
20 Derek Granger: 'The Arts: *Expresso Bongo*', *Financial Times* (25 April 1958), 15.
21 R. B. Marriott: 'James Kenney Returns – as a Potential Star of Musicals', *The Stage* (1 May 1958), 10.
22 Bob Dawbarn: '*Expresso Bongo* Is Hit of 1957–8', *Melody Maker* (5 July 1958), 8.
23 Leslie Mallory: 'Out with Picture Hats – Up with Realism', *News Chronicle* (20 November 1958), 6.

Chapter 8

1 Mike Nevard: 'Spinning Disc: Laugh with the Caveman', *Daily Herald* (2 December 1959), 6.
2 *The Stage* (7 July 1960), 13.
3 E.F.: 'Good as Irma, Not so Dear', *Daily News* (Saturday 19 July 1958), 3.
4 R.M.B.: 'The Mermaid Opens with Rousing, Bawdy Comedy', *The Stage* (4 June 1959), 11.
5 A selective discography is included in David Stafford and Caroline Stafford: *Fings Aint' Wot They Used t'Be: The Lionel Bart Story* (London: Omnibus Press, 2011), 275–8.
6 Lionel Bart: 'Lionel Bart on the "Epic Musical"', *Blitz!* [souvenir programme] (London: Adelphi Theatre, 1962); text reproduced from *The Times* (22 March 1962).
7 Joan Maitland: 'Joan Maitland, Co-Author of the Book', *Blitz!* [souvenir programme] (London: Adelphi Theatre, 1962). Maitland has subsequently been credited as sole author of the book.
8 Sean Kenny: 'Sean Kenny', *Blitz!* [souvenir programme] (London: Adelphi Theatre, 1962).
9 Lionel Bart: 'Lionel Bart on the "Epic Musical"', *Blitz!* [souvenir programme] (London: Adelphi Theatre, 1962); text reproduced from *The Times* (22 March 1962).
10 Ibid.
11 Pauline Grant: [disc notes], *Blitz!* (1962); reproduced, disc notes EMI CD 7 97470 2.
12 Lionel Bart: [programme note], *Maggie May* (London: Adelphi Theatre, 1964).
13 Ibid.
14 Alun Owen: [programme note], *Maggie May* (London: Adelphi Theatre, 1964).
15 [unsigned]: 'Colour and Gaiety', *The Stage and Television Today* (9 November 1961), 9.
16 Lionel Bart: 'Lionel Bart on the "Epic Musical"', *Blitz!* [souvenir programme] (London: Adelphi Theatre, 1962); text reproduced from *The Times* (22 March 1962).
17 Noel Whitcombe [sic]: 'Bongo! The Angry Young Musical', *Daily Mirror* (26 March 1958).
18 Eric Johns: 'Ron Moody: Acting a Means to an End', *Theatre World*, vol. lvi, no. 428 (September 1960), 17, 29.
19 Norman Nadel [Broadway review, *New York World-Telegram*], reproduced in *Oliver!* [programme book], New Theatre [1963].
20 Matt Wolf: 'Oliver!' [review], *Variety* (11 December 1994). https://variety.com/1994/legit/reviews/oliver-4-1200439737/. Accessed 9 September 2022.

Bibliography

Andrews, Malcolm. *Charles Dickens and His Performing Selves: Dickens and the Public Readings*. Oxford: Oxford University Press, 2006.
Anonymous [Robert Hichens]. *The Green Carnation*. New York: Appleton and Company, 1894.
Banfield, Stephen. 'English Musical Comedy, 1890-1924', in Robert Gordon and Olaf Jubin (eds), *The Oxford Handbook of the British Musical*, 117–42. New York: Oxford University Press, 2016.
Bart, Lionel. *Oliver!*. Vocal score. London: Chappell, 1960.
Bart, Lionel. *Oliver!*. Libretto. New York: Tams-Witmark, 1977.
Bordman, Gerald. *American Musical Theatre: A Chronicle*. New York: Oxford University Press, 1978.
Burrows, George. 'Musical Comedy in the 1920s and 1930s: "Mister Cinders" and "Me and My Girl" as Class-Conscious Carnival', in Robert Gordon and Olaf Jubin (eds), *The Oxford Handbook of the British Musical*, 171–97. New York: Oxford University Press, 2016.
Clum, John M. *Something for the Boys: Musical Theatre and Gay Culture*. New York: St Martin's Press, 1999.
Cochran, C. B. *Showman Looks On*. London: J.M. Dent, 1945.
Colin, Saul. 'The Musical in America', *Plays and Players*, 3 (1956): 14–15. [January: Musicals number.]
Colson, Marvin. *The Haunted Stage: The Theatre as Memory Machine. Theater: Theory/Text/Performance*. Ann Arbor: University of Michigan Press, 2003.
Cotton, Billy. *I Did It My Way: The Life Story of Billy Cotton*. London: George C. Harrap, 1970.
Courtneidge, Cicely. *Cicely*. London: Hutchinson, 1953.
Coward, Noël. *Bitter Sweet: An Operette in 3 Acts*. Vocal score. London: Chappell, 1929.
Coward, Noël. *Bitter Sweet*. Libretto. London: Samuel French, 1933.
Coward, Noël. 'Introduction', in *Play Parade [The Collected Plays of Noel Coward]*, vii–xviii. London: Heinemann, 1934.
Coward, Noël. 'Operette', in *Second Play Parade [The Collected Plays of Noel Coward]*, 189–317. Libretto. London: Heinemann, 1939a.
Coward, Noël. *Second Play Parade [The Collected Plays of Noel Coward]*. London: Heinemann, 1939b.
Coward, Noël. *The Noël Coward Song Book*. Introduction and annotations by Noël Coward; illustrated by Gladys Calthrop. London: Michael Joseph, 1953.
Coward, Noël. *Play Parade 5. [The Collected Plays of Noel Coward]*. London: Heinemann, 1958.
Coward, Noël. *Noël Coward: Autobiography: Consisting of Present Indicative, Future Indefinite and the Uncompleted Past Conditional*. Introduction by Sheridan Morley. London: Methuen, 1986.
Dunn, Anthony J. *The Worlds of Wolf Mankowitz: Between Elite and Popular Cultures in Post-War Britain*. Edgeware and Portland: Vallentine Mitchell, 2013.

Ellis, Vivian. *I'm on a See-Saw*. London: Joseph, 1953.
Ellis, Vivian. 'Give Us a Chance!' *Plays and Players*, 3 (1956): 17. [January: Musicals number.]
Ellis, Vivian and Alan Herbert. *Bless the Bride*. Vocal score. London: Chappell, 1947.
Findon, B. W. (ed.). 'Bitter Sweet', *Play Pictorial*, lv, no. 330 (1929a): 37–56. London: The Stage Pictorial Publishing Company Ltd.
Findon, B. W. (ed.). 'Plays of the Month', *Play Pictorial*, lv, no. 329 (1929b): iv–vii. London: The Stage Pictorial Publishing Company Ltd.
Findon, B. W. (ed.). 'Editorial', *Play Pictorial*, lv, no. 330 (1929c): i. London: The Stage Pictorial Publishing Company Ltd.
Furber, Douglas. *From London and New York: Revue Sketches*. London and New York: Samuel French, 1927.
Furber, Douglas. *My Best Sketches*. London and New York: Samuel French, 1935.
Furber, Douglas. *Surely You Can Write a Song?: How to Write Lyrics*. London: Ascherberg, Hopwood & Crew, 1950.
Gänzl, Kurt. *The British Musical Theatre: Vol. 1 1865–1914*. Basingstoke: MacMillan, 1986a.
Gänzl, Kurt. *The British Musical Theatre: Vol. 2 1915–1984*. Basingstoke: MacMillan, 1986b.
Gay, Noel, L. Arthur Rose and Douglas Furber. *Me and My Girl*. Song book. London: Wise Publications, 1994.
Goldworthy, Vesna. *Inventing Ruritania*. New Haven and London: Yale University Press, 1998.
Gordon, Robert, Olaf Jubin and Millie Taylor. *British Musical Theatre since 1950*. London: Bloomsbury, 2016.
Graves, Robert and Alan Hodge. *The Long Weekend*. Introduction by Juliet Gardiner. London: Faber and Faber, 1940/Folio Society 2009.
Green, Stanley. *Broadway Musicals: Show by Show*. 4th edn revised and updated by K. Green. Milwaukee: Hal Leonard, 1994.
Handley-Taylor, Geoffrey. *The Book of Popular Musical Comedies*. V&A Theatre and Performance Collection ML1950 folio. Unpublished manuscript, n.d. [1953].
Harding, James. *Ivor Novello*. London: W.H. Allen, 1987.
Hassall, Christopher. *Edward Marsh – Patron of the Arts: A Biography*. London: Longmans, Green and Co., 1959.
Herbert, A. P. *Tantivy Towers and Derby Day*. Librettos. London: Methuen, 1932.
Herbert, A. P. *Big Ben. A Light Opera in Two Acts*. Libretto. London: Methuen & Co. Ltd., 1946.
Herbert, A. P. *Bless the Bride. A Light Opera in Two Acts*. Libretto. London: Samuel French, 1948.
Herbert, A. P. *Independent Member*. London: Methuen & Co., 1950.
Herbert, A. P. *A.P.H.: His Life and Times*. London: Heinemann, 1970.
Herbert, A. P. *Uncommon Law: Being Sixty-Six Misleading Cases Revised in One Volume*. London: Eyre Methuen, 1977. Edition first published Methuen, 1969.
Hoare, Philip. *Noël Coward: A Biography*. London: Sinclair-Stevenson, 1995 [1996 printing].
Johnson, Laurie and Lionel Bart. *Lock Up Your Daughters*. Vocal score. London: Peter Maurice Music, 1960.
Kersh, Gerald. *Night and the City*. Introduction by John King. London: London Books, 2007. First published 1938 by Jonathan Cape.

Lane, Lupino. *How to Be a Comedian*. 2nd edn. London: Frederick Muller, 1945.
Lehár, Franz. *Die lustige Witwe: Operette in 3 Akten*. Leipzig and Vienna: Doblinger, 1906.
Light, Alison and Raphael Samuel. 'Doing the Lambeth Walk', in Raphael Samuel (ed.), *Patriotism: The Making and Unmaking of British National Identity: III National Fictions*, 262-71. London: Routledge, 1989.
Littlewood, Joan. *Joan's Book: Joan Littlewood's Peculiar History as She Tells It [Minerva]*. London: Mandarin paperbacks, 1995.
Macpherson, Ben. *Cultural Identity in British Musical Theatre, 1890-1939: Knowing One's Place*. Palgrave Studies in Musical Theatre. London: Palgrave, 2018.
Macqueen-Pope, Walter James. *Ivor: The Story of an Achievement*. 2nd edn. London: W.H. Allen & Co., 1954.
Madge, Charles and Tom Harrison. *Britain by Mass-Observation*. Harmondsworth: Penguin Books, 1939.
Mankowitz, Wolf. *The ABC of Show Business*. London: Oldbourne Press, n.d. [?1956].
Mankowitz, Wolf and James More. *Expresso Bongo*. Playscript. London: Evans Brothers, 1960.
Mankowitz, Wolf, Monty Norman and David Heneker. *Make Me an Offer*. Playscript. London: Samuel French, 1959.
Mayes, Sean and Sarah K. Whitlock. *An Inconvenient Black History of British Musical Theatre*. London: Bloomsbury/Methuen Drama, 2022.
McHugh, Dominic. 'Noël Coward: Sui Generis', in Robert Gordon and Olaf Jubin (eds), *The Oxford Handbook of the British Musical*, 445-62. New York: Oxford University Press, 2016.
Mordden, Ethan. *Make Believe: The Broadway Musical in the 1920s*. New York and Oxford: Oxford University Press, 1997.
Mordden, Ethan. *Pick a Pocket or Two: A History of the British Musical*. New York: Oxford University Press, 2021.
Morley, Sheridan. *Spread a Little Happiness: The First Hundred Years of the British Musical*. New York: Thames & Hudson, 1987.
Mundy, John. *The British Film Musical*. Manchester: Manchester University Press, 2007.
Music Critic of The Times (comp.). *Musical Britain 1951*. London: The Times/Oxford University Press, 1951.
Napolitano, Marc. 'Disneyfying Dickens: "Oliver & Company" and "The Muppet Christmas Carol" as Dickensian Musicals', *Studies in Popular Culture*, xxxii, no. 1 (Fall) (2009): 79-102. Popular Culture Association in the South, 2009.
Napolitano, Marc. *Oliver!: A Dickensian Musical*. Oxford and New York: Oxford University Press, 2014.
Napper, Lawrence. *British Cinema and Middlebrow Culture in the Interwar Years*. Exeter: University of Exeter, 2014.
Napper, Lawrence and Michael Williams. 'The Curious Appeal of Ivor Novello', in Bruce Babington (ed.), *British Stars and Stardom*, 42-55. Manchester and New York: Manchester University Press, 2001.
Nicholls, Stewart. 'West End Royalty: Ivor Novello and English Operetta, 1917-1951', in Robert Gordon and Olaf Jubin (eds), *The Oxford Handbook of the British Musical*, 199-223. New York: Oxford University Press, 2016.
Nicholls, Stewart. 'Seduced by Paris: "Irma la Douce" and Its Journey to Broadway', in Olaf Jubin (ed.), *Paris and the Musical: The City of Lights on Stage and Screen*, 110-28. Abingdon: Routledge, 2021.

Noble, Peter. *Ivor Novello: Man of the Theatre*. Foreword by Noël Coward. 3rd edn. London: Falcon Press, 1951.

Norman, Frank. *Much Ado about Nuffink*. London: Hodder and Stoughton, 1974.

Norman, Frank. *Why Fings Went West. A Time Remembered*. London: Lemon Tree Press, 1975.

Norman, Frank and Lionel Bart. *Fings Ain't Wot They Used t'Be*. Playscript. London: Samuel French, 1960.

Novello, Ivor. *'I Lived with You', 'Party', 'Symphony in Two Flats'*. Introduction by Edward Marsh CB CMG CVO. London: Methuen, 1932.

Novello, Ivor. *Proscenium*. London and New York: Samuel French, 1934.

Novello, Ivor and Christopher Hassall. *The Dancing Years*. Vocal score. London: Chappell, 1949.

Novello, Ivor and Christopher Hassall. *The Dancing Years. A Musical Play*. Libretto. London: Samuel French, 1953.

Osborne, John. *Plays One* [Originally published as *Look Back in Anger and Other Plays*]. London: Faber and Faber, 1996.

Parker, John (comp.). *Who's Who in Theatre: A Biographical Record of the Contemporary Stage*, ed. F. Gaye. 13th edn. London: Sir Isaac Pitman & Sons, 1961.

Payn, Graham and Sheridan Morley (eds). *The Noël Coward Diaries*. London: Macmillan, 1982.

Philips, Deborah. *And This Is My Friend Sandy: Sandy Wilson's 'The Boy Friend', London Theatre and Gay Culture*. London: Methuen, 2021.

Platt, Len. *Musical Comedy on the West End Stage, 1890–1939*. Basingstoke: Palgrave Macmillan, 2004.

Platt, Len, Tobias Becker and David Linton (eds). *Popular Musical Theatre in London and Berlin: 1890–1939*. Cambridge: Cambridge University Press, 2014.

Pound, Reginald. *A.P. Herbert*. London: Michael Joseph, 1976.

Robins, Denise. *Murder in Mayfair*. London: Mills and Boon, 1935.

Rose, L. Arthur and Douglas Furber. *Me and My Girl*. Playscript. London: Samuel French, 1954.

Rose, L. Arthur, Douglas Furber and Stephen Fry. *Me and My Girl*. Playscript. London: Samuel French, 1986.

Rose, Rose. *Perchance to Dream: The World of Ivor Novello*. London: Leslie Frewin, 1974.

Scott, Derek B. 'German Operetta in the West End and on Broadway', in Len Platt, Tobias Becker and David Linton (eds), *Popular Musical Theatre in London and Berlin: 1890–1939*, 62–80. Cambridge: Cambridge University Press, 2014.

Scott, Derek B. *German Operetta on Broadway and in the West End, 1900–1940*. Cambridge: Cambridge University Press, 2019.

Sheridan, Paul. *Late and Early Joys at the Players' Theatre*. Illustrated by Paul Sheridan. Foreword by Dame Sybil Thorndike. London: T.V. Boardman, 1952.

Slattery-Christy, David. *In Search of Ruritania: The Life and Times of Ivor Novello*. Milton Keynes: AuthorHouse, 2008.

Snelson, John. '"Ordinary People" and British Musicals of the Post-War Decade', in Robert Gordon and Olaf Jubin (eds), *The Oxford Handbook of the British Musical*, 249–69. New York: Oxford University Press, 2016.

Snelson, John. 'The Waltzing Years: British Operetta 1907–1939', in Michela Niccolai and Clair Rowden (eds), *Musical Theatre in Europe 1830–1945*, 241–66. Turnhout: Brepols, 2017.

Snelson, John. 'Shockwaves at a Distance: Ellis and Herbert's "Bless the Bride"', in Olaf Jubin (ed.), *Paris and the Musical: The City of Lights on Stage and Screen*, 185–201. Abingdon: Routledge, 2021.

Snelson, John. 'The Most Beloved Musical: "Guys and Dolls" in London', in Robert Gordon and Olaf Jubin (eds), *Oxford Handbook to the Global Musical*. New York: Oxford University Press, 2023.

Snelson, John M. *The West End Musical 1947-54: British Identity and the 'American Invasion'*. Thesis. Birmingham: University of Birmingham, 2003.

Stafford, David and Caroline Stafford. *Fings Ain't Wot They Used t'Be: The Lionel Bart Story*. London: Omnibus Press, 2011.

Stephens, Frances. *Theatre World Annual (London) No. 1: A Pictorial Review of West End Productions with a Record of Plays and Players*. Theatre World Annual [1 June 1949-31 May 1950]. London: Rockliff Publishing Corporation, 1950.

Stephens, Frances. *Theatre World Annual (London) No. 3: A Pictorial Review of West End Productions with a Record of Plays and Players*. Theatre World Annual [1 June 1951-31 May 1952]. London: Rockliff Publishing Corporation, 1952.

Stephens, Frances. *Theatre World Annual (London) No. 5: A Pictorial Review of West End Productions with a record of Plays and Players*. Theatre World Annual [1 June 1953-31 May 1954]. London: Rockliff Publishing Corporation, 1954.

Stephens, Frances. *Theatre World Annual (London) No. 11: A Pictorial Review of West End Productions with a record of Plays and Players*. Theatre World Annual [1 June 1959-31 May 1960]. London: Barrie and Rockliff, 1960.

Steyn, Mark. *Broadway Babies Say Goodnight: Musicals Then and Now*. London: Faber & Faber, 1997.

Suskin, Steven. *Opening Night on Broadway: A Critical Quotebook of the Golden Era of the Musical Theatre, Oklahoma! (1943) to Fiddler on the Roof (1964)*. New York: Schirmer Books, 1990.

Suskin, Steven. *Show Tunes 1905-1985: The Songs, Shows and Careers of Broadway's Major Composers*. 2nd edn. New York: Dodd, Mead, 1992.

Suskin, Steven. *More Opening Night on Broadway: A Critical Quotebook of the Golden Era of the Musical Theatre, 1965-1981*. New York: Schirmer Books, 1997.

Taylor, Millie. 'Lionel Bart: British Vernacular Musical Theatre', in Gordon Robert and Olaf Jubin (eds), *The Oxford Handbook of the British Musical*, 483-506. New York: Oxford University Press, 2016.

Trewin, J. C. (ed.). *The Year's Work in Theatre 1948-1949*, 53-5. London: The British Council/Longmans, Green and Co., 1949.

Trewin, J. C. *The Gay Twenties: A Decade of the Theatre*. Foreword by Noël Coward. London: Macdonald, 1958.

Trewin, J. C. *The Turbulent Thirties: A Further Decade of the Theatre*. Foreword by Emlyn Williams. London: Macdonald, 1960.

Vlasto, Dominic. 'The Potency of Cheap Music', in Joel Kaplan and Sheila Stowell (eds), *Look Back in Pleasure: Noël Coward Reconsidered*, 144-62. London: Methuen, 2000.

Wearing, J. P. *The London Stage 1890-1959: A Calendar of Productions, Performers, and Personnel*. 2nd edn. Lanham: Rowman and Littlefield, 2014.

Webb, Paul. *Ivor Novello: Portrait of a Star*. London: Stage Directions, 1999.

Webb, Paul. *Ivor Novello: Portrait of a Star*. 2nd edn. London: Haus, 2005.

Wells, Elizabeth A. 'After "Anger": The British Musical of the Late 1950s', in Robert Gordon and Olaf Jubin (eds), *The Oxford Handbook of the British Musical*, 273-89. New York: Oxford University Press, 2016.

Wells, Elizabeth A. '"Expresso Bongo" and "Make Me an Offer": The "Angry Young Musical" in the 1950s', *Studies in Musical Theatre*, 14 (2020): 163-73. Bristol: Intellect.

White, James Dillon. *Born to Star: The Lupino Lane Story*. London, Melbourne and Toronto: William Heinemann, 1957.
Wilson, Sandy. *The Boy Friend*. London: Andre Deutsch, 1955. With a preface by Vida Hope and illustrations by the author.
Wilson, Sandy. 'A Future for British Musicals', in F. Lumley (ed.), *Theatre in Review*, 185–8. Edinburgh: Richard Patterson, 1956.
Wilson, Sandy. *Boy Friend*. Harmondsworth: Penguin Books, 1959.
Wilson, Sandy. *The Boy Friend*. Vocal score. London: Chappell, 1960a.
Wilson, Sandy. *The Boy Friend*. Playscript. London: Samuel French, 1960b.
Wilson, Sandy. *I Could Be Happy: An Autobiography*. New York: Stein and Day, 1975a.
Wilson, Sandy. *Ivor*. London: Joseph, 1975b.
Wilson, Sandy. *The Roaring Twenties*. Unpaginated. London: Eyre Methuen, 1976.
Wright, Adrian. *A Tanner's Worth of Tunes: Rediscovering the Post-War British Musical*. Woodbridge: The Boydell Press, 2010.
Zweiniger-Bargielowska, Ina. *Austerity in Britain: Rationing, Controls, and Consumption 1939–1955*. Oxford: Oxford University Press, 2000.

Index

Ace of Clubs 11, 28, 125, 135
Adams, Archie Emmett 39
adaptation
    for film 29, 31, 45, 112–13, 131–2, 157
    for stage 33, 48–51, 94–5, 109–11, 156–8, 163
ADC Theatre (Cambridge) 125
Adelphi Theatre (London) 26, 33, 48, 53, 67, 75, 91, 141–2
Afgar 40
After the Ball 28
Aldwych Theatre (London) 21
Alhambra Theatre (London) 64
Altman, Robert 55
Ambassadors Theatre (London) 60
American–British comparison, *see* British–American comparison
An American in Paris (film) 75
Andrews, Julie 110, 111, 136
And So to Bed 88, 92
Annie 94
Annie Get Your Gun 81
Anything Goes 106
The Arcadians 25, 42, 148, 150
Arc de Triomphe 26, 57, 58, 78, 79
Arlette 56
Armitage, Richard 48
Arms and the Girl 75
Askey, Arthur 12–13, 164
Astaire, Adele 42
A to Z (revue) 39, 56, 58

Ballets Russes 76
Barron, Muriel 58
Bart, Lionel
    creative process 140–3, 145–6
    musical eclecticism 146–52
    as pop songwriter 2, 95, 131
    success 3, 5, 10, 140, 155–6
Bassey, Shirley 2, 149
Beat Girl (film) 130

The Beatles 147
Beaton, Cecil 27, 137
Beaumont, Roma 58, 67
The Beggar's Opera 116
Belle, or the Ballad of Dr Crippen 119
Benediction (film) 55
Berlin, Irving 105
Berliner Ensemble 117
Bernstein, Leonard 92
Best Foot Forward 4
Bet Your Life 6, 164
Big Ben 75, 78–9, 83, 89–90, 93, 118
The Bing Boys 53
The Biograph Girl 119
Bitter Sweet, see also Noël Coward
    adaptation of 29–32
    and Coward's identity 14
    creation of 17–18, 20
    and David Heneker 118
    film 7–8, 10, 27, 29–31
    in performance 1–3, 24
    plot 17
    reaction to 3, 19–20, 29
    recordings 31–2
    songs 1, 18, 22–5, 27–32
    temporal interplay 9, 11, 164–5
    theatre and society 43
    waltzes 23–4
Black, George 78
Bless the Bride, see also C. B. Cochran; Vivian Ellis; A. P. Herbert
    Act I finale 86–7
    creation of 76
    creative team 167
    genre 83–8, 95, 162
    plot 75
    reaction to 94–5
    revival 163
    songs 75, 77, 81–2, 84–6
    temporal interplay 165
    and wartime 8, 80–1, 94–5

Blitz! 141, 143, 146, 149, 151–2
Bott, Alan 66
Bourne, Matthew 156
The Boy Friend, see also Sandy Wilson
   comparison with *Expresso Bongo* 133, 152
   film 107, 112–13
   in performance 99, 101, 110–11
   period recreation 97–100, 104–6, 112–13, 165
   plot 97–8, 102
   reaction to 6, 100, 106, 110–11
   in rehearsal 111
   songs 102–5, 110, 112–13
   temporal interplay 9
   theatre convention 101–3, 112
Braham, Philip 39
Brecht, Bertolt 132
Breffort, Alexandre 122
Brewer, Herbert 55
Bricusse, Leslie 120
Brigadoon 137
Bristol Old Vic Theatre 109
Britannia Theatre (London) 41
British–American comparison
   critical contrast 3–7, 93–5, 110–12, 132, 136–8, 155–6
   cultural context 10–12, 20–1, 28, 94–5, 108, 148–9, 156
Broadway–West End comparison, *see* British–American comparison
Brodszky, Max 89
Brohn, William David 157
Brown, Georgia 149
Brown, Lew 50
The Buccaneer 108, 113
Buchanan, Jack 38, 39
Burrows, George 43, 47–8
Bussy, Raymond 31
Butt, Clara 55
Bygraves, Max 2
By Jupiter 4

Cabaret 122, 155, 157
The Call of the Blood (film) 56
Calthrop, Gladys 20
The Camels Are Coming (film) 35
Cardinali, Roberto 31
Careless Rapture 53, 57–8, 79

Carina (opera) 82, 86
Carl Rosa Opera Company 1
Carmen (opera) 1
Carter, Desmond 36
Caryll, Ivan 20
Cats 139, 157
Cavalcade 105
censorship 37–8, 48–9, 68–9, 125–6
Chaplin, Charlie 38, 41
Chappell, William 116, 121
Charlie Girl 48, 119
Charlot, André 18, 35
Charlot's Revue of 1926 19, 35
Charnin, Martin 94
Chu Chin Chow 53
Churchill, Winston Spencer 77, 88
Cinderella (pantomime) 141
class
   contrast of 37–8, 42–3, 45–7, 75, 125, 136, 138, 151, 163
   lower 9, 117, 121, 130, 146–7, 150–1
   upper 18–19, 97–8
Clowns in Clover (revue) 35
Clum, John M. 110–11
Cochran, C(harles) B(lake)
   creation of *Bless the Bride* 75, 79, 167
   and Douglas Furber 39–40
   film rights 8
   and Noël Coward 8, 18–19
   revues 18–19, 39–40, 42, 76
Cochran's 1930 Revue 83
Coe, Peter 142, 156
The Coliseum (London) 8, 39, 70, 81
Collier, Constance 61
Collier, John 108
Comedy Theatre (London) 127
The Constant Nymph (play/film) 56, 58
Conversation Piece 25
Cookman, Anthony 76, 92
Cosh Boy (play/film) 127
Cotton, Billy 34
A Country Girl 43
Courtneidge, Cicely 11–12, 35, 39–40, 73, 78, 164–5
Coward, Noël
   contemporary critique 18–19, 23–4
   influences 17, 20, 26
   integrated scores 17–18, 20–2, 29
   musical style 5, 17–18, 21–2

Index

plays 18
revues 18–20, 25, 27
songs 18–19, 105, 113
theatrical reflexivity 26–7
wartime 27
Cowardy Custard 79
The Crazy Gang 35
Crest of the Wave 4, 53, 57–8, 79, 150
Crisham, Walter 58
The Crooked Mile 109, 117

D'Oyly Carte, Richard 75
Daly's Theatre (London) 20
Damn Yankees 132
The Dancing Years, see also Christopher Hassall; Ivor Novello
creation of 57, 59, 68
'A Masque of Vienna' 69–71, 175 n.31
film 10, 64, 66, 70
'The Leap Year Waltz' 65, 174 n.14
reaction to 53, 67
songs 53, 59–60, 63–5
staging 57, 66, 79
temporal interplay 10, 164
and wartime 8, 10, 66–8, 70
Dare, Zena 58, 136
Davies, Clara Novello 55
Davies, Terence 55
Day, Frances 78
Dear Miss Phoebe 6
Debussy, Claude 55
De La Bère, Rupert 89
Delaney, Shelagh 117
Delysia, Alice 78
Dene, Terry 129
Derby Day (opera) 77, 90
The Desert Song 21
Dickens, Charles 120, 143–4, 152
Die Fledermaus 20
The Dippers (play) 56
Divorce Me, Darling! 106–7
Don Pasquale (opera) 86
Douglas, Lord Alfred 27
Downhill (play/film) 56
The Duke Wore Jeans (film) 130, 140
Duse, Eleonora 76

Eddy, Nelson 30
Elliott, George Henry 99

Ellis, Mary 54, 58, 67, 71
Ellis, Vivian
collaboration 75, 78–9, 167
and Gilbert and Sullivan 77
musical style 5, 82–4, 88
songs 78, 82–3, 88–9
Elsie, Lily 58
Embassy Theatre (London) 101
England, Adele 44–5
Entertainments National Service Association (ENSA) 27, 53
Expresso Bongo, see also David Heneker; Julian More; Monty Norman; Wolf Mankowitz
censorship 125
and contemporary life 8
film 8, 10, 116, 121, 123, 127–31
plot 115
pop culture 117, 129–30, 165
reaction to 116, 132–3, 137
as social comment 8
as Soho musical 116–17
songs 122–6, 128–9, 132, 134–5, 139
theatre innovation 122–4
Eyre, Richard 125
Eyton, Frank 36

Fagan, J(ames) B(ernard) 88
Fall, Leo 84
Feather Your Nest (film) 35
Fellini, Federico 143
Feuer, Cy 110–11
Fields, Gracie 1, 150
film
adaptation from stage 8, 10, 29–31, 45–7, 66, 112–13, 131–2, 139, 143, 153–4
adaptation to stage 144
early film 7–8, 27, 41–2, 56–7, 60–2
influence of 60–2, 107, 112, 127, 152–5, 157–8
youth culture 130–2
Findon, B(enjamin) W(illiam) 5
Fings Ain't Wot They Used t'Be 117, 119, 126, 140–2, 150–1
Finian's Rainbow 4, 130
Flagstad, Kirsten 55
Flanagan and Alan 147

Floradora 139
Follow a Star (revue) 78
Follow that Girl 2, 109
Ford, Florrie 148
Ford, Lena Guilbert 56
Formby, George 35, 164
Francis, Day & Hunter 82
Frears, Stephen 125
Free as Air 115, 133
Fresh Fields 57
Friml, Rudolf 21
Fry, Stephen 48
Furber, Douglas 39–40

A Gaiety Girl 43
Gaiety Theatre (London) 1, 20, 26
Gaitskell, Hugh 88
Gay, Maisie 39
Gay, Noel 7, 33–6, 44, 48
Gay's the Word 6, 57–8, 109, 164
Gánzl, Kurt 33
Gemmell, Don 100
Gilbert, Geo(rge) 36
Gilbert, Jos(eph) 36
Gilbert, Olive 57–8, 67
Gilbert, W(illiam) S(chwenk) 75
Gilbert and Sullivan (Savoy Operas) 7, 20, 77, 93
The Girl Behind the Counter 43
The Girl Friend 105, 110
Glamorous Night 4, 53, 55, 57–8, 79
Globe Theatre (London) 106
The Glorious Years 164
The Golden Moth 56, 58
The Gondoliers 77
Good News 105
The Good Old Days (television programme) 99, 148
Gordon, Robert 109, 139, 148
Gosford Park (film) 55
Grab Me a Gondola 109, 118
Graham, Harry 36
Granger, Derek 133
Graves, George 34, 49
Graves, Peter 58, 67
Graves, Robert 14
Gray, Clifford 36
Gray, Sally 46
Guest, Val 130

Guétary, George 75
Guitry, Sacha 1
Guys and Dolls 28, 125, 135

Hair 152
Hale, Binnie 89
Hale, Sonnie 1
Half a Sixpence 48, 119, 130, 163
Hamlet (play) 12–13
Hammerstein II, Oscar 4
The Happiest Millionaire (film) 130
Harrison, Rex 121, 136
Harvey, Laurence 121
Hassall, Christopher 59–60, 73
Hayter, James 145
Hazell, Hy 137
'Hear Ye, Israel' (Mendelssohn) 56
Heathcliff 132
Heawood, John 99
Hello, Dolly! 155
Henderson, Ray 50
Heneker, David 5, 118–20, 122, 132, 137, 144
Henry V (film) 13
Henson, Leslie 78
Herbert, A(lan) P(atrick)
   collaboration 75, 78–9, 167
   and Gilbert, W. S. 77
   humour 77
   politics 80–1, 83, 88–91, 118
   wartime 77, 89, 91, 162
Her Excellency 12, 164
Hess, Myra 82
Hide and Seek 83
His Majesty's Theatre (London) 1, 2, 21
His Monkey Wife 108
Hitchcock, Alfred 56
Hoare, Philip 19
Hodge, Alan 14
Hollings, Ken 129–30
Holloway, Stanley 136
Hope, Vida 99–100, 110–11
Houdini, Harry 76
The House That Jack Built (revue) 39, 40
Hulbert, Claude 106
Hulbert, Jack 35, 39–40, 78

Il barbiere di Siviglia (opera) 86
I Lived with You (play/film) 57

In Which We Serve (film) 78
Iolanthe 77
Irma la Douce 122, 152

Jacques, Hattie 99–100
Johnny the Priest 117
Johnson, Laurie 141
Joseph and the Amazing Technicolor Dreamcoat 27
Joyland (film) 41

Kálmán, Emmerich 84
A Kayf Up West (play) 144
Kenney, James 127, 134
Kenny, Sean 144, 152–3, 157, 159
Kern, Jerome 4, 82, 106
Kersh, Gerald 128
The Kid from Stratford 12–13, 164
Kill Me Tomorrow (film) 131
King's Head Theatre (London) 94
King's Rhapsody 6, 57–8, 91, 118
The King and I 121
Kiss Me, Kate 148

Lady Windermere's Fan (play) 28
The Lambeth Walk (film) 45
The Land of Smiles 21, 25, 63
Lane, Lupino
    comic technique 37–9, 41–2, 46–7, 163
    creation of Bill Snibson 38–42, 46–7, 50
    creation of *Me and My Girl* 33
    family history 40–1
    film 41, 45
Lane, Sara 41
La Strada 143
Lawrence, Gertrude 39
Laye, Evelyn 24, 29
Lean, David 8, 144, 153
Lee, Jennie 99
Lee, Vanessa 31, 43
Lehár, Franz 21, 24–5, 84
Leicester Haymarket Theatre 48
Lerner, Alan Jay 137
Les Misérables 157–8, 162
Lewenstein, Oscar 126
Lilac Time 21
Lillie, Beatrice 39, 42

The Lily White Boys 117
Lindsay, Robert 50
The Lisbon Story 26
Littlewood, Joan 116–17, 141
Lloyd, Marie 99
Lock Up Your Daughters 140–2, 152
The Lodger (film) 56
Loesser, Frank 125
Loewe, Frederick 137
Lom, Herbert 121
London Casino 53
London Hippodrome 1, 6, 57
London Palladium Theatre 35, 78, 152, 156
London Pavilion Theatre 1, 18, 40
Look Back in Anger (play) 107, 117, 152
Lord Chamberlain, *see* censorship
Love from Judy 6, 109
Love Lies 1
The Love Parade (film) 41
Lubitsch, Ernst 41
Lupino, Wallace 38, 41
Lupino family 40–1, *see also* Lupino Lane
Lyceum Theatre (London) 1
Lynn, Vera 146
Lyric Theatre (London) 118
Lyric Theatre, Hammersmith (London) 118

McCormack, John 40
MacDonald, Jeanette 30–1
McHugh, Dominic 15, 25, 29
Mackintosh, Cameron 152, 156
McLaren, Malcolm 165
MacMillan, Harold 88
Macpherson, Ben 13–14, 25, 43
Macqueen-Pope, W(alter) J(ames) 54–5, 57, 60
MacRae, Gordon 31
Maggie May 141, 143, 147, 151
Magyar Melody 25
The Maid of the Mountains (film) 40
Maitland, Joan 141, 145
Make Me an Offer 117, 119
Mallory, Leslie 137
Mankowitz, Wolf 118–21, 127–9
Man of la Mancha 124

Mariette 1
Marnac, Jane   24, 31
Marquis Theatre (New York)   33
Marsh, Edward   57, 71, 73
Martin, Mary   28
Martin, Millicent   137
Massary, Fritzi   25–6
Master Crook, see *Cosh Boy*
Matthews, Jessie   1
Me and My Girl, see also Douglas Furber; Noel Gay; Lupino Lane; Arthur L. Rose
   censorship   49
   class   9, 42–3, 45–7, 130
   film   8, 41–2, 45–7
   in performance   45–7, 50–1
   'The Lambeth Walk'   36, 42–6, 50–1
   physical comedy   46–8
   plot   33
   revision   48–9, 51
   revival   11, 156, 163, 165
   songs   33, 35, 45, 50–1
Melville, Alan   72
Mendes, Sam   156
Mercanton, Louis   56
Mermaid Theatre (London)   141
The Merry Widow   25, 58, 63
Metaxa, George   31
Monckton, Lionel   20, 60
Monnot, Marguerite   122
Monroe, Marilyn   108
Montgomery, (General Field Marshall) Bernard Law   77
Monty Python's Life of Brian (film)   6
Moody, Ron   156
Mordden, Ethan   20, 112
More, Julian   118, 120, 122, 132, 137
Mr. Cinders   47–8, 78, 83, 101
Mrs Henderson Presents (film)   125
Murder in Mayfair (play)   57, 59
Music Box Theatre (New York)   27
music hall   34–5, 41, 99, 146, 148–9, 153
The Music Man   150
My Fair Lady   2, 91, 109, 115, 121, 136–8, 153

Nadel, Norman   156
Napolitano, Marc   139
Napper, Lawrence   43, 60

Neagle, Anna   30, 164
The New Moon   1, 21
New Theatre (London)   2, 139
Nicholls, Anthony   67
Nicholls, Peter   120
Nicholls, Stewart   57, 72
No, No, Nanette   101, 104–5, 112
Noble, Peter   54–5, 57
Norman, Frank   141–2, 144, 150
Norman, Monty   118–20, 122, 137
Novello, Ivor
   British operetta   25
   contemporary references in musicals   71
   film   60–1
   Ivor Novello Awards   4
   musical influences   55–6, 58, 63–4
   as playwright   56
   portrayal on film   55
   reputation   54–7, 70–3, 173 n.7
   revues   56
   songs   55–6, 58–60, 64–5, 71–2, 105

Oh What a Lovely War   122
O-Kay for Sound   35
Oklahoma!   10, 84, 91, 94–5, 138
Oliver!, see also Lionel Bart
   film   8, 10, 139, 144, 148–9, 152–5, 157–9
   in performance   2–3
   reaction to   3, 139–40, 152, 155, 167
   set design   152–3, 157, 159
   songs   2, 144, 146, 148–58
   theatrical innovation   152–5
Oliver Twist (film)   8
Olivier, Laurence   13
On with the Dance (revue)   18, 78
On Your Toes   4
operetta   18, 20–1, 59, 63
   operette (genre)   18, 83
Operette   26–8, 43
Oranges and Lemons (revue)   100
Ornadel, Cyril   120
Osborne, John   117
Our Miss Gibbs   25, 56
Over She Goes   34
Owen, Alun   141, 147

Pacific 1860   26–8, 43

Index

Paint Your Wagon 137
The Pajama Game 132
Palace Theatre (London) 57, 109
Pal Joey 28, 125, 135
Paprika 25
parody, *see* pastiche
Parr-Davies, Harry 26, 59
pastiche 9, 59–60, 63–4, 77, 85, 101–7, 112, 134, 146–7
past–present comparison, *see* temporal interplay
Patti, Adelina 56
Payn, Graham 28
Peg o' My Heart 34
Pepys, Samuel 88
Perchance to Dream 57–9, 91
Perseverance (or Half a Coronet) 77
Peter Pan 92
The Phantom of the Opera 155, 157, 158, 162
Philips, Deborah 98, 109
Phoenix Theatre (London) 11, 57
Pickwick 120
The Pickwick Papers 120
Pinero, Arthur Wing 42
The Pirates of Penzance 56
Pitt, Archie 1
Platt, Len 36, 43
The Players' Theatre (London) 98–101, 106, 109–10, 148, 149
pop music 2, 4, 95, 107, 115–17, 121–2, 128–32, 134, 140, 142, 158
Poppy 120
Porter, Cole 76, 106, 148
Posford, George 25, 84
Pound, Reginald 77
Presley, Elvis 127
Pretty Peggy 39
Printemps, Yvonne 1, 25
Private Lives (play) 18
Proscenium (play) 57
Puccini, Giacomo 55
Puppets (revue) 56, 58, 105
Purcell, Harold 26
Pygmalion (play) 34

The Queen Was in the Parlour (play) 18

Rape upon Rape (play) 141

The Rat (play/film) 56
Rayner, Minnie 58
Reed, Carol 8, 139
Reinhardt, Max 79
Rent 155
Revill, Clive 156
revival
  operetta 21
  post-war context 13, 81, 93, 104, 133
  repertory prominence 139, 141, 152, 156, 159
  revision 33–4, 49–50, 94, 111–12, 156–7, 163, 168
Reynolds, Alfred 77
Reynolds, Dorothy 2
Richard, Cliff 116, 130–1
The Roar of the Greasepaint – the Smell of the Crowd 152
Roberta 106
Robeson, Paul 40
Robey, George 49
Rock 'n' roll 113, 115, 127, 130–1, 134, 138, 140
Rogers, Eric 157
Romberg, Sigmund 21
Ronald, Landon 55
Rose, L. Arthur 38–40
Rose, Richard 55
Rose Marie 21
Rotten, Johnny 165
'Round the Horne' (radio show) 98
Royal Albert Hall (London) 78
Royal Court Theatre (London) 117, 127
Royale Theatre (New York) 109
Royal Opera House, Covent Garden (London) 1
Rubens, Paul 20, 60
Runyon, Damon 127
Russell, Ken 97, 112–13
the Russian Ballet 1

Sachs, Leonard 99
Sadler's Wells Theatre (London) 31, 93
Sagan, Leontine 79
Sail Away 32
Sailors Three (film) 35
St Dennis, Teddie 45
St Helier, Ivy 31
Salad Days 43, 108–9, 133, 137, 152

Saville Theatre (London)   57, 73, 109, 116, 136, 138
Savoy Theatre (London)   26
Scofield, Paul   121, 137
Secombe, Harry   120, 145
See You Again (revue)   100
See You Later (revue)   100
Serious Charge (film)   131
Set to Music (revue)   27
Shakespeare, William   12–13
Share My Lettuce   115
Shaw, George Bernard   138
Shostakovich, Dmitri   88
The Show's the Thing (revue)   1
Show Boat   105
Shubert Theatre (New York)   12
Silver Wings   34
Sinclair, Barry   55
Slade, Julian   2
Slings and Arrows (revue)   100
Smith, Oliver   137
Soho musicals   107, 116–17, 119, 133, 144–5, 148, 152
The Soldiers of the King (film)   35
Sondheim, Stephen   120
Songbook   120
The Sound of Music   124, 157
Sousa, John Philip   150
South Pacific   4, 6
Splinters revues   39
star casting   11–13, 35, 39–42, 50, 59, 62, 78, 121, 136, 164–5
Stars and Stripes (revue)   39
Steele, Tommy   130–1, 140, 142, 145
Stephens, Frances   3, 6–7, 137
Sterndale Bennett, Joan   99–100
Still Dancing (revue)   78
Stoll, Oswald   8, 39
Stoll Theatre (London)   91
Stolz, Robert   25, 84
Stop Press (revue)   35
Stothart, Herbert   21
Straus, Oscar   1, 84
Streamline (revue)   78
Stuart, Leslie   21
The Student Prince   21
Sullivan, Arthur   75
Summer Holiday (film)   131
Sweeney Todd   120, 155

Symphony in Two Flats (play)   57–8
Tabs (revue)   56
Tales from the Crypt   108
Tantivy Towers (opera)   90
A Taste of Honey (play)   117
Tauber, Richard   21, 25
television   8, 45, 70, 126
temporal interplay   9–11, 25, 84–5, 99–100, 146, 164–5
Tennent, Harry   57
Ternent, Billy   83
Theatre Royal, Drury Lane (London)
    as ENSA headquarters   27, 53
    modern musical   2, 4, 6, 27, 91, 136–7, 153, 156
    Novello show   4, 28, 53, 55, 57, 79
    operetta   1, 21, 63
    stage spectacle   61–2, 157
Theatre Royal, Stratford East (London)/ Theatre Workshop   116–17, 119, 141
Theodore & Co   56
This Year of Grace! (revue)   19, 25, 105
Three Sisters   4
Tilzer, Harry von   148
Time   132
The Tommy Steele Story (film)   130, 140
Tommy the Toreador (film)   130
Too Many Girls   4
Tough at the Top   75, 83, 88, 90
Toye, Wendy   78–9, 162
Travers, Ben   56
Trewin, J(ohn) C(ourtenay)   4
Trinder, Tommy   35
A Trip to Chinatown   148
Tristan und Isolde (opera)   56
The Truth Game (play)   56, 58
Twang!!   143
Twenty Minutes South   43, 109
Twenty to One   34, 36
    character of Bill Snibson   38–9, 42
    class   38–9
    and *Me and My Girl*   33
    physical comedy   39
    verbal comedy   40
Tzelniker, Meier   128

Under the Counter   11–12, 164

Under Your Hat   164
Unity Theatre   141–2

The Vagabond King   21
Valmouth   108, 133
Vaudeville Theatre (London)   2, 26
Victoria Palace Theatre (London)   1, 35, 44
Violetta (Farjeon)   100
Vlasto, Dominic   18
Volpone (play)   141
The Vortex (play/film)   18, 56

Wagner, Richard   55–6
Wake Up and Dream (revue)   1, 39
Wally Pone, King of the Underworld   141
Walton, William   59
Waltz   23–5, 64–6, 84, 86–7, 148–9
Ward, Anthony   156–7
wartime   68–9, 71, 77–8, 80–1, 89
Watergate Theatre (London)   100, 108
The Water Gypsies (film/musical)   78, 83, 88
Watts Jr, Richard   144
Webb, Lizbeth   43, 75
Wedding in Paris   6
Wertham, Fredric   108
Wesker, Arnold   117
West End–Broadway comparison, *see* British–American comparison
West Side Story   109, 116, 117, 137

What Price the Navy (revue)   39
White, James Dillon   34
White Horse Inn   25
The White Rose (film)   56
Wilcox, Michael   29
Wilde, Oscar   27
Will o' the Whispers (revue)   83
Willson, Meredith   150
Wilson, Sandy
  contemporary satire   108
  and intimate revue   100
  on Ivor Novello   59–60, 72
  musical style   5
  Players' Theatre   99–100
  retrospection   97, 104–7
Windmill Theatre (London)   125
Winter Garden Theatre (London)   21
Wodehouse, P. G.   51
Wonderful Life (film)   131
Wood, Peggy   24, 31
Woolf, Julia   82
Woolley, Reginald   99
The World of Paul Slickey   117, 122
Worsley, T(homas) C(uthbert)   132–3
Wyndham's Theatre (London)   101

The Young Ones (film)   131
Ysaÿe, Eugène   82

Ziegfeld Theatre (New York)   29
Zip Goes a Million   6, 11, 109, 164, 167

www.ingramcontent.com/pod-product-compliance
Lightning Source LLC
Chambersburg PA
CBHW051811230426
43672CB00012B/2695